World Religions and Democracy

A *Journal of Democracy* Book

•

BOOKS IN THE SERIES

Edited by Larry Diamond and Marc F. Plattner

Published under the auspices of
the International Forum for Democratic Studies

World Religions and Democracy

*Edited by Larry Diamond, Marc F. Plattner,
and Philip J. Costopoulos*

The Johns Hopkins University Press

Baltimore and London

9 8 7 6 5 4 3 2 1

Chapters in this volume appeared in the following issues of the *Journal of Democracy:*
chapter 6, January 1992; chapter 3, April 1995; chapters 13–15, April 1996; chapter 5,
January 1999; chapter 12, July 1999; Epilogue, January 2000; chapter 1, October 2000;
chapter 20, April 2002; chapters 16–19, April 2003; chapters 8–11, April 2004; chapters
2, 4, and 7, July 2004. For all reproduction rights, please contact the Johns Hopkins
University Press.

The Johns Hopkins University Press
2715 North Charles Street
Baltimore, Maryland 21218-4363
www.press.jhu.edu

ISBN 0-8018-8079-3 — ISBN 0-8018-8080-7 (pbk.)

Library of Congress Control Number: 2004116994

A catalog record for this book is available from the British Library.

CONTENTS

ACKNOWLEDGMENTS

Since 9/11, many people who previously had paid little attention to the issue of religion have become conscious of its political significance. Long before that fateful day in 2001, however, a number of articles in the *Journal of Democracy* had focused on the relationship between democracy and various religious traditions, especially Islam. In the *Journal*'s April 2003 issue we again turned to the subject of Islam, and later that year Johns Hopkins University Press published our volume *Islam and Democracy in the Middle East,* which included a section of essays on the political implications of Islam along with other essays offering analyses of recent political developments in the Middle East. While that book was still in the making, we decided to broaden the *Journal*'s coverage by publishing a cluster of essays on "Christianity and Democracy," and later, individual articles on Confucianism, Hinduism, and Judaism. All this material focused on religion has now been gathered together in the present volume, *World Religions and Democracy*.

We are very pleased to be joined as editors of this book by the *Journal*'s executive editor Philip J. Costopoulos, who has been our primary manuscript editor since we began publishing in 1990. Phil's fine hand and keen mind have been evident in all previous *Journal of Democracy* books, but his role in the case of this volume has been even more central. Thanks to his strong interest in religion and democracy and his extensive knowledge of the topic, he was able to make a major contribution both in the recruitment of authors and in the shaping of the book. Phil was also the principal drafter of the introductory essay.

Some of the contributions to the section on Islam originated in a meeting on 25 September 2002, cosponsored by the International Forum for Democratic Studies (where the *Journal* is based) and the Woodrow Wilson International Center for Scholars, which brought together a group of distinguished Muslim scholars to discuss the issue of "liberal Islam." Special thanks go to Haleh Esfandiari, director of the Middle East Program at the Wilson Center, for helping us to plan and to organize that meeting, and to Abdou Filali-Ansary and Laith Kubba for their very helpful advice. With regards to the section on Christianity, we are much obliged to Timothy S. Shah of the Ethics and Public Policy Center (EPPC) and the Pew Forum on Religion and Public Life, who stimulated our interest in addressing this subject and advised us in recruiting these essays. We are also grateful to the EPPC for hosting and cosponsoring with the *Journal* a June 2004 meeting on "Christianity and Democracy," featuring the authors included here as well as EPPC senior fellow George Weigel.

Once again, we are pleased to have an opportunity to thank some of the many institutions and individuals who have assisted us. The National Endowment for Democracy, the *Journal*'s parent organization, has unfailingly supported our work and respected our intellectual independence. We are deeply grateful to the Endowment's Board of Directors and to its president, our good friend Carl Gershman. Since our founding, the Lynde and Harry Bradley Foundation has provided us with invaluable financial assistance. The members of our editorial board merit our thanks for their indispensable help in identifying issues and topics to be explored in our pages. We are also much indebted to our publisher, the Johns Hopkins University Press (JHUP), and in particular to Henry Tom, an executive editor in its books division. This is the sixteenth book we have published with JHUP, and many more are sure to follow.

The *Journal* has been blessed with an outstanding editorial staff, whose hard work lies behind this and previous *Journal of Democracy* collections. This is the first book for managing editor Maureen Wellman, who efficiently and cheerfully supervised its production. Associate editors Anja Håvedal and Zerxes Spencer made important editorial contributions. Former managing editor Stephanie Lewis, who oversaw the production of eight previous *Journal of Democracy* books, prepared the index for this volume with meticulous precision. We would also like to thank a number of former staff members—John Gould, Jordan Branch, Mark Eckert, Mahindan Kanakaratnam, Kristin Helz, Miriam Kramer, and Annette Theuring—and the many interns who have volunteered their time and effort to assist the editors in their work.

—Marc F. Plattner and Larry Diamond

INTRODUCTION

Philip J. Costopoulos

Despite Alexis de Tocqueville's warnings that a healthy liberal democracy will require a vibrant religious element, the prevailing view over most of the past half-century at least has been that democracy's progress is naturally accompanied not merely by the advance of secularism but by the waning of religion. Social scientists generally embraced secularization theory, which boils down to the idea that modernization advances in lockstep with the decline of religious belief, activity, and organization. This is a version of the historicist notion that religion belongs to the childhood of the human race, and is destined to fade away with the rise of science, mass politics (democratic or otherwise), the sundry dislocations occasioned by urbanization, and other phenomena characteristic of modernity. Such an account may seem to offer a relatively accurate rendering of developments in Western Europe, and the contrary example of the United States, where high levels of religious affiliation and belief persist, has often been chalked up to "American exceptionalism." Influenced perhaps by the West European experience, students of democracy and democratization have paid the whole subject of religion relatively little attention.

There are growing signs, however, of a reversal in this trend as scholars of democracy increasingly grapple with the issues raised by the interactions between democratization and various religious traditions. Before the Second World War, democracy was found almost solely in historically Christian lands. Since then, the second and third global waves of democratization have carried this form of rule (or influences associated with it) to countries inhabited by all the world's major religious communities. It should be anything but surprising that the challenges which flow from the need to work out accommodations between democracy on the one hand and spiritual traditions such as Confucianism, Hinduism, Buddhism, Judaism, and Islam on the other have raised a host of intellectually fascinating and at times politically arduous questions for scholars and politicians alike.

Of course, the greatest spur to renewed interest in the "theological-political" question has been the recent rise in the global salience of Islam, a religion whose adherents form more than a sixth of the world's population and make up the majority in about a quarter of the world's sovereign countries. Students of democratization have had to come to grips with the lagging performance of democracy in majority-Muslim countries generally and its outright absence from the Arab world in particular. Given the enormous influence of Islam in these lands, one can hardly avoid asking whether that religion plays a role in these difficulties. At the same time, friends of democracy within the Muslim world have had to confront the illiberal tendencies fostered by the new prominence of extremist interpretations of their own religious tradition. And the rest of the world has been compelled to take notice by the horrific acts of global terrorism committed by those who claim to be acting in the name of Islam.

Especially across the global South, where a majority of the world's Muslims, Hindus, and Buddhists have always lived and where most of the world's Christians now live as well, religion remains a phenomenon of large and growing significance. Social scientists may not have abandoned the belief—for which there is considerable evidence—that secularization and the decline of religion as a public force remain potent trends. Yet many also recognize that the old linear narrative of "modernization up, religion down" is far too simple and does not begin to capture the complexity of religion's varied circumstances in the contemporary world, or the complicated ways in which secularizing forces (possibly including democratization) and persistent religious commitments and identities can influence one another.

To put it crudely but not altogether unfairly, the world over the last half-century has become more modernized—more urban, more pervaded by scientific technology, and in certain ways and places more secularized—and yet also more democratic and more religious. The spread of democracy and the perseverance and even resurgence of religion and religious identity as motive historical forces have come about even though, according to many if not most twentieth-century intellectuals, this outcome was far from expected.

We have chosen to begin this volume with Alfred Stepan's widely cited essay "Religion, Democracy, and the 'Twin Tolerations'" because it attacks common misunderstandings of the relationship between religion and democracy while providing a globally applicable template for grasping its nature in a way that is true to observed facts. The key to this template is Stepan's idea of the "twin tolerations." These mean that political authorities agree to allow free religious activity within broad and equally applied limits, while religious persons and bodies agree to relinquish claims to wield direct political power even as they remain free to use all available means of peaceful persuasion (including the votes of religious people) in seeking to shape public policy as they prefer. This situation can obtain, stresses Stepan, even when the state recognizes one religion or religious body as somehow the "established" religion of the country, provided that the laws also effectually safeguard religious freedom and toleration for the nonestablished faiths.

The Importance of Differentiation

Behind the "twin tolerations" lies the concept that sociologists of religion call differentiation. As a political reality, this idea hinges on a principled distinction between religious and political authority, based on the understanding that each belongs to a conceptually distinct (albeit interrelated) sphere of human life with its own proper aims, methods, and forms of thought, discourse, and action. This notion is most famously associated with the long and complicated history of Western Christianity—modern secularism is essentially a byproduct of disagreements beneath what Peter Berger (borrowing a term from David Martin) calls the "domes" of historically Christian cultures. Yet Pratap Bhanu Mehta's essay in this volume provides an admirable account of how Hinduism, working from sources and insights very much its own, has grounded a quite similar and salutary sense that religion and politics are both valuable human pursuits which need not and should not be sacrificed to or confused with each other.

Among the implications of the ideas of differentiation and the twin tolerations is one that Stepan points out: Not all types of secularism are created equal. A secularist regime that is not grounded in mutual tolerance between spiritual and political authority, but where the state dictates to or even suppresses religion—think of the USSR, classical Kemalism in Turkey, or Ba'athism in Syria and Saddam-era Iraq—will almost surely not be a liberal democracy. In view of this, one wonders whether a large part of the difficulty in which the Muslim world finds itself today may not be traceable to its unfortunate position poised between various forms of illiberal, command-based secularism on the one hand, and powerful fundamentalist forces (the well-funded Saudi Arabian Wahabis, the Iranian heirs of Khomeini) on the other.

Both secularist and religious authoritarians in the broader Middle East reject differentiation. Thus the region today is a place where the most influential opponents of many illiberal secular regimes may well be radical Islamists who oppose these regimes not out of any principled opposition to illiberalism as such, but rather out of a desire to replace the state's secular illiberalism with a putatively religious brand more to their own liking. Such Islamists may talk of democracy, but upon closer scrutiny it will appear that the version they have in mind departs in key respects from liberal constitutionalism, and may even be a euphemism for theocracy tarted up with populist slogans and a Potemkin parliament (*vide* Iran). Yet a strategy of reinforcing secular police states such as Egypt's, which actively manipulates and seeks to coopt religious opinion—giving wide, state-funded scope to antidemocratic, anti-Western, and anti-Semitic extremism in the process—can have inflammatory consequences of its own. In any event, such a strategy hardly seems likely to offer even indirect help to the cause of liberal democracy or to the long-term project of building a democratic peace.

In the end, the key to helping the Muslim world escape the pincers of illiberal religious fundamentalism and illiberal secular authoritarianism will be to pursue a long-range strategy of helping Muslim societies themselves to squeeze out or erode both these malign forces. This in turn will require promoting the idea of a differentiation that gives due regard to both religious and political authority while rejecting any attempt by one to dominate or interfere unduly with the other. Obviously, such a work of persuasion will be Herculean even under the best of circumstances, and will take a long time to make its effects felt in practice. At the core of this effort must be a vast and incremental process of debate and deliberation among Muslims themselves, but it will be one which the outside world will nonetheless be able to influence through a variety of means.[1]

Voices from the Muslim world that may be described as favoring various versions of the differentiation principle also figure in the present volume. Most of these writers, including Abdou Filali-Ansary, Laith Kubba, and Radwan Masmoudi, comment from points of view sympathetic to the Islamic tradition, and see its teachings as compatible with liberal democracy. Iraq and Afghanistan could become laboratories for something like the experiment in differentiation that such authors explicitly or implicity recommend, though the outcome in both cases is of course fraught with uncertainty.[2]

And yet "differentiation" as an idea at least has the advantage of being free from the disastrous miscommunication, detailed by Abdou Filali-Ansary in the first of the three essays that he has contributed to this volume, which surrounds the terms "secular" and "secularism" in the Arab and wider Muslim worlds. Arabic is not a language in which loan words readily work. Due to an unfortunate mistranslation by a pair of nineteenth-century Muslim polemicists, explains Filali-Ansary, the word "secularism" and its variants (such as the French laïcite) have come to be understood throughout large swaths of the Arabic-speaking and larger Muslim community as simply equivalent to "atheism," "godlessness," or "irreligion." "Differentiation" is a descriptive term coined by social scientists and not a theological or political rallying cry. Yet might its exposition and even (to the extent possible) popularization not help friends of democracy in the Muslim world to steer around the shoals of confusion that now surround the word "secularism"?

One may derive hope from the thought that the process of persuasion on behalf of differentiation has succeeded before. Premodern Christianity was, as Islam is today in most places, an explicitly "public" religion that tended more to reject than to accept differentiation (even if the doctrinal and historical roots for differentiation were there and became partially actualized during episodes such as power struggles between popes and emperors). Liberal secularity, or if you like, a fully realized and widely accepted concept of differentiation, triumphed as a kind of side effect of quarrels within Christendom itself. Neither Martin Luther nor his opponents were trying to advance the cause of anything like differentiation or the twin tolerations. Indeed, Luther and his bitterest foes all wanted to restore a unified Christendom,[3] and would have been as one in rejecting other alternatives. But as so often happens, fate, fortune, providence, or whatever else may stand behind the ironic cunning of history saw to it that they built other than they knew: The struggle for religious-cum-political control in early-modern Europe became the forcing bed of the accommodation between religion and politics on which modern liberal democracy rests.

Liberal secularity, a fully realized and widely accepted concept of differentiation, trimphed as a kind of side effect of quarrels within Christendom itself.

The hope must be tempered for any student of history, however, by knowledge of how large a role violence played in all this. Luther's ninety-five theses (1517) and the response to them touched off more than a century and a quarter of savage religious warfare. By the time the Treaty of Westphalia ended most of the fighting in 1648, wolves were roaming the streets of small German cities. Commentators who speak blithely today about how Islam needs its own Luther and its own "Reformation" should perhaps be careful what they wish for. The twin tolerations were embraced, however haltingly, in the Christian West only after a terrible effusion of blood. Helping the Islamic world and its neighbors avoid such a path in an age of increasingly accessible and portable technologies of mass slaughter is surely one of the most urgent historical tasks human beings have ever faced.

The contributions to this volume by Laith Kubba, Abdou Filali-Ansary, Radwan Masmoudi, and other Muslim-world liberals suggest that the task will have to begin with a serious theological effort on the part of Muslim thinkers. Among their essential contributions will be the effort to distinguish that which is intrinsically Islamic from various historical and cultural accretions or bankrupt folkways that have become powerfully but mistakenly entangled with Islam in too many minds. These excrescences—or "baggage," as Kubba calls them—give illiberal practices such as the second-class treatment of women a false odor of sanctity for some Muslims today, but needlessly so: Islam properly understood neither licenses nor requires them, Kubba argues, and indeed should be read as condemning the injustice that they imply. An enlightened and enlarged exposition of authentic Islamic tradition *by Muslims* and for Muslims must be the first order of the day. Some sneer at Muslim liberals for being a corporal's guard too given to Western ways, but universal (that is to say, neither narrowly Western nor narrowly Muslim) principles are at stake, and small self-conscious minorities with persistence, potent arguments, and a vision have moved history before. Of course, as the Boroumands explain, the violent radicals of groups such as al-Qaeda and Hezbollah also think of themselves as a world-changing minority. For years to come, the contest between their view of Islam and the view embraced by moderate and liberal Muslims will be crucial.

The Eastern Religions

Chaibong Hahm's account of Confucianism is noteworthy not only for its psychological penetration into the core Confucian spiritual experiences and its exquisite sense of historical irony, but also for its author's affinity with Sherlock Holmes. Hahm, like Sir Arthur Conan-Doyle's famous fictional detective in the story "Silver Blaze," recognizes the importance of explaining the "curious incident" of the dog that did *not* bark in the nighttime—in this case, the absence within the Confucian cultural realm of a mass fundamentalist backlash against modernity and modernization.

The answer to this riddle, Hahm suggests, may lie in Confucianism's own lack of differentiation. As a belief system, it is not especially otherworldly or transcendental in character—some scholars consider it not a religion at all but rather an ethical system—and in its classical incarnation it was almost completely identified with East Asia's imperial and monarchical regimes.[4] When these regimes buckled under direct or indirect pressure from expanding Western influences, Confucianism's credibility as a potential source and legitimator of resistance seems to have crumbled to dust along with them. Still, the habits of loyalty and deference to authority that Confucianism had instilled into the characters of generations of Asians proved available for leveraging by the new modernizing states (beginning with Meiji Japan in the late 1860s) that arose on the ruins of the older monarchies.

Francis Fukuyama's discussion of Confucianism vindicates the central idea of much-maligned modernization theory—that economic development and the rise of a commercial middle class are good for democratization. Fukuyama also draws attention to the incipiently quasiliberal but perhaps also somewhat anarchic implications of Chinese (as opposed to Japanese) Confucianism's teaching that one should obey one's nearby father rather than the faraway emperor. Fukuyama's essay, originally published at a time of much discussion about the putatively neo-Confucian "Asian values" pushed by Singapore's official intellectuals, does not find in this now largely dormant line of thought any serious threat to the ideational dominance of modern democratic discourse in East Asia. Like Chaibong Hahm, in other words, Fukuyama is impressed by Confucianism's *lack* of a tendency to generate a fundamentalist backlash despite both that belief system's continuing influence on everyday life and human character in East Asia and the stresses of modernization that East Asians have had to endure over the last century and a half or so.

Pratap Mehta's recounting of Hinduism's dance with democracy necessarily focuses on the experience of India, which is both the world's largest democratically governed country and the home of the vast bulk of the globe's Hindu population. Choosing to take the road less traveled in essays of this sort, Mehta largely refrains from offering a catalogue of democracy-friendly or democracy-compatible Hindu religious teachings, though he does circle back to something like such an account later in his chapter. Instead, he analyzes the complex internal and external dynamics that led India's Hindu majority to embrace democratic constitutionalism in response to a crisis of authority that was political and social as well as spiritual and intellectual. Here too, the encounter with Western (in this case British) colonialism was a crucial catalyst—the sand within the oyster that called forth a pearl of creative response. Fortunately, traditional Hinduism already contained its own brand of the differentiation principle, so there was less room for disastrous misreceptions of the idea of secularism such as the one that Abdou Filali-Ansary describes in his essay "Muslims and Democracy."

Despite his affirmations of Hinduism's political moderation and capacity for creativity under pressure, Mehta is worried. He casts a concerned gaze over a Hindu India where continuing anxieties about identity and secret insecurities about the meaningfulness of traditional beliefs amid the puzzling din of the modern world are fueling a potent political movement devoted to a Hindu brand of narcissistic and illiberal identity politics. Perhaps one may take comfort in the results of India's 2004 elections, in which the party most closely associated with the politics of Hindutva ("Hinduness") lost its governing majority in the national parliament after having failed to win more than about a quarter of the national vote in any polling over the last two decades.

Taken together, the essays by the Dalai Lama of Tibet and Burma's Aung San Suu Kyi demonstrate how people reflecting from within the heart of a religious tradition (in this case Buddhism) can discern what may roughly be called liberal and consensual principles. While nobody would suggest that traditional teachings provide a full-blown theory of contemporary representative democracy, they do provide material for a powerful critique of contemporary autocracy. This is a significant achievement in any cultural context, and all the more so in regions such as East and Southeast Asia, where autocratic regimes have tried to seize the high ground of "traditional Asian values" as part of a larger effort to suggest that democratic liberalism is a foreign import that Asian peoples cannot and should not take as a template.

No observer would claim that the impediments to free self-government in Tibet and Burma have much if anything to do with religion—the former suffered invasion and conquest at the hands of Communist China, while the latter has for decades been under the heel of a kleptocratic military dictatorship that postures as a socialist regime. In the case of Tibet, moreover, the Dalai Lama, believed by many of his countrymen to be a manifestation of the Buddha of Compassion, has used his remarkable spiritual authority to advance the cause of democratic constitutionalism within the government-in-exile that he heads. He is thus not only Tibet's leading Buddhist but also its leading democrat. Remarkably, he has even leveraged his spiritual authority to insist, despite the religious qualms felt by many of his compatriots, that the constitution of Tibet's government in exile include a provision making any incumbent Dalai Lama subject to impeachment.

The Lessons of Jewish and Christian Experience

Of all the contributors to this volume, Hillel Fradkin most directly confronts the phenomenon of religion and democracy both gaining ground in world history over the last half-century or so. Taking the measure of this unexpected turn of events, he asks whether the two are intrinsically, as opposed to episodically, compatible. Searching the wisdom of the Jewish tradition, he finds sober yet not desperate counsel. The Hebrew Bible is not a democrat's handbook. Political sovereignty in its pages comes directly from God—a not altogether democratic view that is also ironically the source of the Bible's protoliberal critique of monarchy. The revelation that God hands down, moreover, is a temporally and communally binding law, not simply a personal gift of faith to individuals. And yet Fradkin locates in scripture an underlying attitude of prudence and moderation in matters political that can be read as leaving ethical space for rule by consent and according to law. The Bible seems to view politics in the way it views so many things, as a flawed enterprise reflective of human failings but also potentially useful in helping to correct or at least mitigate them. Politics as such may fall far short of the glory of God, but the Bible does not see this as grounds for indifference regarding distinctions between more and less just forms of temporal rule.

If Jews today are among the world's staunchest democrats, Fradkin suggests, it may well be because the insights gleaned from this larger political wisdom—combined with their bitter experiences as victims of persecution, genocide, and terror—have allowed them to see with special clarity not only the modest but real possibilities for betterment that liberal democracy offers, but also the abysmal boundlessness of the evils and cruelty against which liberal democracy guards.[5]

Daniel Philpott's essay examines the Catholic role in spreading democracy and challenging autocracy during the third wave of democratization. He identifies the trend toward greater differentiation that swept Catholicism in the wake of the Second Vatican Council (1962–65) as one of the factors that made the Church *more* and not less politically effective in a number of societies. These ranged from some that were heavily and historically Catholic (such as Poland and Spain) to others where Catholics were a distinct but well-organized minority (such as South Korea). Philpott finds that increased role differentiation—a church more focused on a religious mission drawn from the heart of its own theological vision and less concerned with retaining the cloak or remnants of Constantinian or neo-Constantinian establishment—led to greater Catholic effectiveness even in countries where religious observance and commitment were declining, as they have been throughout most of Europe for at least the last quarter-century.

Timothy Shah and Robert Woodberry make a strong case, drawn from quantitative evidence, that of all the religious orientations considered in this volume, Protestant Christianity has done the most to facilitate democratization. This does not mean that other religious traditions are inherently antidemocratic, or that Protestants are ipso facto democrats who have always intentionally promoted democracy. As Shah and Woodberry make clear, Protestants as old as Martin Luther, John Calvin, and Oliver Cromwell and as recent as Zambia's strongman-president Frederick Chiluba have not always been model democrats, to say the least. But the authors also document the ways in which the actions of Protestant religious groups have systematically fostered (either directly or as side-effects) literacy, mass printing, economic development, lower corruption, a sterner sense of individual accountability, a more active civil society, and other factors rightly considered to be conducive to democratization.

To give just a few examples of Protestantism as a directly and indirectly democratic force: The first polity in world history to embrace a systematic policy of opposition (including armed opposition) to slavery and the slave trade was the British Empire in the early nineteenth century. A substantial number of influential Britons had of course long profited from slavery and did not necessarily want to see this change, but they were outlobbied by abolitionist groups that were overwhelmingly and fervently Protestant in nature. The existence of nongovernmental or civil society groups around the globe can be traced to the influence of Protestant missionaries, who both founded such groups to press their favored reforms and stimulated their opponents to form groups of their own (much of the Hindu activism that Pratap Mehta describes was a response to British missionaries' efforts to challenge older Indian practices such as widow-burning and "untouchability").

Shah and Woodberry provide striking figures on the recent and quite amazing growth of Protestantism across the postcolonial global South. The Protestant share of the combined populations of Africa, Asia, and Latin America grew by almost 1,000 percent between 1900 and 2000, for instance, with most of the increase coming during the century's latter decades. But much of this expansion was the work of newer Pentecostal bodies rather than classical Protestant churches, the authors point out, and it remains to be seen precisely what effects Pentecostalism (which differs from older forms of Protestantism in significant ways) will tend to exert on democratization in countries where Pentecostal communities thrive.

In their analyses of Christianity, both Philpott and Shah and Woodberry tell stories that began around the middle of the seventeenth century and reached major points of inflection beginning in or around the 1960s: In the case of Catholicism, the clearly significant turnabout was the Second Vatican Council's embrace of democracy and human rights as belonging to the Gospel message. In the Protestant case, the turn—whose full effects remain unknown—was the shift of the demographic center of gravity to the global South,[6] where democracy's prospects seem far less certain than they do in the northwestern quarter of the globe that forms the native soil of classical Protestantism.

No such timeline can be cited in relation to the journey of Eastern Orthodox Christianity. As Elizabeth Prodromou recounts its itinerary, this third-largest of the four main streams of world Christianity (the fourth is a relatively small and doctrinally distinct branch of Orthodoxy whose experience roughly parallels that of the Eastern Orthodox) has had little historical experience living under democratic conditions, has endured centuries of life under the oppressive rule of non-Christian or aggressively atheistic conquerors, and is apt to find some forms of democratic pluralism unsettling if not downright unfair. And yet her sober analysis is far from gloomy. One draws from it the sense that Orthodoxy is now living uneasily but hopefully through the early stages of a turn toward a more robust accommodation with democracy. Except for those Orthodox believers who lived in the West, no Orthodox Christian population outside of Greece had much or any experience of full-fledged liberal democracy. More of the ice melted in 1989–91, when communism collapsed across Eastern Europe and the former USSR. Since then, some Orthodox authorities have begun to worry about Catholic and Protestant missionary activities in historically Orthodox lands, leading to some of the statism and suspicion of pluralism that Prodromou outlines. But there is nothing like a mass-scale fundamentalist reaction against democracy by Orthodox believers, and one may expect that the larger tide will be toward more rather than less acceptance of democracy and pluralism (including free religious activity) by this wing of Christianity.

Peter Berger, a leading critic of conventional secularization theory among sociologists, sums up the three essays devoted to Christianity by agreeing that Catholicism and Protestantism are hospitable to democracy, and that Orthodoxy is moving, albeit grudgingly, in the same direction. Berger further implies that the basic Protestant view of religious belonging as a species of free association and faith as an individual choice adumbrates the paradigmatic transformation that all religions must undergo (or somehow discover from within their own resources) if they are to exist in something more than an uneasy truce with modern democratic society. This inevitably angers some traditional believers, notes Berger, and understandably so. They see their coreligionists becoming implicitly and functionally "protestantized" (that is, individualistic and voluntaristic in spiritual matters), formal doctrines and official communal self-understandings to the contrary notwithstanding.

Since most world religions, and certainly all the three monotheisms, consider human choice an important but emphatically less than supreme value (it must remain subject to the higher moral order mandated by divine or natural law, for instance), one can sense the tensions that even the quiet and gradual rise of a choice-based attitude toward religion can create. While none of the world religions is intrinsically and absolutely opposed to liberal democracy, it may also be noted that 1) there are various forms of or approaches to each of these religions; 2) not all forms or approaches are equally compatible with democracy; and 3) while it may be impolitic to say this, one form—the functionally "protestantized" kind—may be the most compatible of all, though other approaches may be minimally or moderately compatible as well.

Islam

Islam, as Ernest Gellner once argued, seems to display what might be described as certain broad streaks of intrinsic "protestantization." As Gellner put it:

> The high culture form of Islam is endowed with a number of features—unitarianism, a rule-ethic, individualism, scripturalism, puritanism, an egalitarian aversion to mediation and hierarchy, a fairly small load of magic—that are congruent, presumably, with the requirements of modernity and modernisation.[7]

The question then arises, as Abdou Filali-Ansary points out, as to how Islam wound up at one end of what appears to be a "dynamic of polarization," with democracy or modernity at the other. Islam has features of a "public" religion that makes strong and not necessarily democratic political claims, but it is not historically unique in this regard. Much the same could be said in principle of Judaism and Christianity, and before the current Dalai Lama's reforms Tibetan Buddhism was overtly theocratic. Then too, readers will find in Radwan Masmoudi's sympathetic exposition of the "four pillars of liberal Islam" a reading of the Islamic tradition from within that emphasizes the intellectual support it can provide to "limited government, individual liberty, human dignity, and human rights."

If Gellner and Masmoudi are correct that the answer cannot lie primarily at the doctrinal or structural level, then one must look to the historical or conjunctural level. The essays by not only Filali-Ansary and Masmoudi but also Bernard Lewis, Robin Wright, Abdelwahab El-Affendi, Laith Kubba, and Ladan and Roya Boroumand may be understood as contributions to such an inquiry. Some were written before and some after the terrorist attacks of 11 September 2001, but all focus on the recent past as the place to search for an explanation of, to borrow the title of a post-9/11 book by Lewis, "what went wrong" and what might be done to fix it.

Among the ideas proposed are: encourage internal reformers (Wright); rehabilitate the ideas of Islamic protoliberals such as Ibn Khaldun and Averroës (Filali-Ansary); insist on firm distinctions between what actually belongs to the core of Islamic tradition and what has been taken on over the centuries as un-Islamic and needlessly illiberal baggage (Kubba); stop pretending that one must resolve every thorny theological-political issue right away and focus instead on pragmatic reformist politics as the "art of the possible" (El-Affendi); realize and convey to Muslims the understanding that radical Islamism has more to do with the widespread modern phenomenon of violent, totalitarian illiberalism—with "the spread of bad ideas"[8] from outside the Muslim world—than with anything genuinely "religious" (the Boroumands). None of these is a cure-all, of course, but the problem seems large enough to offer more than one handle, and if a complex but not especially ancient series of conceptual mistakes and misunderstandings is behind at least some of the political troubles in the broader Middle East today, then the unraveling might as well begin with the advocacy of better understandings in the here and now.

A Muslim Democratic Model?

The auguries for improved understanding and discourse might even be warily described as potentially somewhat favorable, at least in principle. An opening could come in Turkey, a country that has long been a site of creative contact as well as destructive conflict between the Muslim world and the West. Today, a politician who has a record of democratic vote-getting and who hails from an Islamic-inspired political party heads a large parliamentary majority and directs the government of the Turkish Republic, the Muslim world's original and still most assertively secular state. In rhetoric that seems to gesture at the West European Christian Democratic tradition, Turkey's Prime Minister Reccep Tayyip Erdoğan has spoken of his own Justice and Development Party (AKP) as a formation of "conservative" (which some commentators take to mean "Muslim"[9]) democrats who are eager to lead Turkey toward membership in the European Union.[10] Although those who accuse the AKP of engaging in tactical dissimulation while secretly harboring a typical Islamist agenda may not yet have made a convincing case, it would be naïve to deny that the AKP contains significant elements that reject the principle of differentiation and do so on what they see as Islamic grounds.

Whether Erdoğan has the will and the ability decisively to resist pro-Islamization pressure from these elements remains to be seen. And even one who believes that Erdoğan is a sincere democrat and not a "stealth" Islamist may wish that he would go farther toward making the case for a full and principled embrace of differentiation in the Islamic context. This might involve explaining systematically that while he and his party seek to moderate the aggressive "command" aspect of classical Kemalist secularism, they also insist on a due differentiation that instills respect for the distinct aims and freedoms of both religious and political life in a free and self-governing society. Differentiation, or secularism rightly understood, would indeed mean a certain kind of benign abstraction from religion by public authorities, but not its denial or confutation, as some might fear.

While among those who are fearful on behalf of religion there surely exists a significant minority of hard-core extremists who will never accept such a "differentiation-friendly" account of Islam and politics, the leeway for persuasion may be larger than many think: In Muslim-majority countries outside the Arab League—that is, in the countries where nearly all the recent competitive electoral activity in the Muslim world has been taking place—militant Islamism has shown itself to be of distinctly limited appeal at the polls. While Islamist outreach, schooling, and organizational efforts (often funded by Saudi and Gulf-region oil money) remain formidable, it may still be possible to convince large numbers of Muslims to make the principle of differentiation (and with it, the twin tolerations) a basic operating assumption in a way that is simply not the case at this time,[11] whatever one believes about the notional possibility of an authentic accommodation between Islam and democratic liberalism on the level of doctrine.

Turkish prime minister Erdoğan's choice of rhetoric that seems to gesture at a comparison of his party with the Christian Democratic, center-right tradition of Europe suggests that he may intuit—or feel the need to speak at times as if he intuits—something like a point that Daniel Philpott makes in his essay on Catholicism. Philpott argues that role differentiation, far from representing a simple surrender of religion's influence, can actually open the way to an *increase* in the efficacy of religious people and institutions. With his eyes still on the prize of entry into the European Union, might Erdoğan not do even more to counsel Muslims in his native Turkey and elsewhere who feel drawn to political life that the path of differentiation—a path that is neither illiberally secular nor Islamist—is a viable route for them to travel?

What might such a path be like? To give one example, traveling it would of course mean continuing to reject any idea of making *shari'a* into public law (something that Turkey's chastened but still potent Kemalist establishment rejects and that the AKP says it does not want anyway). But it might also mean working to change the current state policy, dating back to Kemal Atatürk and the founding of the modern Turkish Republic, under which the government's ministry of religious affairs sets the content of Friday sermons in mosques across the country. One policy is Islamist, the other is illberally secularist. Under the twin tolerations, both would be unacceptable.

To the east of Turkey and its citizens, and like them numbering about 70 million, the people of Iran may be mentally ready—if not yet practically able—to steer their country down the path toward differentiation. Iranians have now suffered a quarter-century of life under an Islamist police state, the negative example of which may have already done more than any mere argument could to persuade them of the virtues of putting distance between religious authority and political power.[12]

The case for the twin tolerations might also be bolstered if opinion leaders and publics throughout the Muslim world can be brought to take more seriously the degree of de facto but theoretically undigested secularization that already characterizes Muslim-majority societies. As Abdou Filali-Ansary points out, the Muslim world today comprises nation-states with bureaucracies, political parties, secular legal codes that cover a vast range of circumstances and matters not compassed by *shari'a* (which was never meant to be public law in the full sense of the word anyway), state-run educational systems, and populations who expect their lot to be self-rule and material betterment rather than the premodern staples of all-pervading hierarchy, mute resignation, and eschatological hope.

Filali-Ansary's first essay contributes to this effort by elegantly unwinding the sad skein of confusions, begun by the traumatic nineteenth-century encounter with European colonialism, which has led to the rise of Islamism. Today, demands for the adoption of *shari'a* as public law are a hallmark of illiberal Islamists everywhere. But as Filali-Ansary explains, outside of matters concerning personal status (regarding which clerics felt they could build prescriptive systems based on what they saw as unambiguous Koranic mandates), *shari'a* in its original, medieval form was intended more as a repository of learned ethical discussions about what it means to be a good Muslim than as a full-fledged set of laws. Moreover, it was meant not as an ideal mark of some rigidly perfect Islamic state or as a license to set up dictatorships of the putatively virtuous, but rather as a "second-best" attempt to place at least some sacred limits on the willfulness and powers of the despots who dominated so many Muslim lands.

How this ancient prudential effort to raise ethical, religious, and quasilegal barriers against abuses of power became a latter-day blank check for the likes of the Taliban and the Saudi religious police is a sad story of intellectual trauma and distortion that has left Muslims who wish to make the case for differentiation with a much steeper hill to climb than would otherwise have been the case. Filali-Ansary does a noble job of leveling this hill in speech; one suspects that bringing the false eminence low in deed will be more difficult, but if thoughts are fathers to actions then his scholarly bulldozing is a good start.

Faith and Freedom: Resurgent but Mutually Uneasy?

Hillel Fradkin's concluding essay, with its reflections on Tocqueville's treatment of religion and democracy in the American experience, sounds a note of caution. Fradkin asks whether transcendent spirituality and modern demotic societies (meaning any society based on a populist theory of legitimation, whether or not it is a full-fledged liberal democracy) are really naturally and unproblematically in harmony with one another. Many democrats and many religious people—who may often be one and the same—would without doubt and quite honorably like to believe that this is so. But is it? Fradkin suggests that the spirit of democracy and the spirit of religion will not in fact be found on the same wavelength most of the time. Democracy is by and large latitudinarian, prone to level distinctions of various kinds, none too respectful of traditional authority, and mostly concerned with the worldly present and future. Traditional religion, by contrast, usually emphasizes hierarchy, received wisdom, the normative character of past events held to be sacred, and the future conceived as a subject for eschatological hopes, not schemes of continuing temporal improvement (which may even be condemned for rejecting sacred limits).

This cautionary comparison suggests that the current resilience or resurgence of democracy and the currently rising saliency of religion that we see around the world are distinct and even somewhat contradictory effects that may nonetheless spring from the same substrate of causes. The complex and even bewildering circumstances of modern life, as many observers have noted, have a leveling and disintegrative character that can breed intense social, intellectual, and spiritual anxieties. Against these gnawing discontents, a renewed, adaptive, and self-conscious religious traditionalism can seem like a bulwark. This may be especially so in the case of people, like many of those now dwelling in the vast new conurbations of the global South, who are only a generation or so removed from far more traditional rural or village-based modes of living. These older and relatively constricted ways of life imposed hardships of their own, no doubt, but also offered certitudes that modern, urban, democratic life is hard-pressed to supply.

In this view, the renewed public prominence of religion appears as a backlash against a larger modernizing and secularizing or differentiating trend to which democratization belongs. One problem with this view is that not all of the new manifestations of public religion are inherently antidemocratic. Some such manifestations (the Taliban movement and other forms of violent Islamism, certain strains of Hindu nationalism, or the tiny Christian "theonomist" movement in the United States) plainly are hostile to liberal democracy. Others, such as Protestant Pentecostalism in Latin America, present a mixed picture. Still others, such as the activism of the Roman Catholic Church since the Second Vatican Council, have plainly favored constitutional democracy.

If religion and democracy are in tension—each ready, at least in theory, to step over the other's "red lines" in the name of its own special claims—is that always necessarily bad? Reading Fradkin suggests a final irony. A religion that conforms too easily to the characteristic prejudices and leanings of democracy—perhaps not least because generations of life under such an egalitarian and permissive regime have worn away the sharper edges of religious asceticism, otherworldliness, and doctrine—may be of less benefit to democracy than a religion that harbors reserves of unease and criticism toward democratic life, even while abjuring any thought of trying to undermine or overthrow liberal democracy in the name of some more virtuous form of commonwealth. A too-smooth religion may even lose altogether its capacity to help sustain democracy by pushing against democratic societies' ordinary penchants for easygoing intellectual and moral latitudinarianism and individualism, as well as such societies' tendency to become engrossed by present pleasures in a world where alarms still sound and where democracy requires not merely supine enjoyment, but active defense in the moral and intellectual as well as the practical realm.

Even here, however, the idea of differentiation may help to guide our thinking, for does it not suggest that a religion too at ease under democracy is by that very token too lacking in differentiation as well? Keeping religion and politics properly differentiated and not too entangled is a subtle and two-way business, in other words, and has implications that go well beyond legal provisions or high-profile public controversies and reach down to the level of the crucial spiritual, moral, and intellectual habits that form a people fit for self-government.

NOTES

1. As Fareed Zakaria has suggested, the West could exert a positive influence simply by pressing harder on regimes such as those in Saudi Arabia and Egypt to

end their support—unofficial as well as official—for Islamic radicalism and extremist incitement generally. See Fareed Zakaria, "Islam, Democracy, and
Constitutional Liberalism," *Political Science Quarterly* 119 (Spring 2004): 15–16.

2. On the new post-Taliban constitution of Afghanistan and the ambiguities it
contains with regard to Islam and various questions of rights, see Barnett R.
Rubin, "Crafting a Constitution for Afghanistan," *Journal of Democracy* 15 (July
2004): 5–19. As Rubin points out, the Afghan judiciary remains dominated by
ulama (Islamic scholars) who have been left in place for largely pragmatic reasons. The predominance of such a group among Afghanistan's judges is a
worrisome portent for those who hope to see the principle of differentiation gain
a purchase in that country, so recently freed from the burden of an especially
odious tyranny rooted in the fanatical rejection of any distinction between religious and political authority.

3. As Professor Vali Nasr of the U.S. Naval Postgraduate School points out,
many Islamists today similarly oppose the traditional authorities of their own religious world and do so in service (as the Islamists see it) to the cause of restoring the
Islamists' own preferred version of a politically and religiously unified "Islamdom,"
which they call the caliphate. Personal e-mail correspondence with author, 14
September 2004.

4. As Chaibong Hahm explains, this situation itself concealed a large irony,
since Confucianism originated as a kind of first philosophy for marginalized intellectuals and only became an official court belief system and basis for the education
of rulers several centuries after its founder's death (circa 479 B.C.E.).

5. The great German-American Protestant theologian Reinhold Niebuhr (1892–
1971) expressed a similar thought reflective of Biblical insight when he famously
wrote—at the time of the Holocaust and the Second World War—that "Man's
capacity for justice makes democracy possible, but man's inclination to injustice
makes democracy necessary." *The Children of Light and the Children of Darkness:
A Vindication of Democracy and a Critique of Its Traditional Defense* (New York:
Scribner's, 1944), foreword.

6. A similar trend has occurred in Catholicism, but that church's greater centralization and global system of organization may dampen the effects of such a shift.

7. Quoted by Samuel P. Huntington, "Democracy's Third Wave," in Marc F.
Plattner and Larry Diamond, eds., *The Global Resurgence of Democracy* (Baltimore: Johns Hopkins University Press, 1993), 19.

8. Ian Buruma and Avishai Margalit, *Occidentalism: The West in the Eyes of Its
Enemies* (New York: Penguin, 2004).

9. For an example of such a comment, see Radwan A. Masmoudi, "A Victory
for the Cause of Islamic Democracy: An American Muslim Analyzes the Surprise
Election in Turkey," available at *www.beliefnet.com/story/116/story_11673_1.html.*

10. Speaking through an interpreter at a public forum hosted by the American
Enterprise Institute in Washington, D.C., on 29 January 2004, Erdoğan referred to
"conservative" rather than "Muslim" democracy. But he also said, "Turkey's democratization is a self-imposed process. . . . the result of the free choice of the
predominantly Muslim Turkish society. I do not claim, of course, that Turkey's
experience is a model that can be implemented identically in all other Muslim
societies. However, the Turkish experience does have a substance which can serve
as a source of inspiration for other Muslim societies, other Muslim peoples."
See *www.aei.org/events/filter.,eventID.735/transcript.asp*; and also the impressions
of Erdoğan and his ideas recorded by a Western journalist familiar with Turkey in
Stephen Kinzer, "Will Turkey Make It?" *New York Review of Books,* 15 July 2004.

Also worth consulting is Soli Özel, "Turkey at the Polls: After the Tsunami," *Journal of Democracy* 14 (April 2003): 80–94.

11. Indeed, Professor Nasr notes, "Modern Islamic thought is more emphatic" than earlier Islamic thought in "rejecting differentiation," which suggests that "modernization has increased rather than decreased Islam's rejection of 'differentiation.'" Personal e-mail correspondence with author, 14 September 2004.

12. One might also posit that support for differentiation in a future Iran could flow from the greater traditional readiness of Shi'ite Muslims to accept the idea that there should be a distinct space between religion and political rule. There are still Iranian ayatollahs, for instance, who reject the late Ayatollah Khomeini's notion of "the supremacy of the Islamic jurist" as a novelty that goes against the relatively "quietist" mainstream of Shi'ite thought.

I

A Conceptual Framework

1

RELIGION, DEMOCRACY, AND THE "TWIN TOLERATIONS"

Alfred Stepan

Alfred Stepan, *Wallace Sayre Professor of Government at Columbia University, is coauthor with Juan J. Linz of* Problems of Democratic Transition and Consolidation: Southern Europe, South America, and Post-Communist Europe *(1996). A much longer and more extensively annotated version of this essay appeared in his book,* Arguing Comparative Politics *(2001).*

Are all, or only some, of the world's religious systems politically compatible with democracy? This is, of course, one of the most important and heatedly debated questions of our times. My goal is to contribute to this debate from the perspective of comparative politics. More specifically, as a specialist in political institutions and democratization, I intend to discuss three questions, the answers to which should improve our understanding of this critical issue.

First, what are the minimal institutional and political requirements that a polity must satisfy before it can be considered a democracy? Building on this analysis, what can we then infer about the need for the "twin tolerations"—that is, the minimal boundaries of freedom of action that must somehow be crafted for political institutions vis-à-vis religious authorities, and for religious individuals and groups vis-à-vis political institutions?

Second, how have a set of longstanding democracies—the 15 countries in the European Union (EU)—actually met these requirements, and what influential misinterpretations of the Western European experience with religion and democracy must we avoid?

Third, what are the implications of the answers to our first two questions for polities heavily influenced by such cultural and religious traditions as Confucianism,[1] Islam, and Eastern Orthodox Christianity—traditions that some analysts, starting from a civilizational as opposed to an institutional perspective, see as presenting major obstacles to democracy?

Before addressing these three questions, let me briefly give some quotations from Samuel P. Huntington's *The Clash of Civilizations and the Remaking of World Order,* an exceedingly influential statement of a civilizational perspective that represents a major competing perspective to my own institutional approach.

Huntington gives primacy of place to Christianity as the distinctive positive influence in the making of Western civilization: "Western Christianity . . . is historically the single most important characteristic of Western civilization."[2] For Huntington, Western culture's key contribution has been the separation of church and state, something that he sees as foreign to the world's other major religious systems. "In Islam," Huntington says, "God is Caesar; in [Confucianism,] Caesar is God; in Orthodoxy, God is Caesar's junior partner." After arguing that "kin cultures" increasingly support each other in "civilizational fault-line" conflicts and developing a scenario of a religiously driven World War III, Huntington warns: "The underlying problem for the West is not Islamic fundamentalism. It is Islam." Regarding Confucianism, he asserts that contemporary China's "Confucian heritage, with its emphasis on authority, order, hierarchy, and supremacy of the collectivity over the individual, creates obstacles to democratization." In discussing post-communist Europe, he says that "the central dividing line . . . is now the line separating the people of Western Christianity, on the one hand, from Muslim and Orthodox peoples on the other." He asks rhetorically, "Where does Europe end?" and answers, "Where Western Christianity ends and Islam and Orthodoxy begin."[3]

For Huntington, civilizations, not states, are now the key units, and he argues that due to the growing importance of "kin cultures" and "civilizational fault-line conflicts," the world's religious civilizations are increasingly unitary and change-resistant. Clearly, a central thrust of Huntington's message is not only that democracy emerged *first* within Western civilization but that the other great religious civilizations of the world lack the unique bundle of cultural characteristics necessary to support Western-style democracy.

If we approach the issue from an institutionalist perspective, will we arrive at a different view of the probable cultural boundaries of democracy?

Democracy and Core Institutions

All important theorists of democratization accept that a necessary condition for completing a successful transition to democracy is free and contested elections of the sort discussed by Robert A. Dahl in his classic book *Polyarchy*. Among the requirements for democracy, Dahl includes the opportunity to formulate and signify preferences and to have these preferences weighed adequately in the conduct of government. For these conditions to be satisfied, Dahl argues that eight institutional guarantees are required: 1) freedom to form and to join organizations; 2) freedom of expression; 3) the right to vote; 4) eligibility for public office; 5) the right of political leaders to compete for support and votes; 6) alternative sources of information; 7) free and fair elections; and 8) institutions for making government policies depend on votes and other expressions of preference.[4]

My colleague Juan J. Linz and I have argued that Dahl's eight guarantees are necessary but not sufficient conditions of democracy. They are insufficient because no matter how free and fair the elections and no matter how large the government's majority, democracy must also have a constitution that itself is democratic in that it respects fundamental liberties and offers considerable protections for minority rights. Furthermore, the democratically elected government must rule within the confines of its constitution and be bound by the law and by a complex set of vertical and horizontal institutions that help to ensure accountability.

If we combine these criteria, it is clear that democracy should not be considered consolidated in a country unless there is the opportunity for the development of a robust and critical civil society that helps check the state and constantly generates alternatives. For such civil-society alternatives to be aggregated and implemented, political society, and especially political parties, should be allowed unfettered relations with civil society.

Democracy is a system of conflict regulation that allows open competition over the values and goals that citizens want to advance. In the strict democratic sense, this means that as long as groups do not use violence, do not violate the rights of other citizens, and stay within the rules of the democratic game, *all* groups are granted the right to advance their interests, both in civil society and in political society. This is the minimal institutional statement of what democratic politics does and does not entail.[5]

What does this institutional "threshold" approach imply about religion, politics, democracy, and the "twin tolerations"? Specifically, what are the necessary boundaries of freedom for elected governments from religious groups, and for religious individuals and groups from government?

Democratic institutions must be free, within the bounds of the constitution and human rights, to generate policies. Religious institutions should not have constitutionally privileged prerogatives that allow them to mandate public policy to democratically elected governments. At the same time, individuals and religious communities, consistent with our institutional definition of democracy, must have complete freedom to worship privately. In addition, as individuals and groups, they must be able to advance their values publicly in civil society and to sponsor organizations and movements in political society, as long as their actions do not impinge negatively on the liberties of other citizens or violate democracy and the law. This institutional approach to democracy necessarily implies that no group in civil society—including religious groups—can *a priori* be prohibited from forming a political party. Constraints on political parties may only be imposed *after* a party, by its actions, violates democratic principles. The judgment as to whether or not a party has violated democratic principles should be decided not by parties in the government but by the courts. Within this broad framework of minimal freedom for the democratic state and minimal religious freedom for citizens, an extraordinarily broad range of concrete patterns of religious-state relations would meet our minimal definition of a democracy.

Let us explore this argument further by moving to our second question. Empirically, what are the actual patterns of relations between religion and the state in longstanding democracies? How have the "twin tolerations" of freedom for democratically elected governments and freedom for religious organizations in civil and political society been constructed in specific democratic polities?

Western Europe and the Twin Tolerations

How should one read the "lessons" of the historical relationship between Western Christianity and democracy? Here I would like to call particular attention to four possible misinterpretations. *Empirically,* we should beware of simple assertions about the actual existence of "separation of church and state" or the necessity of "secularism." *Doctrinally,* we should beware of assuming that any of the world's religious systems are univocally democratic or nondemocratic. *Methodologically,* we should beware of what I will call the "fallacy of unique founding conditions." And *normatively,* we should beware of the liberal injunction, famously argued by the most influential contemporary political philosopher in the English language, John Rawls, to "take the truths of religion off the political agenda."[6]

When discussing the prospects for democracy in non-Western, "non-Christian" civilizations, analysts frequently assume that the separation of church and state and secularism are core features not only of Western democracy, but of democracy itself. For such analysts, a religious system such as Eastern Orthodoxy—where there is often an established church—poses major problems for the consolidation of democracy. Similarly, when an Islamic-based government came to power in Turkey in 1996, there were frequent references to the threat that this presented to Western-style secular democracy. Indeed, military encroachments on the autonomy of the democratically elected government in Turkey have frequently been viewed as an unfortunate necessity to protect secular democracy. Are these correct readings or dangerous misreadings of the lessons of the relationship of church and state in Western democracies?

To answer this question, let us undertake an empirical analysis of the degree to which the separation of church and state actually exists in a specific set of Western countries, all of which for the last decade have satisfied Dahl's eight institutional guarantees and the additional conditions for a democracy that I have stipulated, and have socially and politically constructed the "twin tolerations." First, we should note that, as of 1990, five of the EU's 15 member states—Denmark, Finland, Greece, Sweden, and the United Kingdom (in England and Scotland)—had established churches. Norway, although not in the EU, is another European democracy with an established church. In fact, until 1995, *every* longstanding West European democracy with a strong Lutheran majority (Sweden, Denmark, Iceland, Finland and Norway) had an established church. Only Sweden has begun a process of disestablishing the Lutheran church.

The Netherlands does not have an established church. Yet as a result of heated conflict among Catholics, Calvinists, and secularizing liberal governments over the role of the church in education, the country arrived in 1917 at a politically negotiated "consociational" settlement of this issue. It permits local communities, if they are overwhelmingly of one specific religious community, to choose to have their local school be a private Calvinist or a private Catholic school *and* to have it receive state support.

Germany and Austria have constitutional provisions in their federal systems allowing local communities to decide on the role of religion in education. Germany does not have an established church, but Protestantism and Catholicism are recognized as official religions. German taxpayers, unless they elect to pay a 9 percent surcharge to their tax bill in the form of a Church tax *(Kirchensteuer)* and thereby officially become a member of the church *(Mitglied der Kirche),* do not have the automatic right to be baptized, married, or buried in their denominational church or, in some cases, may find it difficult to gain easy access to the church hospitals or old-age homes that receive state support from the *Kirchensteuer*. Thus the vast majority of citizens in the former West Germany paid the state-collected church tax.

What do contemporary West European constitutions and normal political practice indicate about the role of religious parties in government? Despite what Western analysts may think about the impropriety of religious-based parties ruling in a secular democracy like Turkey, Christian Democratic parties have frequently ruled in Germany, Austria, Italy, Belgium, and the Netherlands. The *only* EU member state whose constitution prohibits political parties from using religious affiliations or symbols is Portugal. Yet I should make two observations about this apparent anomaly. First, the article prohibiting the use of religious symbols by political parties in Portugal is a nondemocratic holdover from the constitution drafted in 1976 by a Constituent Assembly under heavy pressure from the revolutionary Armed Forces Movement and later revised (in 1982) to conform with democratic standards. Second, Portugal has a de facto Christian Democratic Party, the Centro Democrático Social, which operates with full political freedom and is a member in good standing of all the international Christian Democratic organizations.

TABLE 1—THE "TWIN TOLERATIONS"
VARIETIES OF DEMOCRATIC PATTERNS OF RELIGIOUS-STATE RELATIONS

RELATIVELY STABLE PATTERNS			RELATIVELY UNSTABLE PATTERNS
SECULAR, BUT FRIENDLY TO RELIGION	NONSECULAR, BUT FRIENDLY TO DEMOCRACY	SOCIOLOGICALLY SPONTANEOUS SECULARISM	VERY UNFRIENDLY SECULARISM LEGISLATED BY MAJORITY, BUT REVERSIBLE BY MAJORITY
No official religion. Full separation of church and state. No state monies for religious education or organizations. Private religious schools allowed if they conform to normal academic standards. Full private and public freedom for all religions as long as they do not violate individual liberties. Religious organizations allowed to minister to their followers inside state organizations (such as the military and state hospitals). Religious groups allowed full participation in civil society. Organizations and parties related to religious groups allowed to compete for power in political society.	Established church receives state subsidies, and some official religion taught in state schools (but nonreligious students do not have to take religious courses). Official religion accorded no constitutional or quasiconstitutional prerogatives to mandate significant policies. Citizens can elect to have "church tax" sent to a secular institution. Nonofficial religion allowed full freedom and can receive some state monies. All religious groups can participate in civil society. All religious groups can compete for power in political society.	Society largely "disenchanted" and religion not an important factor in political life. Democratically elected officials under no significant pressures to comply with religious dictates concerning their public policy decisions. All religious groups free to organize civil society and to compete for political power, but have little weight or salience.	Antireligious tone in most state regulations (for example, teaching of religion forbidden in state *and* non–state-supported schools; no chaplains of any religion allowed in military organizations or state hospitals). Significant percentage of believers "semiloyal" or disloyal to regime.

In the twentieth century, probably the two most "hostile" separations of church and state in Western Europe occurred in 1931 in Spain and in 1905 in France. Both of these countries, however, now have a "friendly" separation of church and state. In fact, since 1958, the French government has paid a substantial part of the cost of the Catholic Church's elementary school system. Virtually no Western European democracy now has a rigid or hostile separation of church and state. Most have arrived at a democratically negotiated freedom of religion from state interference, and all of them allow religious groups freedom not only to worship privately but to organize groups in civil society and political society. The "lesson" from Western Europe, therefore, lies *not* in the need for a "wall of separation" between church and state but in the constant political construction and reconstruction of the "twin tolerations." Indeed, it is only in the context of the "twin tolerations" that the concept of "separation of church and state" has a place in the modern vocabulary of West European democracy.

A similar caveat should be borne in mind concerning the concept of "secularism." Discursive traditions as dissimilar as the Enlightenment, liberalism, French republicanism, and modernization theory have all argued (or assumed) that modernity and democracy require secularism.

TABLE 2—THE "TWIN INTOLERATIONS"
VARIETIES OF NONDEMOCRATIC PATTERNS OF RELIGIOUS-STATE RELATIONS

STATE PRECLUDES NECESSARY DEGREE OF AUTONOMY FOR RELIGION IN POLITICS		RELIGIOUS GROUPS PRECLUDE NECESSARY DEGREE OF AUTONOMY FOR A DEMOCRATIC GOVERNMENT	
GOVERNMENT-IMPOSED ATHEISTIC SECULARISM	RELIGION CONTROLLED BY ELECTED GOVERNMENT OR QUASIDEMOCRATIC CONSTITUTIONALLY EMBEDDED PROCEDURES	ELECTED GOVERNMENT'S POLICIES SUBJECT TO VETO BY NONELECTED RELIGIOUS OFFICIALS	THEOCRATIC ANTISECULARISM
Right of private worship is forbidden or highly controlled. Right of religious groups to participate in civil society denied. Right of religious groups to compete for power in political society denied. No competitive elections held.	Virtually unamendable constitution declares state secular and gives state officials a major role in regulating public expression of religion. Right of religious groups to actively participate in civil society constitutionally subject to unilateral state control or prohibition. Right of organizations or parties related to religious groups to compete for power in political society constitutionally denied. Relatively competitive elections normally held. Right of private worship is respected.	Constitutional or quasi-constitutional prerogatives accorded to nonelected religious groups to mandate significant policies to democratically elected authorities. Virtually unamendable constitution declares official religion. Official religion receives state subsidies. Competitive elections regularly held. Right of private worship is respected.	Demos cannot participate in selection of highest religious authorities (and thus the highest political authority does not emanate from, and is not responsible to, democratic procedures). No permissible area of private or public life allowed that does not conform to dominant religion. Fusion of religious and political power under religious control.

From the viewpoint of empirical democratic practice, however, the concept of secularism must be radically rethought. At the very least, serious analysts must acknowledge, as Tables 1 and 2 make clear, that secularism and the separation of church and state have no inherent affinity with democracy, and indeed can be closely related to nondemocratic forms that systematically violate the twin tolerations.

The categories in Tables 1 and 2 are not meant to be exhaustive or mutually exclusive, but simply to convey the range of democratic and nondemocratic state-religious patterns. They show that there can be democratic and nondemocratic secularism, democracies with established churches, and even democracies with a "very unfriendly" separation of church and state. One obviously could develop many other categories. My central analytic point stands, however. If we are looking for the defining characteristics of democracy vis-à-vis religion, "secularism" and the "separation of church and state" are not an intrinsic part of the core definition, but the "twin tolerations" are.

More Misinterpretations

Building upon our reading of the empirical context of such phrases as "separation of church and state" and "secularism," we are in a position to see why we should beware of three other major misinterpretations.

1) The assumption of univocality. We should beware of assuming that any religion's doctrine is univocally prodemocratic or antidemocratic. Western Christianity has certainly been *multivocal* concerning democracy and the twin tolerations. At certain times in its history, Catholic doctrine has been marshalled to oppose liberalism, the nation-state, tolerance, and democracy. In the name of Catholicism, the Inquisition committed massive human rights violations. John Calvin's Geneva had no space either for inclusive citizenship or for any form of representative democracy. For more than 300 years, Lutheranism, particularly in Northern Germany, accepted both theologically and politically what Max Weber called "caesaropapist" state control of religion.[7]

Extrapolating from these historical situations, numerous articles and books were written on the inherent obstacles that Catholicism, Lutheranism, or Calvinism place in the way of democracy because of their antidemocratic doctrines and nondemocratic practices. Later, of course, spiritual and political activists of all these faiths found and mobilized doctrinal elements within their own religions to help them craft new practices supportive of tolerance and democracy.

The warning we should take away from this brief discussion is obvious. When we consider the question of non-Western religions and their relationship to democracy, it would seem appropriate not to assume univocality but to explore whether these doctrines contain *multivocal* components that are *usable* for (or at least *compatible* with) the political construction of the twin tolerations.

2) The fallacy of "unique founding conditions." This fallacy involves the assumption that the unique constellation of specific conditions that were present at the birth of such phenomena as electoral democracy, a relatively independent civil society, or the spirit of capitalism must be present in all cases if they are to thrive. The fallacy, of course, is to confuse the conditions associated with the invention of something with the possibility of its replication, or more accurately, its *reformulation* under different conditions. Whatever we may think about Max Weber's thesis in *The Protestant Ethic and The Spirit of Capitalism,* no one who has carefully observed Korea, Taiwan, or Hong Kong would deny that these polities have created their own dynamic form of capitalism.[8] We should beware of falling into the fallacy of "unique founding conditions" when we examine whether polities strongly influenced by Confucianism, Hinduism, Orthodoxy, or Islam can emulate or recreate, using some of their own distinctive cultural resources, a form of democracy that would meet the minimal institutional conditions for democracy spelled out earlier in this essay.

3) Removing religion from the political agenda. In their theoretical accounts of the development of a just society, contemporary liberal political philosophers John Rawls and Bruce Ackerman give great weight to *liberal arguing,* but almost no weight to *democratic bargaining.*[9]

Rawls is particularly interested in how a plural society in which the citizens hold a variety of socially embedded, reasonable, but deeply opposed comprehensive doctrines can arrive at an overlapping consensus. His normative recommendation is that, on major issues of quasi-constitutional import, individuals should be able to advance their arguments only by using freestanding conceptions of justice that are not rooted in one of the comprehensive but opposing doctrines found in the polity. Following this logic, public arguments about the place of religion are appropriate only if they employ, or at least can employ, freestanding conceptions of political justice.

Rawls's argument is both powerful and internally consistent. Yet he devotes virtually no attention to how *actual* polities have consensually and democratically arrived at agreements to "take religion off the political agenda." Almost none of them followed the Rawlsian normative map.

Politics is about conflict, and democratic politics involves the creation of procedures to manage major conflicts. In many countries that are now longstanding democracies, both Western and non-Western, the major conflict for a long period of time was precisely over the place of religion in the polity. In many of these cases, this conflict was politically contained or neutralized only after long public arguments and negotiations in which religion was the dominant item on the political agenda. Thus in the Netherlands, as noted above, religious conflicts were eventually taken off the political agenda of majority decision-making by a *democratic—but not liberal or secular—consociational agreement* that allocated funds, spaces, and mutual vetoes to religious communities with competing comprehensive doctrines.

Achieving such an agreement normally requires debate within the major religious communities. And proponents of the democratic bargain are often able to win over their fellow believers only by employing arguments that are *not* conceptually freestanding but deeply embedded in their own religious community's comprehensive doctrine.

One can expect, therefore, that in polities where a significant portion of believers may be under the sway of a doctrinally based nondemocratic religious discourse, one of the major tasks of political and spiritual leaders who wish to revalue democratic norms in their own religious community will be to advance theologically convincing public arguments about the legitimate multivocality of their religion. Although such arguments may violate Rawls's requirement for freestanding public reasoning, they are vital to the success of democratization in a country divided over the meaning and appropriateness of democracy. Liberal arguing has a place in democracy, but it would empty meaning and history out of political philosophy if we did not leave room for democratic bargaining and the nonliberal public argument within religious communities that it sometimes requires.

Let us now turn to exploring these general arguments in the contexts of cultures heavily influenced by Confucianism, Islam, and Eastern Orthodoxy.

Confucianism: Caesar Is God?

Most scholars of Confucianism would acknowledge that there are significant Confucian cultural components in Taiwan, South Korea, and Singapore. They would probably also say that the Confucian legacy was historically somewhat stronger in Taiwan and Korea than in Singapore.

Most scholars of democratization would acknowledge that Taiwan and Korea now meet the minimal conditions of democracy that I have cited. In my judgment, however, *no* important scholar of democratization would argue that Singapore meets even half of Dahl's eight minimal guarantees. Thus we can say that South Korea and Taiwan are above the threshold for identifying a country as a democracy, while Singapore is below it.

I argued earlier against assuming that any of the world's major religious traditions are univocal. If this argument is right, this means that, within what Huntington calls "kin cultures," we should be on the alert for struggles over meaning. When the former prime minister of Singapore, Lee Kuan Yew, attempted to appropriate "Asian Values" as a fundamental prop of his regime, he was challenged by President Kim Dae Jung of Korea and President Lee Teng-hui of Taiwan. In effect, they both said: "We are democratic. We draw upon some important democratic values found in the Confucian tradition. But you, Lee Kuan Yew, do not have a democracy in Singapore and you rationalize it by drawing upon some nondemocratic values within Confucianism. We are better democrats, and better Confucians, than you, so don't you dare attempt to hijack 'Asian Values.'"[10]

Kim Dae Jung's response succinctly underscores many of the core points of the argument advanced in this essay. He insists that Lee Kuan Yew's version of Asian values is little more than a self-serving excuse for authoritarian rule and devotes two pages to citing Confucian and neo-Confucian tenets that support democracy and legitimate dissent. He then talks of "Lee's record of absolute intolerance of dissent," says that Lee's Singapore is a "near-totalitarian police state," and concludes with an elegant rejection of what I have called the "fallacy of unique founding circumstances," asserting that "the fact that [democracy] was developed elsewhere does not mean it will not work in Asia."

The South Korean and Taiwanese presidents made normative and empirical distinctions that are crucial to modern democratic theory. At the level of the core defining characteristics of modern democracy, we must not be relativists. Any country, in any culture, must meet the same institutional and behavioral requirements. Yet we must also recognize that within the world of democracies there are many subtypes with distinctive secondary characteristics: Some have a large state, some do not; some accept individual values and reject collective values; some accept individual values but also espouse collective values. Many of the secondary values that differentiate Korean and Taiwanese democracy from U.S. democracy (higher saving rates so that the family can look after their own aged, a somewhat more robust role for the state in the economy, and somewhat greater respect for legal authority) draw upon Confucian values, but none of these "Asian values" are necessarily antidemocratic. Indeed, as Presidents Kim Dae Jung and Lee Teng-hui repeatedly and correctly assert, they are part of the distinctive strength of their own subtype of democracy.

Let me close this section on Confucianism with some illustrations of the multivocality of its doctrine and the political struggle to appropriate its meaning. Simon Leys's new translation of *The Analects of Confucius,* with 100 pages of valuable annotations, correctly points out that "state Confucianism repeatedly stressed the Confucian precept of *obedience* while obliterating the symmetrical Confucian duty of *disobedience* to a ruler if the ruler deviates from The Way." Leys stresses other, less hierarchical sayings: "Zila asked how to serve the Prince. The Master said, 'Tell him the Truth even if it offends him.'" Dissent is supported by the Confucian injunction, "A righteous man, a man attached to humanity, does not seek life at the expense of humanity; there are instances where he will give his life in order to fulfil his humanity." Xun Zi, one of the great followers of Confucius, built upon the above injunction when he defined a good minister as one who "follows the way, he does not follow the rules."[11]

Since rulers in the Confucian world strove for centuries to foster acquiescence by selectively emphasizing those elements of the Confucian corpus favoring obedience, the authoritarian legacy of state Confucianism will be diffusely present in new democracies such as Korea and Taiwan for decades to come. Yet this legacy has not prevented the emergence of democratic rule in these countries. Indeed, as we have seen, some of the most important political leaders in the new democracies of Taiwan and Korea have used components of the Confucian legacy in support of their struggle to deepen democracy.

Islam and the "Free-Elections Trap"

There is an extensive body of literature arguing that many key aspects of democracy are lacking in the Islamic tradition. The lack of separation between religion and the state is seen as stemming from the Prophet Mohammed's fusion of military and spiritual authority. The lack of space for democratic public opinion in making laws is seen as deriving from the Koran, in which God dictated to the Prophet Mohammed the content of fixed laws that a good Islamic polity must follow. The lack of inclusive citizenship is seen as originating in interpretations of the Koran that argue that the only true polity in Islam is the fused religious-political community of the *Ummah,* in which there is no legitimate space for other religions. Certainly, with the rise of Islamic fundamentalism these claims have been frequently asserted by some Islamic activists. Especially in the context of the Algerian crisis of 1991–92, this gave rise to scholarly assertions that Islam and democracy are incompatible and to arguments in the West's leading journals of opinion warning against falling into the "Islamic free-elections trap." According to this view, allowing free elections in Islamic countries would bring to power governments that would use these democratic freedoms to destroy democracy itself.

Any human rights activist or democratic theorist must of course acknowledge that numerous atrocities are being committed in some countries in the name of Islam. In Algeria, both the military-state and Islamic fundamentalists are slaughtering innocents. Women's rights are being flagrantly violated by the Taliban in Afghanistan. In the name of Islam, parts of Sudan have been turned into a killing zone. At the aggregate level, a recent attempt to document political freedoms and civil rights around the world concluded that "the Islamic world remains most resistant to the spread of democracy."[12]

It is in this context that Huntington asserted that the West's problem is "not Islamic fundamentalism but Islam." Huntington's vision of Islam's future allows virtually no room for struggling democratic forces to prevail in some key Islamic countries. Indeed, democratic failure is almost "over-determined" in his world of authoritarian "kin cultures" and unstoppable cultural wars. How should empirical democratic theorists respond?

I think we should begin with my hypothesis that all great religious civilizations are multivocal. Although Islamic fundamentalists are attempting to appropriate political Islam, there are also other voices—in the Koran, in scholarly interpretations of the Koran, and among some major contemporary Islamic political leaders. For example, Sura (verse) 256 of the Koran states that "There shall be no compulsion in Religion." This injunction provides a strong Koranic base for religious tolerance.[13]

Political activists, journalists, and even professors sometimes misleadingly equate Islam with Arab culture. They then assert *correctly* that there are no democracies in the Islamic countries of the Arab world, leaving the *false* impression there are no Muslims living under democratic regimes. In fact, however, a case can be made that about half of all the world's Muslims, 435 million people (or more than 600 million, if we include Indonesia), live in democracies, near-democracies, or intermittent democracies.

How do I arrive at the figure of 435 million? By looking at Islam in the entire world and including fragile, even intermittent democracies that may be under military rule at the moment (such as Pakistan) or have been under military rule in the recent past (such as Turkey). I thus include not only the 110 million Muslims in Bangladesh but also Pakistan's 120 million Muslims and the 65 million Muslims in Turkey. I also include India's 120 million Muslims, who have contributed significantly to Indian democracy and are one of the important voices in the world's multivocal Islamic culture. Finally, if we include the at least 20 million Muslims living under democratic regimes in areas such as Western Europe, North America, and Australia, we get 435 million. I believe that the inclusion of this Islamic diaspora is justified if we see Islam as an evolving, constantly changing global culture that is to some degree being "deterritorialized."

The big country that democratization theorists are watching most closely is Indonesia. With its estimated population of 216 million people, roughly 190 million of whom are Muslim, Indonesia is the world's largest Muslim country. Obviously, its attempted transition to democracy faces great obstacles: the worst case of what the economists called "Asian flu"; long-repressed regional demands for decentralization (secession, in the cases of East Timor, Aceh, and Irian Jaya); a constitution written in 1945 during the war of independence that is almost unusable for a democracy; and a military organization that has been centrally involved in national politics since the 1940s and has often exacerbated, or even incited, major communal conflicts. But will the fact that the country is predominantly Islamic significantly increase the chances of democratic failure or breakdown? I do not think there is strong evidence to support such a presumption.

Under Suharto's 32-year rule (1965–98), Indonesia was a military authoritarian regime that increasingly acquired patrimonial (even "sultanistic") dimensions in the 1990s. Islam was never a major part of Suharto's power base, however. Indeed, most analysts during the Suharto period did not consider Islamic fundamentalists as a major obstacle to future democratization.

In any attempt at democratic transition, leadership and organization are extremely important. The two largest and most influential Islamic organizations at the start of the possible transition in Indonesia, Nahdatul Ulama (NU) and Muhammadiyah, both with over 25 million members, were led by Abdurrahman Wahid and Amien Rais, respectively, both leaders in the struggle against Suharto. Amien Rais played a key role in helping to keep the student protests mobilized, relatively peaceful, and focused on democratic demands. After Suharto's fall, he considered leading an existing Islamic political grouping but instead created a new political party, the PAN, that was not explicitly Islamist and included non-Muslims in its leadership.

Abdurrahman Wahid (now president of Indonesia) also created a new political party, the PKB, and throughout the 1999 electoral campaign he argued against an Islamic state and in favor of religious pluralism. Wahid often operated in informal alliances with the most electorally powerful political leader, Megawati Sukarnoputri, and her secular nationalist party, the PDI, which includes secular Muslims, Christians, and many non-Muslim minorities. In Indonesia, Muslim identities are often moderate, syncretic, and pluralist. Muslim women in Indonesia have significantly more personal and career freedom than those in the Middle East. In this context, there was at least some space for a leader like Wahid—despite his weakness as an administrator—to attempt to foster a transition to democracy by constantly arguing that tolerance was one of the best parts of Indonesia's religious tradition.

Despite interethnic and religious conflicts, often tolerated and at times even supported by parts of the armed forces, no Islamic fundamentalist party developed a significant mass following in the year following Suharto's fall. In June 1999, in the freest election in over four decades, the two leading Islamic fundamentalist parties, the PBB and the PK, polled only 2 percent and 1 percent of the total popular vote, respectively.

Democracy in Indonesia has certainly not yet become the "only game in town." Outbreaks of religious violence on a number of the country's more than 2,000 inhabited islands continue to cause dangerous tensions and breakdowns of law. Nonetheless, against great initial odds, democracy is still on the agenda in Indonesia, two years after the fall of Suharto.

Let us now turn to Bangladesh, Pakistan, and Turkey. All of them have, or recently had, military regimes, but in recent times they all at some time have been at or above the threshold of being democracies. The 1996 election in Bangladesh satisfied all of Dahl's eight institutional guarantees. Voter turnout, at 73 percent (with women around 76 percent), was 13 percent higher than in any general election in the nation's history. Interestingly, the fundamentalist Islamic Party (JI) trailed far behind three other parties, winning only 3 seats. The JI seems to have polled worst among women.[14]

Pakistan was founded by Mohammed Ali Jinnah as an Islamic republic and has some features of Islamic law in its constitution. It is important to stress two points, however. First, the most democratically troubling features of Islamic law were imposed under General Mohammed Zia ul-Haq's military rule. Second, during the recent period of electorally competitive, civilian rule, there were no significant new impositions of Islamic law. There was also some curtailment of the reach of Islamic law as the electoral performance of Islamic fundamentalist parties weakened.

Until the October 1999 military coup, there had been five consecutive elections in Pakistan since 1988. Did the results strengthen or weaken the thesis of an "Islamic free-election trap"? In increasingly competitive elections, the largest revivalist or fundamentalist Islamic party, the IJI, came in second in 1988 and won a plurality in 1990 and 1993. In 1996 and 1997, however, the total vote for all the Islamic fundamentalist parties combined fell to less than 15 percent. In the 1997 election, which observers considered the freest and most open of Pakistan's recent elections, Islamic fundamentalist parties only won two seats in the National Assembly. In an excellent analysis of the relationship of Islamic revivalist parties and competitive elections in Pakistan since independence, S.V.R. Nasr contends that competitive politics, far from being a "trap," actually "encourages the flowering of the diversity of Muslim political expression and prevents the reduction of the political discourse to revivalism versus secularism."[15] Violent and fundamentalist Islamic groups are still active in Pakistan, to be sure, but their strength owes more to secret subsidies they receive from Pakistan's notorious Inter-services Intelligence Agency (ISI) than to the votes they receive in elections.[16]

Thus Huntington's implication that elections in predominantly Islamic countries will lead to fundamentalist majorities who will use their electoral freedom to end democracy gets no support from our analysis of electoral and political behavior in the world's three largest Islamic countries. Even in Iran, the "free-election trap" thesis has recently been refuted by events. Although the theocratic hard-liners continue to control state television and to close opposition newspapers, and the "Council of Guardians" still vets all candidates, the antifundamentalist opposition won at least 70 percent of the vote in the 1997 presidential election, the municipal elections of 1999, and the parliamentary elections of 2000. Iran is thus becoming increasingly multivocal.

Let me conclude my reflections on Islam and democracy by briefly considering the case of Turkey and the questions it raises regarding secularism and democracy. From June 1996 to June 1997, Turkey had its first prime minister representing a de facto Islamic party, Necmettin Erbakan of the Welfare Party. Soon after Erbakan took office, the Welfare Party was accused of violating Turkey's secular constitution. In the face of these charges and of pressure from the military, Erbakan resigned, and the Constitutional Court subsequently outlawed the Welfare Party.

Leading Western scholars have spoken as if there were a Western-style separation of religion and state in Turkey, sometimes suggesting that the policies promoted by Turkey's founder Kemal Atatürk were modeled on French secularism. In fact, however, the Atatürk tradition has been directed toward controlling religious expression so that it conforms with state goals. If Turkey really had either a complete separation of church and state or complete secularism, it would not need 50,000 civil servants in its Directorate of Religious Affairs to manage religious schooling.

The Turkish constitution of 1982 was drafted during a period of military rule by a committee vetted by the military. It was approved by a plebiscite, but no one was permitted to campaign against ratification. Article 2 asserts that the Turkish Republic is secular. Article 4 states that Article 2 can never be changed, not even by Constitutional amendment. Article 24 asserts that "education and instruction in religion and ethics shall be under state supervision and control," and adds, in a clause used to ban the Welfare Party, that "No one shall be allowed to exploit or abuse religious systems."

How does the operational definition of "secularism" drawn up by the military in 1982 and appealed to in the months leading up to Erkaban's forced resignation in June 1997 compare with secularism as it is practiced in democracies elsewhere? I think it is clear that Turkey's constitution is more restrictive both of freedom of religious expression within civil society and of freedom of organization within political society than that of any longstanding Western democracy.

I believe that in Turkey (as in Pakistan and probably Indonesia as well) the greatest obstacle to democracy is posed not by Islam but by military and intelligence organizations unaccountable to democratic authority. It has sometimes been suggested that in Islamic countries so many unique issues arise that democratization theory does not really apply. But our analysis of Indonesia, Bangladesh, Pakistan, Turkey, and even post-1997 Iran demonstrates the pitfalls of focusing only on the problems for democracy related to Islam, while neglecting the overall sociopolitical, military, ethnic, economic, and international contexts.

Eastern Orthodoxy: A Strong Obstacle?

What can we say about Eastern Orthodoxy and democracy? It must be acknowledged that Roman Catholicism and Protestantism played a more powerful role in recent civil-society resistance movements, especially in communist Europe, than did Orthodoxy. Why? And what does this mean, and *not* mean, for the future of democracy in countries where Orthodoxy is the dominant religion? The major explanation for this variance cannot lie in Orthodoxy's core religious doctrine: For their first millennium, Eastern and Western Christianity shared the same theological doctrines. The critical differences in recent patterns of resistance to the state by Orthodoxy and Roman Catholicism are due more to their organizational forms and the parts of their common multivocal tradition to which they have given the most emphasis.

Let us look comparatively at the question of civil-society resistance. As a transnational, hierarchical organization, Roman Catholicism can provide material and doctrinal support to a local Catholic church to help it resist state oppression. To the extent that the Catholic church may resist the state, it can support a more robust and autonomous civil society. Juan J. Linz and I have analyzed how the Catholic church provided such support in Poland, Lithuania, Chile, Brazil, and (during Franco's last years) in Spain. Protestantism, with its emphasis on individual conscience and its international networks, also played a role in supporting civil-society opposition to a repressive state in East Germany and Estonia. In the 1970s and 1980s, Protestantism and especially post–Vatican II Catholicism chose to give important weight to the "prophetic mission" that calls for individuals to speak out against worldly injustice no matter what the consequences.

With respect to resistance to the state, Eastern Orthodox Christianity is often organizationally and ideologically in a relatively weak position because the church is a *national* (as opposed to a *transnational*) organization. In such "caesaropapist" systems, the state often plays a major role in the national church's finances and appointments. Such a church is not really a relatively autonomous part of civil society because, in Weber's words, there is a high degree of "subordination of priestly to secular power." Under Stalin, the role of secular power in the USSR often meant the participation of the KGB in the highest religious councils of Orthodoxy.

As Weber and others have emphasized, Orthodoxy places more stress on liturgy than action and encourages "quietism" as a response to the world. In the structural context of caesaropapism and the liturgical context of quietism, the "prophetic" response to injustice, while doctrinally available in Orthodoxy's multivocal tradition, is seldom invoked.

Despite all of the above, however, I do not believe that Eastern Orthodoxy is an inherently antidemocratic force. If the leaders of the state and political society are committed to democracy and follow democratic practices, Orthodoxy's caesaropapist structures and quietist culture should lead to loyal support of democracy by the Orthodox church, as has been the case in Greece since 1975. If the leaders of the state and political society are antidemocratic, however, the democratic opposition in civil society normally will not receive substantial or effective support from a national Orthodox church.

Let me illustrate these points by discussing the Greek case. Greece and the Greek part of divided Cyprus are the only Orthodox-majority countries that, for the last five years, have met all the criteria for democracy discussed earlier in this essay. From 1967 to 1974, Greece was under authoritarian military rule. What was the role of the Orthodox church vis-à-vis the military dictatorship and the democratic transition? Three points are worth highlighting. First, there were two military juntas, one established in 1967 and one established in November 1973. Within months of coming to power, each junta had managed to arrange the appointment of a new archbishop to head the Greek Orthodox Church. This would have been impossible in Poland. Second, no scholarly work on the Greek dictatorship accords any significant formal or informal role to Orthodox church resistance to the dictatorship. Third, once democracy was instituted in 1974, the church (except for efforts to preserve some minor church prerogatives) did nothing significant to oppose, resist, or stall the eventual consolidation of democracy, and it has been broadly supportive of the democratic government. Indeed, the Greek Orthodox Church has been much less critical of left-wing democratic governments in Greece than the Catholic Church has been of left-wing democratic governments in Poland.

Greece has an established church. But as we have seen, so do Iceland, Denmark, Finland, Norway, and England. The democratic task in Greece after 1974 required not the disestablishment of the church, but the elimination of any nondemocratic domains of church power that restricted democratic politics. Greek democrats have done this and the Greek Orthodox Church has accepted it. Not only does democracy not require a disestablished church, it requires that no constraints be put on the rights of Eastern Orthodox Christians to argue their case in the public arena. Greek democracy has respected this area of legitimate autonomy of religion. There have been some changes both within state-society relations and within the Orthodox church that have made the "twin tolerations" easier to sustain. The constitution crafted in 1975 is somewhat clearer than the previous Greek constitutions had been about democratically appropriate areas for state action vis-à-vis religion, and for the established church's action vis-à-vis other religions and the elected government. Moreover, there is growing sentiment within the Orthodox church that it would be religiously more robust and better able to play an independent role in civil society if it were less dependent on the state.[17]

Unfinished Business

All the world's major religions today are involved in struggles over the twin tolerations. For Hinduism in India and Judaism in Israel, religion-state conflicts are now especially politically salient. In the first two decades of their independence after World War II, India and Israel were under the political and ideological hegemony of secular political leaders and parties. By the 1990s, however, both these secular political traditions were challenged by opposition movements that drew some of their support from forces seeking to redraw the boundaries of the "twin tolerations" to accomodate more fundamentalist and less tolerant visions of the polity.

In Israel, the state was originally a nationalist state for the Jewish people, but there are growing demands for it to be a religious state as well. There are also demands to make citizenship for the Arab minority less inclusive, and even to amend the Law of Return so as to give Orthodox rabbis the authority to determine whom the state of Israel recognizes as a Jew.

In India, after the 1998 and 1999 general elections, the Hindu revivalist BJP formed the government, in alliance with regional parties. Although it also contains more moderate elements, the BJP is pressured by its associated shock troops in uncivil society, such as the neofascist RSS, who want eventually to utilize the majority status of Hindus to make India a state that would privilege Hindu values as they interpret them.

A major force opposing the BJP and the RSS is the Gandhian-Nehruvian strand of Hinduism, which insists that both India and Hinduism are multivocal and that the deepest values of Hinduism must respect the idea of India as a diverse, tolerant state rather than a nation-state of Hindus. Gandhi and Nehru knew that since India was a multicultural, multireligious, and multicommunity state, "nation-state building" would make it harder, not easier, to build democracy.

India is 17 times poorer than any OECD democracy. The support for democracy in India under such difficult conditions cannot be understood without an appreciation of the tremendous strength that Gandhi drew from some traditional Hindu religious values and styles of action in his peaceful struggles for independence, democracy, an end to "untouchability," and respect for Muslims.

If India, with 600 million non-Hindi speakers, 14 languages that are spoken by at least 10 million people, and a minority population of about 120 million Muslims, is to remain a democracy, the voices of those who wish to make India a Hindu and Hindi nation-state must be countered by an ever stronger Gandhian voice speaking for India as a multireligious home to a billion people.

A more complete study of the themes raised in this brief essay would not only discuss religions I have omitted, but would analyze in much greater detail the emergence of the twin tolerations in the West. The establishment of state-sponsored churches in Scandinavia and Britain, while initially a way of securing political control of the church, eventually led not only to the "twin tolerations," but also, in the long run, to the "sociologically spontaneous secularization" of most of the population. Why?

Liberal scholars might also want to reconsider how liberal the anticlerical movements in France and Spain really were. What was the political effect of this liberalism from above? In Spain in the early 1930s, did liberal and socialist anticlericalism justify the tearing down of walls separating civil cemeteries from Jewish cemeteries? If the 1905 French liberal model of expropriating Jesuit property had been followed in the United States, Georgetown and many other Jesuit universities would have been expropriated. Would this have contributed to the strengthening of liberalism in the United States?

Another important area for further research is the role of the state in generating religious toleration. Scholars, especially sociologists of religion, have focused their attention on society-led movements toward tolerance, but at some critical moments state-led policies, such as those structured by Emperor Ferdinand I at the Peace of Augsburg of 1555, were crucial for ending society-led religious conflicts. Likewise, it was the Ottoman state that crafted the millets, with their extraordinary tolerance for religious self-government by minority national religious communities. There are many more examples of state-led tolerance, as well as state-led intolerance, that we need to study.

Finally, even the separation of church and state originally mandated by the U.S. Constitution's First Amendment ("Congress shall make no law respecting an establishment of religion, or prohibiting the free exercise thereof") is misunderstood today by many U.S. citizens. The amendment did not prohibit the 13 original states from having *their own established religions*. It merely prohibited the Congress from establishing one official religion for the United States *as a whole*. In fact, on the eve of the revolution, only three of the 13 colonies—Rhode Island, Pennsylvania, and Delaware—had no provision for an established church. Even after the revolution, the South Carolina constitution of 1778 established the "Christian Protestant Religion." Four New England states continued for some time to maintain state-subsidized, largely Congregational, churches. The eventual political construction of the West's strongest wall separating church and state, along with the social emergence of one of the West's most churchgoing, and most fundamentalist populations, is yet another "crooked path" of toleration and intoleration that needs further study and reflection.

NOTES

1. Confucianism is actually a cultural and philosophical tradition, not a religious tradition, in that it is "this-worldly" rather than "other-worldly" and has no priests or church. Nonetheless, many observers, from Max Weber to Samuel P. Huntington, treat it as one of the world's major religious-civilizational traditions, and I will do so in this essay.

2. Samuel P. Huntington, *The Clash of Civilizations and the Remaking of World Order* (New York: Simon and Schuster, 1996), 70.

3. Quotations come from Ibid., pp. 70, 217, 238, 28, and 158, respectively.

4. See Robert A. Dahl, *Polyarchy: Participation and Opposition* (New Haven: Yale University Press, 1971), 1–3.

5. For a much more extensive discussion and for references concerning these additional criteria, see Juan J. Linz and Alfred Stepan, *Problems of Democratic Transition and Consolidation: Southern Europe, South America and Post-Communist Europe* (Baltimore: The Johns Hopkins University Press, 1996), ch. 1.

6. John Rawls, *Political Liberalism* (New York: Columbia University Press, 1993), 151.

7. For Max Weber's discussion of caesaropapism, see Max Weber, *Economy*

and Society, Guenther Roth and Claus Wittich, eds., (Berkeley: University of California Press, 1978), 1159–63.

8. Max Weber, *The Protestant Ethic and the Spirit of Capitalism,* Talcott Parsons, trans., (New York: Charles Scribner's Sons, 1958). Weber, however, is careful not to commit this fallacy himself.

9. See John Rawls, *Political Liberalism;* and Bruce A. Ackerman, *Social Justice in the Liberal State* (New Haven: Yale University Press, 1980).

10.For this exchange, see Fareed Zakaria, "Culture is Destiny: A Conversation with Lee Kuan Yew," *Foreign Affairs* 73 (March–April 1994): 109–29; Kim Dae Jung, "Is Culture Destiny? The Myth of Asia's Anti-Democratic Values," *Foreign Affairs* 73 (November–December, 1994): 189–94; and Lee Teng-hui, "Chinese Culture and Political Renewal," *Journal of Democracy* 6 (October 1995): 3–8. The quote from Kim Dae Jung is from p. 192 of his article in *Foreign Affairs.*

11. *The Analects of Confucius,* Simon Leys, ed. (New York: W.W. Norton, 1997). For Leys' discussion of state Confucianism, see p. 108; for state Confucianism's obliteration of the symmetrical duty of disobedience, see pp. 134–36. The quotations are from pp. 136, 75, and 193, respectively.

12. Adrian Karatnycky, "The 1998 Freedom House Survey: The Decline of Illiberal Democracy," *Journal of Democracy* 10 (January 1999): 121.

13. For examples of these voices, see the expanded version of this essay, "The World's Religious Systems and Democracy: Crafting the 'Twin Tolerations'," in Alfred Stepan, *Arguing Comparative Politics* (Oxford: Oxford University Press, forthcoming 2001).

14.See Yasmeen Murshed and Nazim Kamran Choudhury, "Bangladesh's Second Chance," *Journal of Democracy* 8 (January 1997): 70–82.

15.S.V.R. Nasr, "Democracy and Islamic Revivalism," *Political Science Quarterly* 110 (Summer 1995): 279.

16.See, for example, Sumit Ganguly, "Pakistan's Never Ending Story: Why the October Coup Was No Surprise," *Foreign Affairs* 79 (March–April 2000): 2–7. To be sure, there have been many unfortunate events in Pakistan, such as Pakistani covert support for the Taliban fundamentalist revolution in Afghanistan, but it would appear that the major source of such support was from the military and intelligence systems acting somewhat autonomously. Recent conflicts with India in Kashmir have a similar origin.

17.For a spirited analysis of how Orthodoxy, contra Huntington, is consistent with democracy and capable of politically significant internal change, see Elizabeth H. Prodromou, "Paradigms, Power, and Identity: Rediscovering Orthodoxy and Regionalizing Europe," *European Journal of Political Research* 30 (September 1996): 125–54.

II

Eastern Religions

2

THE IRONIES
OF CONFUCIANSIM

Hahm Chaibong

Hahm Chaibong, *professor of political theory at Yonsei University, is currently on leave serving as director of the Division of Social Sciences Research and Policy at the United Nations Educational, Scientific, and Cultural Organization (UNESCO). He is the author of* Confucianism, Capitalism, and Democracy *(2001, in Korean) and coeditor (with Daniel A. Bell) of* Confucianism for the Modern World *(2003).*

The ideal modern polity is a securely unified nation-state that boasts a free-market economy and a democratic political system. Outside of Western Europe, its former settler colonies, and Japan, the effort to adopt or develop all these essential features of well-ordered modernity has often been a frustrating struggle. Some countries have achieved national unity but have yet to experience significant economic and political development. Others have succeeded in achieving a degree of prosperity, but have yet to undergo a democratic transition. Still others have even established democracies, but usually of the worrisomely fragile sort that look likely to buckle under the inevitable buffets of time and circumstance. Precious few countries have managed to gather unity, prosperity, and democracy into one stable edifice.

The East Asian countries that have been strongly influenced by Confucianism—the loosely organized tradition of spiritual and ethical teachings associated with the Chinese sage Confucius[1] (ca. 551–479 B.C.E.)—offer an interesting variation on the theme of halting development in the so-called Third World. Consider how they have fared as regards the three modern challenges of unity, prosperity, and democracy. First, all the Confucian countries of the region, including massive China as well as the smaller societies of Taiwan, the two Koreas, Vietnam, and Singapore, have succeeded in establishing powerful, centralized, bureaucratic states undergirded by robust national sentiments. Second, many of them have succeeded, often dramatically, at the task of generating economic growth: Taiwan, South Korea, and

Singapore have become famous as "tigers" while more recently China has been astonishing the world in this field. Third, South Korea and Taiwan have not only maintained stable governance and economic development, but have made full-fledged transitions to democracy with all that implies in the way of free and regular elections, peaceful handovers of power, a vibrant civic life proceeding freely under freely made laws, and the panoply of rights and liberties that make democracy liberal and distinguish it from a mere dictatorship of the majority. If one puts Japan back into the picture, it becomes apparent that, aside from Western Europe and the lands of its wider historic ambit, no region has been more successful than East Asia when it comes to achieving political and economic modernization.

What explains the exceptional performance of the region as a whole? Ever since the Newly Industrializing Countries (NICs) of East Asia began recording high economic-growth rates in the 1970s, Confucianism has been cited—and debated—as a possible cause.[2] Questions of causation are notoriously slippery, but no one can deny that there is a strong observed correlation between a society-wide Confucian legacy and a capacity for rapid and sustained economic development. China is only the most recent case out of several stretching back all the way to late nineteenth-century Meiji Japan. Many scholars have also noted the connection between Confucianism and the "developmental states" of this region.[3] In this account, the Confucian emphasis on loyalty and tradition of strong centralized bureaucratic rule, based upon relatively meritocratic civil-service examinations, has buttressed modern nation-states.

When the topic is Confucianism and *democracy,* however, the story takes on a different tone. Even among those who affirm the association between Confucianism on the one hand and state-building and economic development on the other, there is a strong consensus that Confucianism correlates negatively with self-government and modern political liberty. The continuing repressiveness of the regimes in China and Singapore, to say nothing of Vietnam and North Korea, deepens this impression. For many intellectuals, the "Asian values" discourse of the 1990s—much of which originated in Singapore and peaked not long before the East Asian financial crisis late in that decade—created the impression that Confucianism, whatever its happy economic effects, is an antidemocratic worldview.[4] In their effort to find alternatives to the "liberal-individualistic" version of democracy, the proponents of Asian values made Confucianism seem all too open to use by governments that fell well short of the democratic mark. Given this, Samuel P. Huntington's remark is perhaps understandable: "Confucian heritage, with its emphasis on authority, order, hierarchy, and supremacy of the collectivity over the individual, creates obstacles to democratization."[5]

Is Confucianism so fundamentally opposed to democracy that the former must be overcome before the latter can take root? Are Japan, South Korea, and Taiwan just lucky exceptions? Is the democratization of Singapore and China, not to mention Vietnam and North Korea, a forlorn hope?

The Encounter with Modernity

Confucian civilization was the last of the world's major cultural realms to come into sustained contact with Western modernity. While lands and peoples shaped by Islam, Hinduism, and Buddhism had come to know the West much earlier through some combination of trade, travel, intellectual exchange, invasion, conquest, and colonization, it was not until the nineteenth century that the Confucian world had to begin contending with modern civilization. The initial reaction of the Confucian world—one it shared with most other civilizations—was emphatic rejection of Western influence and ways. Fiercely proud of the culture and tradition that they had spent centuries cultivating, Confucian elites in China, Korea, and Japan all denounced and resisted the onslaught of the Western "barbarians."

Total resistance, however, did not last long. Defeat at the hands of Britain in the Opium War (1839–42) led China's rulers to have a try at reforming their dying imperial system. Throughout the late nineteenth and early twentieth centuries they labored to salvage aspects of Confucian tradition while adopting modern technologies, methods, and institutions. Mostly they failed. By the time a republican revolution ended the Ching dynasty in 1911, few in China advocated carrying on with Confucian learning and institutions in any form. With the May Fourth Movement of 1919, there began a long assault on the traditional modes of thought that Confucianism typified. Adherents of the nationalist and the communist models of modernity would struggle for control over the next three decades, with Confucian traditionalism thoroughly sidelined.

Under the Tokugawa Shogunate (1603–1868), Japan adopted an isolationist stance qualified only by limited trade with Korea and a Dutch enclave in Nagasaki. The U.S. gunboat diplomacy carried out by the 1853 visit of Commodore Matthew Perry's "black ships" to Tokyo Bay sparked an intense intra-Japanese debate over how to deal with the foreigners and their technologically formidable civilization. A civil war in the late 1860s settled the dispute. The winners favored reopening the country and learning from the West. Their toppling of the Tokugawa regime and restoration of imperial rule under Emperor Meiji (whose adopted name means "enlightened government") set Japan decisively on the path to modernization.

Vietnam as well initially rejected Western encroachment. The Vietnamese state that first threw off Chinese rule in the tenth century C.E. and fitfully extended its sway southward over most of the country's present-day territory was a centralized, Confucian-influenced entity. From the seventeenth century onward, succeeding dynasties tried to isolate their lands as much as possible from European influence, permitting only a single Portuguese trading mission near what is now the port of Da Nang, as well as limited Catholic missionary activity. Until the triumph of French colonialism in 1885, Vietnam's ruling system had remained Confucian in nature, with Confucian-style civil-service examinations enduring as late as 1921. Yet colonialism's arrival had represented a decisive victory for modernity. After 1885, even the most dogged elements in the anticolonial resistance would never return to Confucian tradition, but would instead adopt Western ideas and ideologies such as Marxism and nationalism in the very act of framing resistance to Western rule. In the seventeenth century, a French Jesuit missionary transcribed written Vietnamese from Chinese-style characters into a modified version of the Roman alphabet, and not even Ho Chi Minh ever tried to undo the change. Similarly, Vietnam's pursuit of modernization under whatever guise has never involved a reversion to Confucian ways.

The Yi dynasty that ruled nineteenth-century Korea also spurned the West. Prince Regent Tae Won-gun (r. 1864–73) oversaw a centuries-old, thoroughly Confucian state in a land so resolutely closed off that it was known as the Hermit Kingdom. He rejected Western trade and diplomatic overtures and persecuted Roman Catholics. Several times in the late 1860s and 1870s, Korean shore defenses resisted punitive or probing expeditions by French and later U.S. naval forces. Common folk and elites alike supported their country's Confucian civilization. An energetic minority of modernizers managed to stage what they hoped would be a Meiji-like coup in 1884, but they soon failed. The heavy price to be paid for such antimodern attitudes became clear in 1910, when a rapidly industrializing Japan, fresh from victorious wars against China and Russia, invaded and seized the Korean peninsula, ruthlessly exploiting it until Japanese power was crushed in the Second World War. Korea since then has been divided between a communist-totalitarian North and a once authoritarian but now democratic-capitalist South. Deep as their differences may run, neither has ever looked back from modernity to a premodern Confucianism.

What is striking about the history of East Asia over the last century and a half is Confucianism's relative feebleness as a wellspring of resistance. When compared to traditional beliefs or value systems in other civilizations that have had jarring encounters with modernity, Confucianism barely registers as a source of organized opposition to new and foreign ways. East Asian societies did produce theoretical critiques and practical movements aimed at stopping one or another aspect of political, economic, or social modernization. Yet after the initial "Confucian reaction" failed, these countermodern trends almost always drew their inspiration from Western ideologies (such as anarchism or the aforementioned Marxism and nationalism) and not from Confucian figures, writings, or institutions. How could Confucianism, seemingly so firmly entrenched in all these lands for six centuries or more, have become so irrelevant so easily? How was it that a civilization which had sunk deep philosophical and ethical roots and undergirded key political, economic, and social institutions could be so soon forgotten? Why is there no "Confucian fundamentalist" reaction despite the rapid and at times brutal modernization and "secularization" of East Asia?

One reason is that Confucianism took so much of the blame for the humiliations that the region's countries suffered at Western hands. Confucian institutions and values, many critics claimed, blocked the kinds of sweeping changes that would have made resistance feasible, and that arguably saved Japan from foreign domination. But this explanation raises another question, for there is a related dynamic of reform and reaction, seen in other regions and cultures, which East Asia has never experienced in a sustained or far-reaching way. In many places other than East Asia, tense encounters or outright conflicts with technologically superior Westerners led to humiliations: The Ottoman-Mameluke army's defeat by Napoleon's much smaller French force at the Battle of the Pyramids in July 1798 might be thought of, for instance, as a rough cognate of China's defeat in the Opium War or Tokugawa Japan's inability to make Commodore Perry's squadron leave Tokyo Bay. Such setbacks spurred efforts to imitate or borrow Western ways in the name of contending against the West on a more equal footing. As Bernard Lewis says in regard to the Muslim world,

> Some of the movements of revolt against Western rule were inspired by religion and fought in the name of Islam. But the most effective at that time— those that actually won political independence—were led by Westernized intellectuals who fought the West with its own intellectual weapons. Sometimes indeed they fought the West with Western help and encouragement.[6]

After the first wave of imitative innovation for the sake of resistance there often came a second, fundamentalist wave. Antimoderns reacted against the imitative reforms and their discomfiting effects or side-effects, taking aim not only at foreigners and foreign influences, but also at domestic actors associated with modernization. To fundamentalists, adopting repugnant Western ways as the price for resisting Western political domination seemed to pose an intolerable dilemma. Caught on its horns, the antimoderns lashed out against both the West and its local imitators-cum-competitors. (Islamic fundamentalists, for instance, hate not only foreign "infidels" but also the relatively modernist secular autocrats who rule so many Muslim countries in the name of nationalist or national-socialist ideologies with roots in resistance to Western colonialism.) The Confucian culture realm has seen modernization aplenty, often of a wrenching sort, yet has never witnessed the rise of a second-order, mass-based fundamentalist backlash like those seen in many other parts of the world. Why not? At least part of the answer lies in the peculiar way in which Confucianism has traditionally been organized institutionally. One of the features that distinguish Confucianism from other religions (if indeed Confucianism is properly classified as a religion, a point which scholars still debate) is its obvious lack of visible and autonomous institutional structures. Instead it takes the form of what sociologists call a "diffused" religious or quasireligious system. There is no priesthood or clerisy whose sole mission is to preserve and propagate Confucian tenets, perform Confucian rituals, and uphold the Confucian "faith."

The Twin Pillars of Family and State

Instead, traditional Confucianism rests on two pillars: the extended family and the state. Classically and ideally, the male head of the Confucian family is the closest analogue to a priest, since to him above all falls the duty of cultivating reverence toward ancestors. The officials of the state (who are also, significantly, the heads of families) are the leading students of Confucianism, whose very mastery of the great Confucian texts, as proven in competitive examinations, raises them to important public posts. The family's due is filial reverence (*xiao* in Chinese, *hyo* in Korean, and *kou* in Japanese). The state's due is political allegiance (*zhong* in Chinese, *chung* in Korean, and *chu* in Japanese). These virtues of filiopiety and loyalty are arguably the two Confucian desiderata *par excellence,* the values that give life to the family and the polity. Confucianism recognizes no realm separate from the family and the state that can be enshrined in a separate institution and guarded by an independent clergy.

Confucianism did not become the cognate of an "orthodoxy" or "established religion" in China, Korea, or Vietnam because monarchs chose to support some clergy-like body of Confucian adepts. Rather, the monarchies that ruled these countries were Confucian institutions through and through. Likewise, since Confucianism makes no distinction between the sacred and secular or eternal and temporal realms, the Byzantine or Eastern Orthodox Christian notion of caesaropapism—of religious and political authority as different types of rule nonetheless exercised by a single person—is another concept that simply does not exist in Confucianism. Questions such as those of the "city of God" versus the "city of man"; of the "two swords" of temporal and spiritual authority, respectively; of "the throne and the altar"; or of how to follow Jesus' command to render unto Caesar what is Caesar's while rendering unto God what is God's have never haunted the Confucian imagination, for the sacred-secular dichotomy that they all assume is a premise which Confucian thought simply does not share.

The reverencing (worship may be too strong a word) of ancestors that is ubiquitous in Confucian theory and practice is a sign of how grand a place the family occupies in the Confucian scale of values. The patriarch's role was to ensure the family's continuity across the generations by guaranteeing its physical, political, economic, and social well-being. This project could require passing the civil-service examination and rising in the official bureaucracy, through employment in which a man could not only serve his state but secure the fortunes of his family. A Confucian patriarch also nurtured family piety in a highly self-conscious way by presiding over rituals held to honor the ancestors in household shrines. In these rites, Confucianism assumed its most liturgical and religious form. Through them, the living generation of the extended family or clan remembered and reaffirmed its place along the continuum afforded by the ever-receding generations of ancestors, on the one hand, and the ever-extending generations of descendents to come, on the other.

This linchpin of the Confucian family-and-state system was the ideal Confucian scholar-bureaucrat. Steeped in the Confucian classics as preparation for government service, he also oversaw the cult of the family and its ancestors. Perhaps the closest parallel to such a hieratic official in the Western tradition would be the ancient Greek or Roman male who was both the master of his household and a citizen of his city. The parallel is imperfect, for while the classical citizen was expected to prize his city's good even above his family's, the Confucian literati were offered no such clear rule for resolving tensions between family piety and political loyalty. Hence balancing the claims of the family and the state, not of the sacred and the secular, became the central preoccupation of Confucian political theory and practice.

Because of Confucianism's "secular" nature, the advent of modernity did not bode well for it. The coming of the modern nation-state model to East Asia deprived Confucianism of one of the two institutional supports that had sustained it for centuries. The family continued to be the single most important repository and transmitter of Confucian values, but in the larger political order the family could not by itself sustain the predominance of Confucian ways. The widespread impression that Confucianism had shown itself powerless to protect traditional regimes against Western encroachment caused a crisis of loyalty, with allegiances shifting relatively quickly to the new modern state. The hollowing out of the old Confucian order and the rise of the modern state was the deeper process that underlay the myriad civil wars, revolutions, rebellions, and coups that swept East Asia from the mid-nineteenth century on.

There was irony at work as well, for while the modern state swept Confucian polities aside, that very same state also owed much of its triumph to the Confucian value of loyalty. The case of Japan, the most important model for other East Asian countries since the second half of the nineteenth century, reveals how modernizing elites hit upon the idea of fostering potent synergies between Confucianism and the new nation-state. In Japan, modernizing change traveled under the guise of a restored monarchy. The return of the monarchy's authority, if not its real power, in the person of Emperor Meiji gave nationalist feeling a strong focus and rallying point, just as those who engineered the restoration hoped it would. The imperial house became the symbol of the nation and provided continuity and coherence amid reforms that turned traditional Japanese life upside down. The abolition of the old class system, the adoption of compulsory universal education and military service, the establishment of modern property rights, and the promulgation of a written constitution (modeled on Prussia's and granted by the emperor in 1889)—changes so deep and disturbing that they provoked manifold rebellions by peasants as well as samurai—all went forward in the emperor's name. At the same time, Confucian values played a role, as in the 1890 imperial rescript on education that not only made schooling mandatory and universal but also ordered it to inculcate family piety and loyalty to the emperor.[7]

The Meiji strategy of using distinctively Confucian cultural resources to buttress a powerful modern state associated with nationalist ideology was suppressed in Japan after that country's defeat in the Second World War. Yet the strategy would prove handy to such modernizing Asian strongmen as South Korea's Park Chung Hee, Taiwan's Chiang Kai-shek and Chiang Ching-kuo, and Singapore's Lee Kuan Yew. In all these cases, Confucian rhetoric extolling filiopiety and political loyalty accompanied the building of a strong, centralized, intrusive, and bureaucratic state capable of generating momentum for modern industrial development.[8] Today, the nominally Marxist rulers of China, Vietnam, and North Korea seem to be adopting this approach, despite prior communist claims that Confucianism is "reactionary."

For the most part, East Asia's modern nation-states have been hugely effective at fostering growth. The sheer speed and success of economic modernization under authoritarian governments ready to quell dissent may have helped to stop any possible fundamentalist reaction before it could start. In Japan and South Korea, the only serious critique has been Marxist. The very success of industrialization and urbanization provided fodder for leftist denunciations of consumerism and various capitalist derelictions and excesses. Because Confucianism never took the form of anything resembling a church (in the broad sense of a religious body conceptually and institutionally distinguishable from the state), the modern nation-states that have arisen in Confucian or post-Confucian societies are as close as one can come to pure specimens of the "secular state" idealized by modern liberal theorists. But without a church to champion a realm of awareness or action over against the realm controlled by the state, these societies also found themselves inordinately threatened by state totalitarianism. The modern state, in effect, became a new and more powerful type of emperor in a region where no popes or "turbulent priests" had ever been on hand to challenge even the older and weaker representatives of the imperial breed. This has meant that East Asia has mostly had to do without the liberalizing influence of what Alfred Stepan calls the "twin tolerations," whereby the political and the religious authorities strike a double-barreled bargain that bolsters freedom as they agree to avoid dictating to one another.[9]

The historically Christian West developed its "twin tolerations" only after enormous difficulty and violence, including the Wars of Religion that wracked Europe from the 1520s to 1648. Yet these very conflicts were instrumental in midwifing the liberal and secular ideals that undergird modern democracy. More recently, the role that the Roman Catholic Church has played in helping to overthrow repressive regimes and defend human rights from communist Poland to the Marcos-era Philippines and East Timor under Indonesian misrule shows how effective a church that stands apart from and at times even defies the state can be at promoting democracy, tolerance, and pluralism.

In Confucian societies, the lack of an independent and culturally indigenous "church" aided the rise of the state and with it socioeconomic modernity, yet left this same state too often unchallenged by countervailing authoritative sources. The new state could define the whole public realm as the nation, and then claim that state control of this realm drew justification from the government's role as supreme bearer of national goals and aspirations. Post-Confucian states freely articulated and imposed national ideologies. The Japanese state even invented its own religion, Shintoism. Underlying legitimacy came from the overriding goal of preventing foreign domination, Western or otherwise (not all the imperialism in East Asia has come from the West, as any review of Korean or Vietnamese history will attest). Meiji Japan marched under the slogan "rich nation, strong army." Korea's Park Chung Hee, the Kuomintang party of Nationalist China, and many others echoed that call. At its worst, this could decay into brutal militarism of the sort that swept aside democratic groups such as the Japanese "liberty and popular rights" movement of the "Taisho Democracy" era (1912–26) before the third decade of the twentieth century. The authoritarian-imperialist path down which Japan's militarists drove their country ended in mushroom clouds. But the U.S. occupation of 1945 to 1952 gave liberal democracy a powerfully assisted new start amid the ashes, with results that endure today. In Kim Il Sung's North Korea, Mao Zedong's China, and Ho Chi Minh's Vietnam, post-Confucian communist states committed far greater assaults on freedom than were seen in the capitalist-authoritarian states of Taiwan, South Korea, and Singapore at their worst. Both the totalitarianism of the communist states and the authoritarianism of the capitalist states may be described as being, in part at least, legacies of Confucianism.

How, given the power of the state and the politically problematic Confucian heritage, did democracy replace authoritarian capitalism in Japan, South Korea, and Taiwan? The importance of economic development and the rising middle classes that it underwrites cannot be gainsaid, especially given the absence or relative weakness of religious supports for an autonomous civil society and a tradition of opposition to government authority.

Japan's path through militaristic hypernationalism and the loss of a catastrophic war to a recovery of nascent liberal-democratic traditions with roots in the Meiji period is a unique tale. South Korea's case, too, has its *sui generis* aspects. South Korea is the only country in East Asia where a large share of the populace—almost half—professes Christianity. Korea's churches, Protestant as well as Catholic, have played a major role in democratization since the 1970s.[10] Clerics such as Seoul's Catholic archbishop Stephen Cardinal Kim, Christian youth-group members, Christian students, and other Christian citizens have often been at the forefront of those peacefully challenging official repression and calling for democracy.

Taiwan's special circumstance is the "ethnic" cleavage between the Kuomintang mainlanders who fled to the island to escape Mao's forces in 1949 and the "native" Taiwanese whom the mainlanders found there. The natives have provided a ready-made basis for political opposition to Kuomintang dominance, with feeling especially dwelling on the natives' greater tendency to favor a clear and final declaration of independence from China. In a roughly similar fashion, interregional tensions within ethnically homogeneous South Korea helped to fuel oppositional politics and hence democracy.

Democracy "Despite" Confucianism?

One thing notable about all these forces for democratization is how little any of them have to do with Confucianism. We have seen how Confucianism has served the cause of (usually authoritarian) state-building and the cause of economic development. Can Confucianism ever serve democracy? Indeed, is it compatible with democracy at all, or does democratization require the rejection of Confucian ways?

In practice, Confucianism has always seemed to flourish best under autocracy. In China, Korea, and Vietnam, Confucian political theory served the monarchy. The post-Confucian states that have harnessed Confucianism for their own ends are far from exceptional in this regard. Yet at the same time, Confucian history features many examples of opposition to despotism. Confucianism, we must remember, privileges not warriors and kings, but literati or scholar-bureaucrats. They are the true defenders of civilization and the most fit to govern. Yet others have more power. The potential for tension with rulers should be apparent.

This is nowhere better illustrated than in the opening lines of Confucianism's most famous book, the *Analects:*

> The Master [Confucius] said: "Having studied, to then repeatedly apply what you have learned—is this not a source of pleasure? To have friends come from distant quarters—is this not a source of enjoyment? To go unacknowledged by others without harboring frustration—is this not the mark of an exemplary person *(junzi)*?"[11]

On the surface, this appears to be an exhortation to study hard, maintain good human relations, and be humble. Read from the perspective of a classical Confucian *junzi,* flourishing at a time when he and his fellow literati held elite official positions throughout East Asia, these words read like a calm counsel to a certain kind of *noblesse oblige:* As a leader of others, one must never stop studying or seeking self-improvement, and as an acknowledged member of society's elite, one does well by being friendly and unassuming. Yet when Confucius uttered this teaching, he and his peers and students were anything but elite figures. On the contrary, they were functionaries hired by monarchs and grandees to work as scribes and clerks, to perform rituals meant to show off the splendor of royal and noble households, and to tutor aristocratic offspring.

Only when we grasp this can we understand the third exhortation, which recommends inner calm in the face of recognition denied. Unless they deliberately disguise themselves, emperors and nobles are never in danger of going unrecognized. Their grand clothes, conveyances, retinues, and houses ensure them recognition, whether they deserve it or not. Elites live in state; Confucius and his fellow literati live in shade. They study arduously and constantly to master the ancient texts and rituals that form the essence of civilization, yet find themselves condemned to remain a nameless, powerless servant class. With this exhortation, Confucius is telling his fellow scribes to be proud of themselves, to maintain a steady self-respect even though the outside world and its rulers will never justly recognize them.

The meaning of the second exhortation then also becomes clear. The literati are civilization's keepers, a band of brothers with ideas that can repair the world. Yet only their peers rate them accurately. Thus a visit from a true friend—one of those rare people with whom one can share one's deepest hopes, dreams, and frustrations—is a joyous occasion indeed. When friends are not at hand, what is a scholar to do other than practice the rituals and seek the true meaning of the classics? As keepers of the faith, the literati must constantly hone their skills and refine their understanding of the civilizing mission that the powerholders neglect. This also explains the first exhortation, to study and then apply the fruits of study. Whatever the unwise ruling classes do, the learned sage must stand ready to advance the cause of civilization if he gets the chance.

Properly understood, then, this opening passage from the leading Confucian text is not a string of calm moral commonplaces, but rather a postcard from the edge, the agonized *cri de coeur* of a frustrated, over-looked intellectual whose true grasp of civilization, its desperate plight, and the means to save it is shared by no one or almost no one with any power. Perhaps the supreme irony in all of Confucianism's ironic history is that this "voice in the wilderness" teaching eventually became the supreme established orthodoxy of the East Asian world. What happened to bring about such a dramatic reversal? Four centuries after Confucius died, the Han emperors of China made Confucian teachings the center of the official religion. The vast empire needed highly educated bureaucrats, and Confucian scholars formed the biggest pool of available talent. The Confucian classics dominated the training of aspiring bureaucrats, whose lives were focused on doing well in the civil-service examination, which tested mastery of Confucian lore. A political theory replete with exhortations to filiopiety, loyalty, and the rule of virtue was just what the empire was looking for as it went about molding a docile corps of administrators.[12]

King's Men or King's Conscience?

Thus was the put-upon Confucian literatus reborn as one of the grand scholar-bureaucrats who ran China on the emperor's behalf. Yet the Confucian mandarins' sense that they were not merely the king's men but also the true bearers and defenders of civilization never completely left them. In fact, the more deeply the imperial system entrenched itself, the stronger this consciousness became. Many literati continued to challenge the emperor's right to rule. In the eleventh century, a new "neo-Confucian" account claimed for the literati a much more central role in governing the empire.

Despite Confucian criticisms of imperial claims, Confucians never imagined a political system other than monarchy. In this, they were hardly an exception. Yet Confucianism did attempt, within the confines of the monarchical system, to limit autocratic prerogatives and excesses. Confucian family piety, to name one example, can be understood at least in part as flowing from a wish to counterbalance the claims of the imperial state. Another important Confucian institution was the "classics mat." Most literally put into practice in Korea, this was a mandatory series of lectures—often consisting of three two-hour talks per day—through which leading literati instructed the crown prince in key Confucian texts and themes. Even sitting kings and emperors sometimes submitted to such tutoring, which became an important traditional means of teaching rulers such central Confucian values as moderation, self-discipline, and concern for the welfare of one's subjects.

Another set of institutions designed to check the monarch's power were the Confucian-inspired "private academies" that literati set up as alternatives to state-run higher education. These academies extended Confucian instruction to places where the state's resources did not reach. More important still, they offered havens where Confucian doctrines could be more or less freely discussed, and sometimes became power bases for alumni serving in the imperial administration. In Korea, certain Confucian academies became so influential that kings sometimes took the extraordinary step of waiving the required civil-service examination in order to recruit academy graduates directly into the royal service. During the regency of Tae Won-gun, the abolition of these private academies came to symbolize the "reforms" that sought to strengthen the power of the monarchy.

Under Confucian "community compacts," moreover, whole groups of adjacent villages could reorganize themselves on the basis of Confucian teachings. Literati drew up these compacts, which typically reinforced their superiority over villagers. Yet the compacts diffused Confucian teachings outward and down along the sociopolitical scale. Over time, such a compact could become the basis for autonomous local rule. There were many cases of compacted communities becoming so independent that they would reject magistrates sent by the central government as unwanted interlopers in local affairs.[13]

Few or no traditional religions, considered in their "pristine" state (that is, before they come under pressure to reach some sort of accommodation with modernity), seem to offer a particularly promising purchase to liberal-democratic principles and ideals. Confucianism was actually exceptional in the degree to which, at least in theory, it took a stand against absolutism and autocracy. Yet Confucianism never had much more than gossamer-thin institutional means with which to buttress principled opposition to monarchs who had armies of soldiers and legions of officials at their beck. That slenderness of practical means, plus the ease with which state power could coopt Confucian ideals such as loyalty, meant that any Confucian-inspired attempt to check autocratic power would be an uphill battle.

The history of Confucianism is a tale of powerful central states repeatedly appropriating key Confucian tenets for state ends. Indeed, the premodern autocracies of East Asia might be looked upon as global pioneers in the art of coopting belief systems to serve a political agenda. Modern autocracies in East Asia have followed suit. But in another, admittedly more subdued light, Confucianism appears to have always borne within itself the theoretical basis for a stance of opposition to or at least suspicion of state power. It will not do to think of the Confucians as protodemocrats: They never recognized anything like the right of the common man to have a say in how he was governed. But by the same token, it might make a certain amount of sense to call the Confucians protoliberals, at least in a functional sense. For they did care—in large part, of course, because they cherished their *own* authority as men of superior wisdom—about keeping the king from thinking that he could simply do as he pleased.

What does this mean then, in terms of the relationship between Confucianism and democracy? In East Asia, democracy is plainly a recent import from the West. Here we note the final irony in an essay that has listed several: Confucianism is not very democratic, nor democracy as such very Confucian. Yet it may be that liberal democracy has now, in some East Asian countries (soon to be joined, one hopes, by others), opened up a free space in which Confucianism can truly come into its own for the first time ever. Confucianism in the past was always bound up with political autocracies and social hierarchies that barred it from imagining a political arrangement under which the Confucian tradition of serious thought and ethical reflection could give free rein to its own potential. Liberal democracy, which tames and balances the power of the state and frees the realm of spiritual awareness from undue political entanglements, may be just what Confucianism has been looking for.

The oppositional potential of Confucianism has been proven time and again in China, Japan, and South Korea. The spontaneous rise of students and intellectuals in these post-Confucian countries whenever the opportunity arose is a clear demonstration of this potential. In South Korea, the students and intellectuals were instrumental in bringing down authoritarian regimes. The Tiananmen Square student protestors whom the Chinese communist regime suppressed so brutally in 1989 made a point of using Confucian as well as Western symbols and rhetoric to press their case for freedom, justice, and self-government in the world's largest country.

This record suggests a harmony between the currents of democratization and those of a renewed and freer Confucianism. In that sense, Japan, South Korea, and Taiwan may not be the exceptions within East Asia after all, for no cultural influence in this region runs deeper or wider than Confucianism. This is not a matter of expecting "Confucianism" in some concrete institutional sense to stand up to tyrants and bring about democracy. Confucianism is just not built that way, and the tyrants in question command, as we have seen, powerful post-Confucian states that Confucian values and habits helped to build. Yet Confucianism has already done indirect work in paving the way for democracy by helping to build the region's coherent nation-states, by speeding these states down the path to economic development, and by showing a potential for stirring opposition to illiberal, undemocratic regimes. One may expect that if East Asia continues predominantly to tread the path of economic modernization—and all indications are that it will—then prospects for democratization will improve, and with them the opportunities for a truer flowering than the Confucian tradition has ever had within its reach. So after the "First Epoch" of classical Confucianism and the "Second Epoch" of neo-Confucianism, we may witness the rise of a "Third Epoch" featuring a "free at last" Confucianism whose self-renewal and self-realization will have been directly made possible by the triumph of democracy across East Asia.

NOTES

1. Also known as Kung Fu-tzu or Master Kong.

2. David Aikman, *Pacific Rim: Area of Change, Area of Opportunity* (Boston: Little, Brown, 1986); Roy Hofheinz, Jr., and Kent E. Calder, *The Eastasia Edge* (New York: Basic, 1982); Gilbert Rozman, ed., *The East Asian Region: Confucian Heritage and Its Modern Adaptation* (Princeton: Princeton University Press, 1991); and Tu Wei-ming, ed., *Confucian Traditions in East Asian Modernity: Moral Education and Economic Culture in Japan and the Four Mini-Dragons* (Cambridge: Harvard University Press, 1996).

3. Chalmers A. Johnson, *MITI and the Japanese Miracle: The Growth of Industrial Policy, 1925–1975* (Stanford: Stanford University Press, 1990); and *Japan: Who Governs? The Rise of the Developmental State* (New York: W.W. Norton, 1996).

4. On the "Asian values" debate, see Francis Fukuyama, "Confucianism and Democracy," *Journal of Democracy* 6 (April 1995): 20–33; the symposium on "Hong Kong, Singapore, and 'Asian Values'" by various authors in the April 1997 issue of the same publication; and Mark R. Thompson, "Whatever Happened to 'Asian Values'?" *Journal of Democracy* 12 (October 2001): 154–65.

5. Samuel P. Huntington, *The Clash of Civilizations and the Remaking of World Order* (New York: Simon & Schuster, 1996), 238.

6. Bernard Lewis, *What Went Wrong? The Clash Between Islam and Modernity in the Middle East* (New York: Perennial, 2003), 61–62.

7. See, for example, Samuel Hideo Yamashita, "Confucianism and the Japanese State: 1904–1945," in Tu Wei-ming, ed., *Confucian Traditions in East Asian Modernity*, 132–54.

8. For a more detailed argument on this point, see Chaibong Hahm and Wooyeal Paik, "Legalistic Confucianism and Economic Development in East Asia, *Journal of East Asian Studies* 3 (September–December 2003): 461–91.

9. Alfred C. Stepan, "Religion, Democracy, and the 'Twin Tolerations,'" *Journal of Democracy* 11 (October 2000): 37–57.

10. Korean Protestants—Presbyterians and Baptists especially—have played an important role as change agents ever since the late nineteenth century, when many intellectuals turned to Christianity as an alternative to Confucianism. Over the last century and more, Christians have founded numerous universities, schools, and hospitals that continue to flourish across South Korea.

11. Roger T. Ames and Henry Rosemont, Jr., *The Analects of Confucius: A Philosophical Translation* (New York: Ballantine, 1998), 71.

12. Hahm Chaibong, "Family Versus the Individual: The Politics of Marriage Laws in Korea," in Daniel A. Bell and Hahm Chaibong, eds., *Confucianism for the Modern World* (Cambridge: Cambridge University Press, 2003), 334–59.

13. Chang Yun-shik, "Mutual Help and Democracy in Korea," in Daniel A. Bell and Hahm Chaibong, eds., *Confucianism for the Modern World,* 90–123.

3

CONFUCIANISM
AND DEMOCRACY

Francis Fukuyama

Francis Fukuyama *is professor of international political economy at the Johns Hopkins School of Advanced International Studies and author, most recently, of* State-Building: Governance and World Order in the 21st Century *(2003). This essay originally appeared in the April 1995 issue of the* Journal of Democracy.

The caning for vandalism last year of American high-school student Michael Fay by the Singaporean authorities underscored the challenge now being put forth by Asian societies to the United States and other Western democracies. The issue was not simply whether Singapore, as a sovereign state, had the right to subject an American expatriate to its laws and legal procedures, but a much more fundamental one. In effect, the Singaporeans used the case of Michael Fay to argue in favor of their brand of authoritarianism, charging that American democracy, with its rampant social problems and general disorder, could not be regarded as a model for an Asian society. This claim forms part of a larger argument that Singaporeans, beginning with former prime minister Lee Kuan Yew, have been making for some time now to the effect that Western-style democracy is incompatible with Confucianism, and that the latter constitutes a much more coherent ideological basis for a well-ordered Asian society than Western notions of individual liberty.[1] While Singaporeans have been the most outspoken proponents of this view, many people in other Asian societies, from Thailand to Japan, have come to share their beliefs. The standing of the United States in Asia has already been affected: on the issue of using trade policy to pressure China into bettering its human rights record, Washington had few allies in the region, and it was forced to back down on its threat of withdrawing China's most-favored-nation (MFN) status.

Are Confucianism and Western-style democracy fundamentally incompatible? Will Asia formulate a new kind of political-economic order that is different in principle from Western capitalist democracy?

The fact is that there are fewer points of incompatibility between Confucianism and democracy than many people in both Asia and the West believe. The essence of postwar "modernization theory" is correct: Economic development tends to be followed by political liberalization.[2] If the rapid economic development that Asia has experienced in recent years is sustained, the region's democratization will continue as well. In the end, however, the contours of Asian democracy may be very different from those of contemporary American democracy, which has experienced serious problems of its own in reconciling individual rights with the interests of the larger community.

Modernization Theory Confirmed

Although it is no longer considered "politically correct" to advocate modernization theory, it has actually stood the test of time relatively well. In a seminal article published in 1959, Seymour Martin Lipset noted the empirical correlation between a high level of economic development and stable democracy.[3] Although the thesis that economic development gives rise to political liberalization has been debated endlessly since then, it was strengthened considerably with the democratic transitions that began in the mid-1970s, and it is more valid today than it was when it was first enunciated.[4]

The correlation between development and democracy is nowhere better illustrated than in Asia. The states of the region have established stable democratic institutions roughly in the same order in which they began to develop economically, beginning with Japan and extending now to South Korea (which held its first completely free elections in 1992) and Taiwan (which is scheduled to hold free legislative elections at the end of this year). There have been a number of failed prodemocracy movements in China, Thailand, and Burma, but even these cases reveal a link between development and democracy. In the Chinese and Thai cases, in particular, the leaders of the prodemocracy movements tended to be relatively well educated, "middle-class," and cosmopolitan citizens—the type of individual that began to emerge during earlier periods of rapid economic growth. The only anomaly in this picture is the Philippines, which, despite having the lowest per-capita income of all the noncommunist states in Southeast Asia, has been a democracy since the election of Corazon Aquino in 1986. Clearly, though, democracy would never have come to the Philippines had it not been for the direct influence of the United States; moreover, democratic practice is not well institutionalized there, and the country retains a semifeudal authority structure in the countryside and features one of Asia's few remaining communist insurgencies. It would not be surprising, in fact, if Philippine democracy were suddenly to collapse, a scenario that is difficult to imagine in South Korea or Japan.

Although modernization theory proposed a correlation between development and democracy, it was hazy on what the causal connections between the two phenomena were. Some proponents, such as Talcott Parsons, argued that democracy was more "functional" than authoritarianism in a modern industrialized society.[5] I have argued elsewhere that the linkage between the two cannot be understood in economic terms.[6] That is, the fundamental impulse toward liberal democracy springs from a noneconomic desire for "recognition." The relationship between economic modernization and democracy is therefore indirect: Economic modernization raises living and educational standards and liberates people from a certain kind of fear brought on by life close to the subsistence level. This permits people to pursue a broader range of goals, including those that remained latent in earlier stages of economic development. Among those latent urges is the desire to be recognized as an adult with a certain basic human dignity—a recognition that is achieved through participation in the political system. Poor peasants in the Philippines or El Salvador can be recruited by landlords to take up arms and form death squads, because they can be manipulated relatively easily on the basis of their immediate needs and are accustomed to obeying traditional sources of authority. It is much more difficult to persuade educated, middle-class professionals to obey the authority of a leader simply because he is wearing a uniform.

The case of Japan seems to provide further confirmation of the proposed link between development and democracy. Japan, of course, has been a formal democracy since General MacArthur imposed a democratic constitution on the country during the U.S. occupation. Nevertheless, many observers both within and outside of Japan have noted that Western-style democracy, with its emphasis on public contestation and individualism, did not seem to sit well with traditional Japanese culture. Some commentators even went so far as to argue that, despite its democratic legal structure, Japan was not a democracy in the Western sense at all, but rather a mildly authoritarian country run by an alliance of bureaucrats, Liberal Democratic Party (LDP) officials, and business leaders.[7]

The political upheaval that has occurred in Japan since the fall of the LDP government in July 1993, however, would seem to bear out some of the premises of modernization theory. The Japanese people deferred to the authority of the bureaucracy-LDP-business triangle for much of the postwar period because that alliance delivered a high rate of economic growth to a nation that had been devastated by the Pacific war. Like many an authoritarian leadership, however, it ultimately failed to hold up its end of the bargain: it presided over the creation and subsequent puncturing of a "bubble economy" in the 1980s, and suffered from creeping and pervasive corruption. There is no guarantee that such a system will be self-correcting in the absence of popular "feedback loops"; moreover, as the Japanese population grew wealthier and more able to take its prosperity for granted, its willingness to defer to the political leadership and overlook abuses diminished. Although it is very difficult to predict the outcome of Japan's current political struggle, it seems unlikely that the old ruling triangle will carry its power and authority intact into the next generation.

Modernization theory came under heavy attack in the 1960s and 1970s from two principal sources. First, Marxist critics argued that capitalist democracy was not the proper goal of political and economic development, and that modernization theorists were apologists for an unjust global economic order. Another group of critics, who might be labeled "cultural relativists," argued that modernization theory was Eurocentric and did not take account of the diversity of ends dictated by the world's different cultures. While the Marxist critique is less prominent today owing to the collapse of communism, the relativist critique remains very powerful, and has intimidated many people out of arguing for the existence of a universally valid development path whose ultimate outcome is free-market democracy.

Some of the criticisms to which modernization theory was subjected did have a certain amount of validity. Clearly, for the theory to retain its strength, it would have to be modified somewhat in light of subsequent experience. The developmental history of England or the United States cannot be held up as a standard against which subsequent experiences must be measured. It is evident that there is not a single path to modernity: the "late" modernizers have taken a very different route to development (with the state playing a more powerful role) than earlier ones. Indeed, it is difficult to come up with a universally valid rule for the sequencing of political and economic liberalization. Although many states, particularly in Asia, have succeeded in following the "authoritarian" transition to democracy, it would have been absurd to propose that the former communist regimes in Eastern Europe delay democratization until their economies were liberalized.[8] Moreover, there is considerable variation in the way that both capitalism and democracy are implemented: Japanese corporations and labor markets are structured very differently from those in the United States, and there is no reason to think that Japanese and American practices will converge any time soon. Finally, the time frame required for economic development to produce conditions favorable to stable democracy is longer than anyone anticipated forty years ago: Sustained economic growth is difficult to achieve, and democratic institutions are even harder to create.

Nonetheless, a significant connection between development and democracy has been borne out over the past fifty years. Few of the original formulators of modernization theory are still around to defend it and willing to do so.[9] But they gave up too easily. If we define democracy and capitalism sufficiently broadly, and are not dogmatic about the means by which either one can be achieved, then the experience of the Asian nations can be seen as proof of the underlying hypothesis.

Asia's Confucian Traditions

Despite the positive relationship that has obtained between development and democracy in the past, many observers today would argue that Asia will not continue to democratize in the future, or that the form democracy takes there will be so specifically rooted in Asian traditions as to be unrecognizable to Westerners.

The most prominent proponent of an Asian alternative to democracy has been former Singaporean prime minister Lee Kuan Yew. Singapore under Lee developed a model of what might be called a "soft" or paternalistic form of authoritarianism, which combined capitalism with an authoritarian political system that suppressed freedom of speech and political dissent while intervening, often intrusively, in its citizens' personal lives. Lee has argued that this model is more appropriate to East Asia's Confucian cultural traditions than is the Western democratic model. In fact, he has said that Western-style democracy would have deleterious effects in a society like that of Singapore, encouraging permissiveness, social instability, and economically irrational decision making.

Many Western authorities on democracy would agree with this assessment of the relationship between Confucianism and democracy. Samuel P. Huntington, for example, has written that "Confucian democracy" is a contradiction in terms:

> Almost no scholarly disagreement exists regarding the proposition that traditional Confucianism was either undemocratic or antidemocratic. . . . Classic Chinese Confucianism and its derivatives in Korea, Vietnam, Singapore, Taiwan, and (in diluted fashion) Japan emphasized the group over the individual, authority over liberty, and responsibilities over rights. Confucian societies lacked a tradition of rights against the state; to the extent that individual rights did exist, they were created by the state. Harmony and cooperation were preferred over disagreement and competition. The maintenance of order and respect for hierarchy were central values. The conflict of ideas, groups, and parties was viewed as dangerous and illegitimate. Most important, Confucianism merged society and the state and provided no legitimacy for autonomous social institutions at the national level.[10]

According to Huntington, the only Asian countries to experience democracy prior to 1990 were Japan and the Philippines, and democratic transitions there were possible only because both countries were influenced directly by the United States and were less Confucian than other Asian societies.

In my view, the arguments of both Huntington and Lee greatly overstate the obstacles that Confucianism poses to the spread of a political system that is recognizably democratic in a Western sense. The most striking area of apparent incompatibility between democracy and Confucianism is the latter's lack of support for individualism or a transcendent law that would stand above existing social relationships and provide the ground for individual conscience as the ultimate source of authority. Despite this important difference, it is not clear that a Confucian society is incapable of creating workable democratic institutions that meet democracy's essential requirements.

Let us begin with the ways in which Confucianism is obviously compatible with democracy. First, the traditional Confucian examination system was a meritocratic institution with potentially egalitarian implications. In traditional China, the examination system was not— for various reasons—truly open to all who were qualified (neither, of course, are Harvard and Yale). In their modern form, however, the examination systems implemented in many Confucian societies as gateways into higher-educational systems and bureaucracies are significant paths to upward mobility that reinforce the relatively egalitarian income distributions that prevail throughout much of Asia. The second main area of compatibility is the Confucian emphasis on education itself. Although an educated populace is seldom noted as a formal requirement of democracy, in practice a society's general level of education has been an important underpinning of democratic institutions. Without a high level of literacy, people cannot know about and therefore participate in democratic debate; moreover, as indicated above, education tends to make people wealthier and more concerned with noneconomic issues such as recognition and political participation. Finally, like most Asian ethical systems, Confucianism is relatively tolerant. In the past, Confucianism has coexisted with other religions, notably Buddhism and Christianity; while Confucianism's record of tolerance is not perfect (witness the periodic persecutions of Buddhists in China), it is arguably better than that of either Islam or Christianity.

The compatibility of Confucianism with modern democracy goes even deeper than this, however, and in ways that are less often recognized. Huntington describes Confucianism as if it were comparable to Islam, being essentially a doctrine that unified the political and social spheres and legitimated the state's authority in all areas of life. Yet to say that Confucianism merely strengthens the group against the individual and the state against all subordinate organizations or institutions vastly oversimplifies the doctrine's real impact. The scholar of Confucianism Tu Wei-ming distinguishes between what he calls "political Confucianism," which legitimates a hierarchical political system culminating in the emperor, and what he calls the "Confucian personal ethic," which regulates day-to-day life.[11] In China, political Confucianism was very much tied to the imperial system and its supporting bureaucracy of gentlemen-scholars. This system was abolished with the overthrow of the Qing dynasty in 1911. Despite efforts by the Communists in Beijing and other Sinitic governments overseas (such as that of Singapore) to appropriate the legitimacy of the imperial system, the continuity of political Confucianism has been disrupted in a fundamental sense. Tu argues that in fact the more important legacy of traditional Confucianism is not its political teaching, but rather the personal ethic that regulates attitudes toward family, work, education, and other elements of daily life that are valued in Chinese society. It is these attitudes, rather than inherited ideas about political authority, that account for the economic success of the overseas Chinese.

One could go even further and argue that the essence of traditional Chinese Confucianism was never political Confucianism at all, but rather an intense familism that took precedence over all other social relations, including relations with political authorities. That is, Confucianism builds a well-ordered society from the ground up rather than the top down, stressing the moral obligations of family life as the basic building block of society. Beyond the traditional Chinese family, or *jia,* are lineages and larger kinship groups; the state and other political authorities are seen as a kind of family of families that unites all Chinese into a single social entity. But the bonds within the immediate family take precedence over higher sorts of ties, including obligations to the emperor. In classical Chinese Confucianism, one's obligation to one's father is greater than to the police; in a famous story related about Confucius, "The king boasted to Confucius that virtue in his land was such that if a father stole, his son would report the crime and the criminal to the state. Confucius replied that in his state virtue was far greater, for a son would never think of treating his father so."[12] (The Chinese Communists tried to change this state of affairs, but that is a different story.) Of course, in a perfectly ordered Confucian society, such conflicts between rival obligations should not occur. But occur they do, and while in classical Chinese dramas these conflicting obligations were often portrayed as a source of anguish, the superior authority of the family was made quite clear in the end.

In this respect, Chinese Confucianism is very different from the version that evolved in Japan when neo-Confucianism was imported into the country after the end of the Song dynasty (960–1279 C.E.). The Japanese modified Chinese Confucianism in certain strategic ways to make it compatible with their own imperial system. In China, even the emperor's authority was not absolute; it could be undermined altogether if his own immorality caused him to lose the "mandate of heaven." The succession of Chinese dynasties over the centuries is testimony to the impermanence of Chinese political authority. Japan, by contrast, has been characterized by a single, unbroken dynastic tradition since the mythical founding of the country, and no political equivalent of the loss of the "mandate of heaven" ever emerged by which a Japanese emperor could lose his throne. The Japanese were careful not to allow the political dictates of Confucianism to impinge on the prerogatives of the emperor and the ruling political class. Hence in Japan obligations to the emperor were superior to obligations to one's father, and a son facing the dilemma of reporting on his father would be required to favor the state over the family. In Chinese Confucianism, the family (or lineage) is a bulwark against the power of the state; in Japan, the family is a much weaker rival to political authority. Hence Huntington's characterization of Confucianism as inevitably supporting state power over subordinate social groups applies much more readily to Japanese than to Chinese Confucianism. Yet it is Japan, rather than China, that has been democratic for the past 45 years.

Granite and Sand

This contrast between Chinese and Japanese Confucianism has given rise to several important differences between the two countries' political cultures—differences that should have implications for the prospects of Western-style democracy. Given the strength of intrafamilial bonds within a traditional Chinese society, ties between people unrelated to each other are relatively weak. In other words, in a Chinese society there is a relatively high degree of distrust between people who are not related. The Chinese may be characterized as family-oriented, but they are not group-oriented, as the Japanese are frequently said to be. The competition between families frequently makes Chinese society appear more individualistic to Western observers than Japanese society, and is the basis for the famous remark that while the Japanese are like a block of granite, the Chinese are like a tray of sand, with each grain representing a single family.

Because of the primacy of the family in China, political authority there has always been weaker than in Japan, and political instability much closer to the surface. Chinese families have traditionally been suspicious of government authority, and many Chinese family businesses—both in the People's Republic of China (PRC) and among the overseas (or Nanyang) Chinese—go through elaborate machinations to hide their affairs from the tax collector and other officials. Nationalism and national identity have traditionally been much weaker in China than in Japan: there is little sense in China of the "us-against-them" mentality that has at times characterized Japanese nationalism. In business relationships and even political affiliations, loyalties to family, lineage, and region frequently take precedence over the mere fact of being Chinese. It has often been remarked that the level of citizenship is lower in China than it is in many other societies: provided the state leaves them alone, most Chinese do not feel any particular obligations to the larger society in which they live. And there is certainly no generalized moral obligation to do right by strangers simply because they are human beings, as there is in Christian culture. Because they lack the intense feeling of natural unity that the Japanese have, the Chinese find political instability, in a sense, more psychologically threatening.

Paradoxically, the weaker Chinese deference to authority creates a greater need for an authoritarian political system in Chinese societies. Precisely because state authority is less respected in China, the danger of social chaos emerging in the absence of an overt, repressive state structure is greater there than in Japan. The fear of China's fragmenting and becoming dangerously unstable was clearly one of the factors motivating the Chinese Communist leadership in its crackdown on the prodemocracy movement at Tiananmen Square in June 1989. Fear of disintegration is what continues to make China's rulers reluctant to liberalize the political system significantly. One is led to suspect that the emphasis on political authoritarianism in Singapore and other Southeast Asian states is less a reflection of those societies' self-discipline—as they would have outsiders believe—than of their rather low level of spontaneous citizenship and corresponding fear of coming apart in the absence of coercive political authority. In Japan, by contrast, it is not necessary for the state to legislate against failing to flush public toilets or writing on walls, because the society itself has absorbed and internalized such rules.

The relationship between Confucianism and democracy, then, is far more complex than many commentators have indicated. Chinese Confucianism, in particular, does not legitimate deference to the authority of an all-powerful state that leaves no scope for the development of an independent civil society. If civil society is weak in China, that weakness is due not to a statist ideology, but rather to the strong familism that is basic to Chinese culture, and the consequent reluctance of the Chinese to trust people outside of their kinship groups. The problem that will confront the institutionalization of democracy in China in the future will not be a culturally ingrained deference to state authority, but a sense of citizenship too feeble to generate spontaneous coherence or call forth sacrifices for the sake of national unity. As in other familistic societies in Southern Europe or Latin America, there will be a need to bring the "morality of the street" more in line with the morality of the family.

The experience of communism in the PRC has done nothing to alter these cultural attitudes, despite decades of anti-Confucian indoctrination. Indeed, the importance of family obligations in the PRC has, if anything, deepened over the past few generations. The traditional Chinese family, after all, was essentially a defensive mechanism that served to protect its members against an arbitrary and capricious state:

although one could not trust the local authorities, one could trust members of one's own family. Nothing in the chaotic political experience of China in the twentieth century has led the average Chinese to change this evaluation of relative risks. Hence we see even members of the communist elite in China securing educations, foreign bank accounts, and safe havens for their children in the event that the communist political edifice comes crashing down.

The statist, group-oriented attitudes toward authority that Huntington believes to be characteristic of Confucianism per se are more properly characteristic of Japan and Japanese Confucianism, and were indeed manifest in Japan in an extreme form during the 1930s. As a result of the disastrous experience of the Second World War, nationalism and statism have been delegitimized, and replaced by a workable democracy. Traditionally deferential attitudes toward political authority continued to be evident, however, in the long-unchallenged rule of the bureaucracy-LDP-business triangle in the postwar period. As noted earlier, however, it is not clear that these attitudes will continue to pose an insurmountable barrier to a more participatory, Western form of democracy featuring multiparty contestation for power.

The ways in which Confucian culture—both Chinese and Japanese—differs significantly from the Christian and democratic culture of the West have to do with the status of the individual. Although Chinese familism may appear individualistic in some respects, it is not the same as the individualism that undergirds the Western ideal. That is, individuals in China do not have a source of legitimate authority on the basis of which they can revolt against their families and the web of social ties into which they are born. Christianity provides the concept of a transcendent God whose Word is the highest source of right. God's laws take precedence over all other obligations—remember that God required Abraham to be willing to sacrifice his son—and this transcendent source of morality is what enables an individual in the West to repudiate all forms of social obligation, from the family all the way up to the state. In modern liberalism, the Christian concept of a universal God is replaced with the concept of an underlying human nature that becomes the universal basis of right. Liberal rights apply to all human beings as such, just as God's law did in Christianity, transcending any particular set of real-world social obligations. While not all of today's American human rights advocates working for organizations like Asia Watch or Amnesty International would describe themselves as believing Christians, they all share their Christian culture's emphasis on universal rights and, consequently, individual conscience as the ultimate source of authority. This, it is safe to say, does not have a counterpart in any Confucian society. It is this difference that is at the root of contemporary disagreements between Americans and Asians over human rights policy.

In evaluating the claim of a fundamental incompatibility between Confucianism and liberal democracy, we should remember that many experts once thought that Confucianism presented insuperable obstacles to capitalist economic modernization as well. While Huntington argues—correctly—that modern liberal democracy grew out of Christian culture, it is clear that democracy emerged only after a long succession of incarnations of Christianity that were inimical to liberal tolerance and democratic contestation. All in all, the obstacles posed by Confucian culture do not seem any greater than those posed by other cultures; indeed, when compared to those of Hinduism or Islam, they appear to be much smaller.

An Attitudinal Shift

The upshot of all this is that Confucianism by no means mandates an authoritarian political system. In Singapore, the current political authorities are appealing to Confucian traditions somewhat dishonestly to justify an intrusive and unnecessarily paternalistic political system. Other Confucian societies like Japan and South Korea have been able to accommodate a greater degree of political participation and individual liberty than Singapore without compromising their own fundamental cultural values, and Taiwan is moving rapidly in the same direction. I see no reason why Singapore should not be able to follow this path. If economic modernization does lead to demands for greater recognition, it will be the next generation of Singaporeans who will be voicing the strongest demands for greater political participation and individual freedom—not because these are Western values, but because they meet the needs of a middle-class, well-educated populace.

On the other hand, virtually no one in Asia today believes it likely that Asian societies will ultimately converge with the particular model of liberal democracy represented by the contemporary United States, or, indeed, that such a state of affairs is remotely desirable. This represents quite a change from the early postwar period, when many people—and not just in Asia—believed that the United States was the exemplar of a modern democracy, to be revered and emulated. This attitudinal shift can be traced to two subsequent developments. The first was East Asia's spectacular economic growth, which many people attributed to the region's Confucian traditions. The second was a perceived decline in the American standard of living, measured not in terms of per-capita GDP, but rather in terms of growing crime, the breakdown of the family, a loss of civility, racial tensions, and illegal immigration—problems that showed no sign of abating. In the view of many Asians, individualism was far too rampant in American society and was leading to social chaos, with potentially devastating economic and political consequences. Thus some began to argue that a "soft" authoritarian system—rooted in

Confucian principles and characterized by less individual liberty and more social discipline—not only would result in faster economic growth, but would create a much more satisfying society in terms of overall quality of life.

There is both an element of truth and a great deal of exaggeration in this Asian analysis of what currently ails the United States. It is true that the individualism deeply ingrained in the theoretical principles underlying the U.S. Constitution and legal system has no counterpart in Asian culture. It is thus no accident that American political discourse is framed largely in terms of conflicting individual rights. Yet as Mary Ann Glendon has pointed out, this "rights talk" is a dialect unique to the United States, with its Lockean and Jeffersonian traditions; in most modern European countries, individual rights are carefully balanced in constitutional law against responsibilities to the community.[13] Moreover, even in the American tradition, the inherent individualism of the constitutional-legal system has always been counterbalanced in practice by strongly communitarian social habits. This high degree of communal participation derived originally from religion (that is, the sectarian form of Protestantism dominant in the United States) and later from the communal habits of America's ethnic groups as well. Alexis de Tocqueville noted in the 1830s that Americans were very good at associating with one another and subordinating their individualism to voluntary groups of one type or another.

It is only in the past couple of generations that the balance between individualism and communalism in the United States has been tipped decisively in favor of the former. For a variety of historical reasons, communal institutions have grown weaker—or have been deliberately undermined by the state—while the number and scope of basic individual rights to which Americans feel they are entitled have steadily increased. The causes of the problem—and possible solutions to it—are well beyond the scope of the present essay, but the result has been a diminution of the appeal to Asians of the American model of democracy. Nor are Asians alone in this view; judging from the positive reaction that many Americans exhibited to the caning of Michael Fay in Singapore, this model has become much less appealing to Americans themselves.

Finding a Balance

To many Asians, the social problems currently plaguing the United States are problems of liberal democracy per se. To the extent that this perception continues, the future of democracy in Asia will depend less on the theoretical compatibility or incompatibility of Confucianism with democratic principles than on whether people in Asia feel that they want their society to resemble that of the United States.

Asia is therefore at a very interesting crossroads. It is quite possible that the modernization hypothesis will continue to be borne out in the future, and that rising per-capita incomes and educational levels in the region will be accompanied by an increasing democratization of political systems. As noted above, this is because there is a universal tendency of human beings to seek recognition of their dignity through a political system that allows them to participate as adult human beings. On the other hand, people's choices are strongly influenced by the alternatives that they see directly at hand, and if East Asia continues to prosper and the United States makes little or no progress in solving its economic and social problems, the Western democratic model will become less and less attractive. Japan's experience will be critical. If Japan emerges from the current recession with its people believing that the country's economic problems were the result of the accumulated inefficiencies of the period of LDP domination, then there will be a sustained impetus for reform of the political system and enhanced prospects for a more genuinely democratic Japan. Yet there is a real possibility that the reform effort itself will become the scapegoat for Japan's economic woes, in which case a sentiment favoring restoration of a more authoritarian kind of political system may take root.

I do not have any particular prediction to make, concerning either Japan or Asia as a whole. What I hope to have shown, however, is that there is no fundamental cultural obstacle to the democratization of contemporary Confucian societies, and there is some reason to believe that these societies will move in the direction of greater political liberalization as they grow wealthier. We should regard assertions that authoritarian political systems are necessarily more Confucian than democratic systems with a certain amount of skepticism. In fact, Confucian values might work quite well in a liberal society (as they clearly do for many Asian immigrants to the United States), where they can serve as a counterbalance to the larger society's atomizing tendencies. On the other hand, the particular form that Asian democracy will ultimately take is unlikely to be identical to the model represented by the United States. If Asia's Confucian traditions allow it to find an appropriate and stable balance between the need for liberty and the need for community, in the end it will be a politically happy place indeed.

NOTES

1. See, for example, Lee's interview with Fareed Zakaria in *Foreign Affairs* 73 (1994): 109–27.

2. The basic texts outlining early postwar modernization theory include Daniel Lerner, *The Passing of Traditional Society* (Glencoe, Ill.: The Free Press, 1958), and the various works of Talcott Parsons, especially *The Structure of Social Action* (New York: McGraw-Hill, 1937), (with Edward Shils) *Toward a General Theory of*

Action (Cambridge: Harvard University Press, 1951), and *The Social System* (Glencoe, Ill.: The Free Press, 1951). In this tradition were the nine volumes sponsored by the American Social Science Research Council between 1963 and 1975, beginning with Lucian Pye's *Communications and Political Development* (Princeton: Princeton University Press, 1963) and ending with Raymond Grew's *Crises of Political Development in Europe and the United States* (Princeton: Princeton University Press, 1978).

3. Seymour Martin Lipset, "Some Social Requisites of Democracy: Economic Development and Political Legitimacy," *American Political Science Review* 53 (1959): 69–105.

4. For empirical evidence, see Larry Diamond, "Economic Development and Democracy Reconsidered," *American Behavioral Scientist* 15 (March–June 1992): 450–99.

5. Talcott Parsons, "Evolutionary Universals in Society," *American Sociological Review* 29 (June 1964): 339–57.

6. See my *The End of History and the Last Man* (New York: The Free Press, 1992), esp. pt. 2, and "Capitalism and Democracy: The Missing Link," *Journal of Democracy* 3 (July 1992): 100–110.

7. See especially Karel van Wolferen, *The Enigma of Japanese Power* (London: Macmillan, 1989).

8. On this subject see Barbara Geddes, "Challenging the Conventional Wisdom," *Journal of Democracy* 5 (October 1994): 104–18; and Minxin Pei, "The Puzzle of East Asian Exceptionalism," *Journal of Democracy* 5 (October 1994): 90–103.

9. One exception is Lucian Pye. See his "Political Science and the Crisis of Authoritarianism," *American Political Science Review* 84 (March 1990): 3–17.

10. Samuel P. Huntington, "Democracy's Third Wave," *Journal of Democracy* 2 (Spring 1991): 24.

11. Tu Wei-ming, *Confucian Ethics Today: The Singapore Challenge* (Singapore: Curriculum Development Institute of Singapore, 1984), 90.

12. Quoted in Marion J. Levy, *The Rise of the Modern Chinese Business Class* (New York: Institute of Pacific Relations, 1949), 1.

13. Mary Ann Glendon, *Rights Talk: The Impoverishment of Political Discourse* (New York: The Free Press, 1992).

4

HINDUISM AND SELF-RULE

Pratap Bhanu Mehta

Pratap Bhanu Mehta *is president of the Center for Policy Research in New Delhi. He has taught government at Harvard, and is author of* The Burden of Democracy *(2003). The present essay originally appeared in the July 2004 issue of the* Journal of Democracy.

Discussions of this or that religious tradition and democracy often begin by listing democratic values such as equality, liberty, toleration, rights, and the like and then asking to what extent they can find support—or at least noncontradiction—within the tradition's teachings. While such exercises can be useful in saving a religion from caricature, they generally shed little light on the actual—and often paradoxical—dynamics that link the world's diverse array of spiritual traditions with the ideas and practices of modern democratic politics.

This is so for a number of reasons. First, a tradition's teachings—even if wonderfully rich and complex in themselves—may have a historically indeterminate relationship to questions of social organization. Hinduism's emphasis on the importance of coming to know and develop one's fullest potentialities, for example, would seem to be a promising resource for the democratic imagination. Yet the long sweep of Hindu history records few attempts to "connect the dots" between such spiritual teachings and sociopolitical attitudes. Then too, the real point in such matters is not what a tradition teaches, but how and what its adherents think and feel. Humans are not merely passive products of culture or religious doctrine, but agents who constantly and actively imagine and reimagine their beliefs and social worlds. Third, and perhaps most important for present purposes, to the extent that religious ideas matter, they do so in ways that are often unintended and paradoxical. As Max Weber argued, it was not Calvinist Christianity's overt teachings but their unlooked-for side effects that powered the rise of capitalism in northwestern Europe. To neglect such complexities is to risk misrepresenting both how a given tradition works in practice and how its beliefs might be related causally to a political order such as democracy. In this spirit, I will forgo offering a "democracy-relevant" catalogue of Hindu teachings and sources, and will try instead to suggest how democracy came to be produced and legitimized through a complex series of negotiations among Hindus.

It has often been remarked that the word "Hindu"—which comes from the same root as the name of the modern-day country of India—is not a term of self-identification, but rather a catchall description used by visitors from the west who originally meant it as shorthand for "those who live east or south of the Indus River." Even at the time of Alexander the Great such people were comparatively numerous and exhibited great and obvious diversity, so the question "Who is a Hindu?" has long had currency. A congeries of movements over the years have sought to explain and create a unified Hindu identity. In the modern period, most critically, a single Hindu legal identity began to emerge as a product of state formation (first colonial and then sovereign) in the nineteenth and twentieth centuries.

Among the most remarkable chapters in the story of how the state has midwifed and defined Hindu identity was a case that the Indian Supreme Court resolved with a landmark 1966 ruling following almost two decades of litigation.[1] The Court made the Swami Narayana sect of Bombay comply with a 1947 law that had opened Hindu temples to all worshipers, including members of "untouchable" hereditary castes. The ruling denied the sect members' claim that they were non-Hindus and hence exempt from having to admit the despised castes. The Court worried that letting a Hindu sect evade the reach of progressive laws would stifle efforts to reform Hinduism at large. The Court emphasized Hinduism's historic capacity for internal reform, its progressive outlook, its flexibility, it compatibility with social equality, and its extraordinary tolerance. Hinduism, the Court taught, is not only consistent with democracy, progress, equality, and social reform, but requires a commitment to these things.

The Court's opinion not only bore directly on the issue of who counts as a Hindu, but also struggled with the task of defining Hinduism itself (the Court came up with a seven-item list of Hindu essentials). The invidious caste distinction at the heart of the case was itself a reminder of the complicated transformations that Hinduism has had to undergo in order to become compatible with democracy. The caste system with all its interdictions, exclusions, and regulations is one of the most elaborately and egregiously hierarchical social conceptions that humans have ever entertained. Dominant interpretations of Hinduism long legitimized caste. A society preoccupied with it would hardly seem to be a promising ground for democracy, individual freedom, or equality. While it is true that freedom and equality remain subject to political contestation in India, the striking thing is that this most hierarchically ordered of societies should have so readily embraced, in principle at first and then increasingly in practice, the principles and the procedures of liberal democracy.

The speed of the change in these millennia-old customs is also stunning. Universal suffrage first arose as a topic of discussion in the early 1890s. By the mid-1920s, the major movements representing Hinduism had accepted the principle. Since India's independence from Britain and partition from Pakistan in 1947, the overall direction of political change has been toward greater power for the numerically vast but long-downtrodden lower castes. They now occupy the political center of gravity in the world's largest democracy. All of this comes to seem even more remarkable when one reflects that in the first half of the twentieth century, no social theory extant anywhere would have advised the introduction of universal suffrage in a poverty-ridden, caste-bound, and largely illiterate society.

Democracy and Cricket

"Democracy," runs a revealing Indian quip, "is like cricket—a quintessentially Indian game that just happens to have been invented elsewhere." Adopting democracy in India required a radical transformation of Hindus' self-understanding, not least because it required them to make real a polity which was, at that time, barely even imaginable. One can readily see how Hindus would have had to satisfy themselves that democracy was at least not against Hindu traditions. What surprises is the extent to which Hindus went beyond this: The early twentieth century on the subcontinent saw a torrent of literature contending that Hinduism required a positive commitment to democracy. Some arguments, including Gandhi's, sought to prove that *swaraj* (self-rule) in all its senses was at Hinduism's core.[2] Others tried to show that a certain conception of democratic practice had always been central to Indian society.[3]

Crucial to such trailblazing writings was Hinduism's complex encounter with colonialism. The presence of the British Raj and all that it signified put pressure on Hindu traditions and forced Hinduism to rearticulate its own principles. Such rethinkings are matters of active human choice, and the directions they take can be unpredictable. Colonial rule was legitimized by the ideas that subject peoples or societies were in some sense backward and that they were not *nations*, and hence had no claim to recognition as sovereign entities. A sense of this backdrop is crucial if one wants to understand how Hinduism has been reframing itself since the nineteenth century. In part the process has been defensive: There have been attempts to show that Hinduism is the source of all that modernity prizes, from democracy to science. Whatever one thinks of such hermeneutical exercises, the key thing politically is that they have had the effect of legitimizing new values in Hindu terms. To claim, even if on historically dubious grounds, that one's tradition is a source of democracy is after all to acknowledge democracy's stature and legitimacy. In its encounter with other traditions, of which liberalism and enlightenment were a subset, Hinduism became aware that if it failed to claim as its own certain values identified with progressive modernity, it would remain vulnerable both to outside criticism and to defections from within its own ranks. Reform may flow from high principle, but it may also arise out of a tradition's sense of what it needs to do to survive external and internal challenges.

The imperative of creating a nation required new and more horizontal forms of mobilization. Nationalism, as Liah Greenfeld points out, is the crucible of modern democracy.[4] Any coherent anticolonial critique must assume that the colonized society can be a self-governing nation. Indians could demand self-determination only by appealing to the authority of a new presence in the social imaginary called "the Indian people." But this would require: 1) privileging their status as members of this people—as citizens of a nation struggling to be born, in other words—over older and more restrictive forms of identification such as sect, clan, or caste; and 2) granting this people at least a modicum of participatory access. Thus did anticolonial nationalism tend to carry secular and democratic ideas along in its logical train.

As important as the imperatives of social reform and nationalism were, however, they would not have been enough to make Indians feel an elective affinity for democracy had certain longstanding features of Hinduism not been present. The notion that democracy fits nicely into, or even can somehow be said to spring from Hindu tradition may have begun as part of a defense against colonialist claims, but there are features of Hinduism that bolster this line of thought. There is something to be said for the idea that Hinduism has a certain supple, plural, or open quality. As the Indian Supreme Court confessed in a recent ruling:

> [W]e find it difficult, if not impossible to define Hindu religion or even adequately describe it. Unlike other religions in the world, the Hindu religion does not claim any one prophet; it does not worship any one God. It does not subscribe to any one dogma: it does not believe in any one philosophic concept: it does not follow any one set of religious rites or performances; in fact, it does not appear to satisfy the narrow traditional features of any religion or creed.[5]

Hinduism, moreover, is a tradition whose source texts contain a great deal of what might be called skepticism. As the *Mahabharata* says:

> There are many different Vedas, the law books are many, the advice of one sage is necessarily different from that given by others. The real rules of duty remain buried in a dark cave. The only path is the way in which great men [or in some readings, "a great many men"] have lived their lives.

Within primal Hinduism, in short, the question of authority was open to a remarkable degree. Hinduism's complex encounter with colonialism—

and with modernity more generally—both tested that openness and made it possible for Hindus who grasped the inner and outer challenges that their tradition was facing to leverage the tradition's openness in constructive ways.

Hindu Law and the Debate About Reform

Yet not all was by design. Decisive accidents and momentous side effects played a role as well. One such side effect began its cascading career in 1765, when the British East India Company started to consolidate Hindus into a single *legal* community. In 1772, mostly for reasons of expediency and out of a hope that respecting local ways would help to legitimize its rule, the Company directed its civil courts to adhere "invariably" to Koranic law with respect to Muslims and to the *shastras* (Hindu scriptures) with respect to Hindus "in all suits regarding inheritance, marriage, caste and all other religious usages or institutions." Though administered by ordinary courts, these laws—unlike criminal statutes—were not applied equally across Company territory, but according to differences of personal status related to membership in religiously defined social groups.

For help in navigating the complexities of native law, the British institutionalized the role of Hindu and Muslim legal experts trained in the interpretation of normative traditional texts. Over time, differences of opinion among these experts, as well as the Company's suspicion that some experts were being deliberately misleading, led to efforts to regularize their training under Company supervision as well as to codify religious law in the form of standard legal digests. Particularly in the case of Hindu texts, this meant unearthing, studying, and most importantly publicizing original and ancient religious sources.

The implications were enormous. First, the process of codification remade the very idea of what counted as Hindu tradition. British officials generally privileged some written *shastras* over others, and tended to privilege *shastras* as a whole over unwritten customs. An explicit legal code based on ancient Sanskrit-language writings displaced the fluidity and variability of customary law. This project, undertaken to serve the official purposes of British judges and administrators, caused the standardization and homogenization (sometimes regressive, sometimes progressive) of social and religious practices in accord with ancient norms often identified with the priestly Brahmins, Hinduism's highest caste. The project also reified the equation of tradition and religion in such a way that all future debate on social and legal reform would take tradition, albeit variously construed, as normative.[6]

The codification project also sparked debates over who had authority to do the codifying, and why. A crucial episode in the long contest came in 1891, the year that saw the promulgation of the Age of Consent

Act, which said that no female under 12 years old could be given in wedlock (as across most of the world, the long-dominant custom in India had been marriages arranged under the authority of patriarchs). The Act met with bitter and concerted opposition. It was the first piece of social legislation that colonial authorities had passed since 1856, when Governor-General Lord Dalhousie had banned *suttee* (widow-burning) on the eve of the Great Indian Mutiny. In 1859, after the violent suppression of this massive uprising—which had been partly a backlash against British changes to native customs—Britain had declared a prudential policy of nonintervention in subcontinental religious matters. By 1891, nationalists had committed themselves to the defense of native traditions. Even India's Westernized intellectual classes were less willing to cooperate with the British in the cause of reform.

Some of the opposition to British-led reform was simply reactionary. But another strain of feeling opposed less the substance of this or that reform than the British part in it. Partha Chaterjee, whose analysis of these episodes is the most impressive I have seen, argues that the emergent nationalist imagination was dividing society into two domains: the outer, material and public domain; and the inner, spiritual domain of the private. The outer domain was the realm of public institutions, economics, technology, and civil society. This domain was the social space where creative borrowing from the West could take place. The inner domain was supposed to remain the ambit of tradition and a distinct cultural identity. In this sphere, which was taken to include religion and family life, nationalists rejected emulation of the West and sought to preserve what they saw as venerable cultural traditions. Crucially, nationalists believed that the nation as a whole was entitled to claim sovereignty over this inner domain.[7] Opposition to British reforms such as the Age of Consent Act bespoke this shift in the "agency of reform from the legal authority of the colonial state to the moral authority of the national community."[8] Nationalists felt that the task of authenticating, articulating, codifying, and reforming tradition should belong to the entire nation.

The nationalists had two goals: to throw off colonial subordination, and to take distinctively "national" traditions out of the realm of the un–self-conscious and merely customary in order that the nation itself might claim them to further its self-realization as an autonomous entity deserving of sovereignty. Of course, who exactly might be said to constitute the nation and on what terms was and is deeply contested. The general expectation among Indian nationalists seems to have been that each of the subcontinent's various subcommunities would take charge of revivifying and reforming its own traditions and customs.

Such thinking helped to inspire a spate of Hindu and Muslim reform movements that swept floodlike across early twentieth-century British India. The idea was to enact substantive reforms, and to refashion communal identities in the process. Muslim reformers sought to replace the variegated array of customary practices followed by their coreligionists in various parts of India with a common and reformed Muslim personal law. This effort culminated in the passage of the Shariat Application Act of 1937. At about the same time, wide-ranging Hindu reform movements were paving the way for Hinduism's modernization. The precise agendas of such movements and the furious controversies that they generated need not detain us here. What is crucial is that these movements were not just challenging the authority of the colonial state to interpret native traditions, but were opening up these religions to a far-reaching self-examination. This was a contest over doctrine, authority, and identity.

Authority and Ambivalence

But who *did* have the authority to speak for indigenous traditions, and why? That never became clear. Hindus in particular had unique issues of their own to wrestle with as they tried to answer this question. One issue was Hinduism's own ambivalence about politics. As one of the most astute analysts of Indian political thought puts it, "Kingship remains, even theoretically, suspended between sacrality and secularity, divinity and mortal humanity, legitimate authority and arbitrary power, dharma and adharma."[9] Political power and spiritual authority were firmly separated, as exemplified by the traditional distinction between the priestly Brahmins and the Kshatriya (warrior) caste. The king inhabited the realm of necessity where politics had its own autonomy and internal logic that brooked no outside interference. But the king drew his legitimacy from his service to the "spiritual order," just as the priests depended upon the king for physical protection. The upshot is that Hindu thought's version of the separation of church and state has never been quite stable. And yet politics, even when dependent upon religion for earthly legitimization, has never in Hindu thought taken on messianic or apocalyptic significance. The world of the political is significant, but it can never become an arena for what Eric Voegelin called "the immanentization of the eschaton."

In practice, this Hindu capacity to imagine and honor the political without expecting it to give meaning to everything or comprehensively relieve the human estate has been of great service in defining the secular space that liberal democracy requires. A steady respect for the proper autonomy of different spheres of human action and a sober refusal to pine for a single ethical order that can render the world whole are aspects of the Hindu moral imagination that not only reinforce democratic politics, but also help to set healthy boundaries for it. When Hindus claim that democracy has been a "natural" outgrowth of Hinduism, they may be gesturing at something like this account of Hindu political prudence and moderation. The Hindu tendency to see politics as an autonomous but limited sphere obviates the need to impose a single doctrinal orthodoxy, and permits a well-advised toleration of various forms of social existence. Indeed, Hindu intellectuals' discussions of democracy often seem to equate it with a kind of group pluralism: Sarvepalli Radhakrishnan's influential *Hindu View of Life* mostly sees democracy as a matter of ensuring that each group "should be allowed to develop the best in it without impeding the progress of others."[10]

Yet contrary to what Radhakrishnan and other neo-Hindu apologists have claimed, traditional Hindu intellectual pluralism long coexisted with the imposition of the most rigid social orthodoxy and hierarchy. Different groups were tolerated only so long as they stayed well within certain none-too-broad boundaries and conventions. While the specific distribution of power and authority among castes could be fluid, and while protests against caste hierarchies flared from time to time, premodern Hinduism on the whole remained bound up with the phenomenon of caste. Many Hindu reformers, such as Swami Vivekanada (1863–1902), thought that political democratization might be the only sure means of improving the lot of historically marginalized groups, since their ranks were so large and democracy does so much by majority rule. The empowerment of India's lower castes goes on still, and still encounters resistance.

Hinduism may have been hierarchical, but it was at the same time so plural that Hindu society was nearly impervious to projects for imposing centralized uniformity. Even after colonialism and then statehood brought a measure of centralization, the pluralism of Hindu group life continued to spin such a complex web of crisscrossing cleavages that no single group could hope to dominate, a circumstance indirectly propitious for liberal democracy. To gain power required building alliances whose very formation would tend to rub the sharpest edges off a group's own claims. Hinduism's skeptical streak and sophisticated approach to ethical reflection, moreover, precluded dreams of reducing the complexity of Hindu society to an imposed conformity of allegedly "pure" thought or belief.

Another unique aspect of the Hindu situation was the impact of Islamic conquests in the subcontinent during the centuries before the British achieved dominance. Hindus had lived under a congeries of regional and local rulers, including the Muslim Mughal emperors. There is nothing in Hindu history like the Islamic caliphate whose specter still haunts the imagination of the Muslim world. The absence of any historical model of a kingdom that represented Hindus as Hindus made it easier to experiment with new political forms and gave leeway for fresh thinking about political questions. This "do-it-yourself" quality of the Hindu experience may also help to explain why so many Hindus have been and continue to be fascinated by the idea that democracy is somehow a "Hindu" system that springs from Hindu sources and represents Hindus as such.

Hinduism has mostly known only local forms of authority, whether embodied by Brahmins in some areas or by other dominant castes elsewhere. Modern times brought all-Indian political forms (first the Raj, then the Republic) and an all-Indian consciousness to go with them. As state consolidation made strides, traditional forms of authority became ever more limited in their sway. There was no way that appeals to such fading and fragmented sources of authority could legitimize anyone's hope to rule the huge new entity being created across the vast land between the Himalayas and Ceylon. With traditional authority dropping out of the picture, in practice the sole recourse for all those hungering and thirsting after political legitimacy and credibility was popular mobilization in some guise or other. Only democracy, in other words, could fill the void left by the older authorities' ineluctable ebb.

As internal and external pressures for change mounted, Hindus had to face them without any institution that had *prima facie* authority to direct the reforms: Hinduism lacks not only a caliphate but a Vatican as well. What agency was there, then, with the power and the legitimacy to undertake the overhaul of religious traditions? What would be a credible representative and institutional process through which a task of such magnitude and sensitivity could be carried out? In postindependence India, the answer turned out to be obvious: Only the modern state, with institutions legitimized by universal suffrage, could take up the work of reforming Hinduism. The modern Indian state is secular in the obvious sense of the term. It accords equal citizenship to people of all religious descriptions—modern India's Muslim population is outstripped in numbers only by those of Indonesia and Pakistan, while Christianity has been present on the subcontinent since apostolic times and Buddhism originated there. The state favors no establishment of religion. Yet the Indian Constitution has been rightly called a charter for the social reform of Hinduism: The secular, democratic government of this Hinduism-suffused society is the authoritative vehicle for the reform of Hinduism. Perhaps secularism, like cricket and democracy, is a quintessentially Indian game that just happens to have been invented elsewhere.

The Indian state thus not only aims to reform Hindu practices, but also enjoys an authorization of sorts from Hindus to do so. In the Indian context, therefore, it is legitimate for state institutions such as the Supreme Court and the Lok Sabha (parliament) to concern themselves with reforming or eliminating invidious socioreligious practices such as second-class treatment of "untouchables." Faced with the challenge "Who shall decide?" Hindus in effect answered: "We all will, and the federal Republic of India will be our means."

The Extremist Security Blanket

Although many would argue that Hindu moral theory furnishes arguments which strengthen democracy, Hindus have generated their own brand of intolerance. While the processes of reform within Hinduism led it inexorably toward democracy, many see in Hindu nationalism a threat to the democratic idea. Given the history just recounted, the heterogeneity of Hinduism itself, and the sense in which Hinduism has made modernity its own, it is unlikely that any Hindu mass movement will ever be able to set up anything close to a theocracy in the usual Western sense of the word. It is not insignificant that even Hindu nationalism seems to feel a need to legitimize itself as a secular ideology: Movement apologists typically claim that they are not against secular principles as such, but only upset that Hindus, India's majority, are asked to accept secularist limits while minorities receive numerous exemptions based on religious identity.

This line of rhetoric, with its narrative of complaint against perceived subjugation, indicates a crisis within Hinduism. While there is much that is still religiously vital about Hindu piety and the remarkable account of life and creation that Hindu teachings provide, being a Hindu is increasingly coming to be identified with participation in the invention of a communal identity that can now fully, and often furiously, discharge its role in history. It is an identity constituted by a sense of injury, a sense of always having been on the losing side, of being a victimized innocent. This narrative strings together Mughal rule with the loss of territorial integrity during partition. It draws sustenance from the all too real threat posed by international Islamist jihadism and plays upon the sentiment that modern secularism itself is a contrivance biased in favor of minorities. Much of the understanding of history that sustains this sense of injury is false or oversimplified. But of greater import is that Hindu identity is coming in many ways to rest upon a sense of resentment that puts minorities at risk and threatens liberal democracy.[11]

Some say that beneath the shouted certitudes of religious or ideological extremism may often be heard the small but persistent whisperings of doubt and insecurity. Could this be so in India today? Do too many of the subcontinent's Hindus (the Hindus of the diaspora are another matter) fear that their religion can no longer prove its worth through its achievements, its intellectual vitality, or the hopeful creativity it nurtures, and so must hug its resentments that much harder? Do anger and extremism, in other words, weave a kind of security blanket for those who wonder about the meaning and relevance under complex modern conditions of their religious tradition (and the questions this raises about their own commitment to it), but who for various reasons prefer what may well be the easier course of seeking enemies without rather than answers within?

In practice, the most immediate threats to democracy from Hindu nationalism have taken the form of efforts by nationalist intellectuals and activists to set benchmarks for national identity. The book that has most influentially stated the nationalist case, V.D. Savarkar's *Hindutva*,[12] begins by asking: "What is India?" The author, who is an intellectual godfather to India's important Bharatiya Janata Party (BJP), rehearses various answers that have been proffered (India is a civilization; India is a community formed by a shared history; and the like). In each case, he shows that the answer either raises more questions than it settles or avoids the issue. Appeals to "common history," for instance, ignore the reality that "history" in the relevant sense is not a set of brute facts about the past, but rather an elective human interpretation: Only people who already think of themselves as having something in common, argues Savarkar, will see themselves as possessors of a common history. Much the same could be said of political institutions: They do not constitute unity so much as reflect it. We also learn that neither language nor (perhaps surprisingly) religion can supply the answer: India is home to a profusion of tongues and religions, and the Hinduism of the majority is internally quite diverse.

Calling the various bluffs behind these alternative accounts of India, Savarkar argues that only the concept of nationhood can command the necessary respect at home and abroad and summon the collective endeavor that history demands of all aspirants to national status. But what makes a nation? In Savarkar's logic, whatever the people share in a nation worthy of the name has to be something that is beyond beliefs, social practices, culture, political institutions, or history. It must be something that exists over and above all the divisions that cleave along these lines, something that is more enduring than political vicissitudes and religiocultural differences.

What could that be? Here Savarkar invokes the trope of blood, of common kinship. Surely a sort of common racial descent unites Indians; whatever their differences, they are as one in a common blood. Savarkar is looking for a way of giving India an identity that can encompass all other differences. His answer is that being Indian means essentially possessing a common ethnicity, which he names Hindutva or "Hinduness." This is what all Indians have in common, including Muslims, Christians, Sikhs, Jains, and Buddhists. For Savarkar and the many to whom he appeals, the call of blood or the race answers the question of what it is to be an Indian. If this vision meets with opposition, he adds, it is because many communities such as the Muslims do not acknowledge who they really are. Rather than giving moral priority and their highest allegiance to their true identity, they direct their devotion beyond India. Rather than acknowledging their common descent, they seek to differentiate themselves. But a benchmark of Indian identity is refusing to follow foreign gods.

The Blind Alley of Identity Politics

What to make of all this? The first thing to note is that Savarkar's opening question is a trap. It does not admit of a natural answer. It only exposes the fragility of any conception of identity. It will lead inevitably to a contest over an authoritative definition, a contest in which the strong will bear it away. Moreover, any process of creating an identity will lead to the creation of that identity's "other." Indeed, the difficulty for most minorities in India now is that their "otherness" is overdetermined. If Indian identity is about fidelity to a religion, they are excluded. If it is about belonging to the single race envisaged by Savarkar, those who do not acknowledge such a race are excluded. If we say Indian identity is constituted by some values, say toleration, then some may be accused of failing to exemplify those values. In short, every attempt to come up with a benchmark or a litmus test for Indian identity will cause mischief. I suspect that simply counterposing some other and more liberal conception of Indian identity will not be enough to match the BJP and the other forces of Hindutva that are now entrenched in politics and society. But the root of the problem is not Hindutva. The root of the problem is the obsession with identity that makes the ideology of Hindutva seem possible and even sensible. The wisest course is to go to first principles in order to reject the fatal allure of the identity question altogether.

Politically, what the 800 million Hindus, 120 million Muslims, and all the other groups in India need to do if democracy is to be sustained is not so much to invent a new conception of Indian identity—even one that emphasizes pluralism and tolerance—as to frame a social contract within which they can peacefully manage their fundamental differences. Hindus, in other words, need not ask "What do we share?" but rather "How can we live together when we disagree about what we share, or even share nothing at all?" The challenge, contra Savarkar, is not to find or invent a basis of unity; the challenge is to live on the basis of difference. Liberal democracy is about managing differences, and not mythically or violently willing them away. It can be of enormous help with this project, indeed must lie very near its heart if the project is to have good prospects for long-term success.

And succeed it must, for any attempt to produce an authoritative conception of India, whether informed by Hindutva or any other ideology, will be fraught with exclusion and violence. So long as Indian political discourse is driven by a need to benchmark collective identity, some subset of citizens will always be at risk. The threat posed to minorities comes not only from this or that conception of nationalism, but from the inherently dangerous and ill-advised character of the quest for a benchmarked identity.

At the end, we are left wondering: Has democracy been good for Hinduism? Has Hinduism been good for democracy? Hindus should recognize that democracy has served them well in creating conditions for a creative response to the crisis of authority that Hinduism, like just about every other global religious tradition, has experienced in modern times. Hinduism over the past century has scored an immense historical achievement by having found ways to cope, ideologically at least, with

so many features of modernity, many of which Hinduism has even succeeding in making its own in remarkably original ways. But now is not
the time—as if there ever could be one—to rest on laurels won. For
Savarkar and the other heralds of Hindutva have gained a wide hearing
for the dangerous pitch they are making. Hindus must guard against
letting their sense (or more precisely, senses) of identity be hijacked by
a self-pity cult that preaches chimerical tests of "Hinduness." Here the
spiritual traditions of Hinduism may be of help, indeed may be the best
or perhaps the only antidote to the tragic narrowing of Hindu horizons
that the apostles of Hindutva intend. Hindu metaphysics at its best
teaches that a "rage for order" of the not-so-blessed kind—a mania for
making false or needless distinctions and calling oneself this rather
than that—may cause one to overlook a wealth of positive possibilities
that reside within the self, including its capacity to transcend the egotistical "I" and proclaim "From oneness and duality and opposites I am
free. I am He."[13]

Hindus have nerved themselves for the last half-century and more to
follow democracy's lively allure, and they have endowed the second-
largest country on Earth—home to nearly a sixth of all the planet's
people—with a liberal constitutional order. Now Hindus must keep their
nerve by turning away from the blind alleys and dead-end roads of
identity politics. To help themselves stay on wiser pathways, they should
recall a lesson from their own tradition that Ralph Waldo Emerson—a
non-Hindu who saw and loved much that is great in Hinduism—so no-
bly expressed when he insisted that "No society can ever be so large as
one man."[14] Surely there is no better counsel than this against the collective narcissism that is now emerging, in one guise or another, as the
worst threat to democracy in India and around the globe.

NOTES

1. *Shastri Yagna Purushdasji* versus *Muldas Bhunadardas Vaisya, All India Reporter (SC)*, 1966, 1119.

2. See Anthony Parel, ed., *Gandhi on Freedom and Self Rule* (Totowa, N.J.: Rowman & Littlefield, 2000).

3. Bruce McCully, "The Origins of Indian Nationalism According to Native Writers," *Journal of Modern History* 7 (September 1935): 295–314.

4. Liah Greenfeld, *Nationalism: Five Roads to Modernity* (Cambridge: Harvard University Press, 1992).

5. *Prabhoo* versus *Kunte, All India Reporter (SC)*, 1996, 1113.

6. In campaigning to ban widow-burning, for example, the leading native foe (Ram Mohan Roy) held that the custom had never enjoyed clear approval from the most authoritative traditional scriptures, which he said actually recommended as-
cetic widowhood. British reformers conceded scriptural warrant for immolation,

but argued that the current material and social motives of relatives and even the widows themselves had undermined the scriptures' assumptions that widows would be acting freely and for purely spiritual reasons. All the reformers took indigenous tradition, not universal progress, as the vital ground upon which to make their case for change (widow-burning was banned in 1829). Reform had become a means of conserving tradition.

7. Partha Chatterjee, *The Nation and Its Fragments: Colonial and Postcolonial Histories* (Princeton: Princeton University Press, 1995), 34.

8. Karuna Mantena has greatly clarified my understanding of this history.

9. J.C. Heesterman, *The Inner Conflict of Tradition* (Chicago: University of Chicago Press, 1985), 111.

10. Sarvepalli Radhakrishnan, *The Hindu View of Life* (London: Unwin, 1960), 70.

11. Other religions besides Hinduism are tempted by their own versions of such a narrative, of course. Alarmingly prominent versions of Islam tout feelings of resentment against the West, while more marginal yet by no means invisible Christian elements in the United States traffic in the idea that Christianity is under siege. (Interestingly, both Muslim and Christian extremists tend to place Jews high on their respective lists of enemies.) These narratives of victimization and resentment bespeak a wider failure of these religions to endow everyday life under the complex conditions of modernity with a sense of meaning or purpose, and also a refusal by significant currents within each religion to accept the facts of difference.

12. Vinayak Damodar Savarkar, *Hindutva: Who Is a Hindu?* (Bombay: RSS Publications Division, 1999).

13. "Maitreyi Upanishad," in J. Patrick Olivelle, trans., *The Samnyasa Upanishads: Hindu Scriptures on Asceticism and Renunciation* (New York: Oxford University Press, 1992), 165.

14. Ralph Waldo Emerson, "New England Reformers," in Brooke Atkinson, ed., *Complete Essays and Other Writings of Ralph Waldo Emerson* (New York: Modern Library, 1950), 456–57.

5

BUDDHISM, ASIAN VALUES, AND DEMOCRACY

His Holiness the Dalai Lama

The Dalai Lama, the spiritual and temporal leader of the Tibetan people, fled Chinese-occupied Tibet into exile in India in 1959. One of the world's great exponents of nonviolence, His Holiness was awarded the Nobel Peace Prize in 1989. The following essay is based on a lecture that he delivered on 10 November 1998 at George Washington University in Washington, D.C. The lecture, one in a series entitled "The Democratic Invention," was cosponsored by the Mário Soares Foundation, the Luso-American Development Foundation, and the International Forum for Democratic Studies.

While democratic aspirations may be manifested in different ways, some universal principles lie at the heart of any democratic society— representative government (established through free and fair elections), the rule of law and accountability (as enforced by an independent judiciary), and freedom of speech (as exemplified by an uncensored press). Democracy, however, is about much more than these formal institutions; it is about genuine freedom and the empowerment of the individual. I am neither an expert in political science nor an authority on democracy and the rule of law. Rather, I am a simple Buddhist monk, educated and trained in our ancient, traditional ways. Nonetheless, my life-long study of Buddhism and my involvement in the Tibetan people's nonviolent struggle for freedom have given me some insights that I would like to discuss.

As a Buddhist monk, I do not find alien the concept and practice of democracy. At the heart of Buddhism lies the idea that the potential for awakening and perfection is present in every human being and that realizing this potential is a matter of personal effort. The Buddha proclaimed that each individual is a master of his or her own destiny, highlighting the capacity that each person has to attain enlightenment. In this sense, the Buddhist world view recognizes the fundamental sameness of all human beings. Like Buddhism, modern democracy is based on the principle that all human beings are essentially equal, and that each of us has an equal right to life, liberty, and happiness. Whether we are rich or poor, educated or uneducated, a follower of one religion or another, each of us is a human being. Not only do we desire happiness and seek to avoid suffering, but each of us also has an equal right to pursue these goals. Thus not only are Buddhism and democracy compatible, they are rooted in a common understanding of the equality and potential of every individual.

As for democracy as a procedure of decision making, we find again in the Buddhist tradition a certain recognition of the need for consensus. For example, the Buddhist monastic order has a long history of basing major decisions affecting the lives of individual monks on collective discourse. In fact, strictly speaking, every rite concerning the maintenance of monastic practice must be performed with a congregation of at least four monks. Thus one could say that the Vinaya rules of discipline that govern the behavior and life of the Buddhist monastic community are in keeping with democratic traditions. In theory at least, even the teachings of the Buddha can be altered under certain circumstances by a congregation of a certain number of ordained monks.

As human beings, we all seek to live in a society in which we can express ourselves freely and strive to be the best we can be. At the same time, pursuing one's own fulfillment at the expense of others would lead to chaos and anarchy. What is required, then, is a system whereby the interests of the individual are balanced with the wider well-being of the community at large. For this reason, I feel it is necessary to develop a sense of universal responsibility, a deep concern for all human beings, irrespective of religion, color, gender, or nationality. If we adopt a self-centered approach to life and constantly try to use others to advance our own interests, we may gain temporary benefits, but in the long run happiness will elude us. Instead, we must learn to work not just for our own individual selves, but for the benefit of all mankind.

While it is true that no system of government is perfect, democracy is the closest to our essential human nature and allows us the greatest opportunity to cultivate a sense of universal responsibility. As a Buddhist, I strongly believe in a humane approach to democracy, an approach that recognizes the importance of the individual without sacrificing a sense of responsibility toward all humanity. Buddhists emphasize the potential of the individual, but we also believe that the purpose of a meaningful life is to serve others.

Many nations consider respect for the individual's civil and political rights to be the most important aspect of democracy. Other countries, especially in the developing world, see the rights of the society—particularly the right to economic development—as overriding the rights of the individual. I believe that economic advancement and respect for individual rights are closely linked. A society cannot fully maximize its economic advantage without granting its people individual civil and political rights. At the same time, these freedoms are diminished if the basic necessities of life are not met.

Some Asian leaders say that democracy and the freedoms that come with it are exclusive products of Western civilization. Asian values, they contend, are significantly different from, if not diametrically opposed to, democracy. They argue that Asian cultures emphasize order, duty, and stability, while the emphasis of Western democracies on individual rights and liberties undermines those values. They suggest that Asians have fundamentally different needs in terms of personal and social fulfillment. I do not share this viewpoint.

It is my fundamental belief that all human beings share the same basic aspirations: We all want happiness and we all experience suffering. Like Americans, Europeans, and the rest of the world, Asians wish to live life to its fullest, to better themselves and the lives of their loved ones. India, the birthplace of Mahatma Gandhi and of the concept of *ahimsa,* or nonviolence, is an excellent example of an Asian country devoted to a democratic form of government. India demonstrates that democracy can sink strong roots outside the Western world. Similarly, our brothers and sisters in Burma, Indonesia, and China are courageously raising their voices together in the call for equality, freedom, and democracy.

The fact that democratic reforms are on the rise around the globe, from the Czech Republic to Mongolia, and from South Africa to Taiwan, is testimony to the strength of the ideals that democracy embodies. As more and more people gain awareness of their individual potential, the number of people seeking to express themselves through a democratic system grows. These global trends illustrate the universality of the desire for a form of government that respects human rights and the rule of law.

The Case of Tibet

I am deeply committed to the political modernization and democratization of my native Tibet and have made efforts to develop a democratic system for Tibetans living in exile. In 1963, I promulgated the democratic constitution of Tibet, and our exiled community has, under difficult circumstances, responded well to the challenge of this experiment with democracy. In 1969, I declared that whether the institution of the Dalai Lama should continue to exist depended on the wishes of the Tibetan people. And in 1991, our legislature, the Assembly of Tibetan People's Deputies, adopted the Charter of Tibetans in Exile, which expanded the Assembly's membership and transferred from me to it the power to elect the Cabinet. While this Charter was modeled on constitutions from established democracies, it also reflects the unique nature of the Tibetan culture and system of values: It protects freedom of religion, upholds the principles of nonviolence, and emphasizes the promotion of the moral and material welfare of the Tibetan people.

In 1992, in order to guide our efforts to have an eventual impact on Tibetans living in Tibet, I announced the Guidelines for Future Tibet's Polity. This document is based on my hope that, before too long, we will achieve a negotiated settlement with the Chinese government granting full autonomy to the Tibetan people. I believe that, once such an agreement is reached, it is the Tibetans inside Tibet who will bear the major responsibility for determining Tibet's future governance and that the officials presently serving in positions of leadership in Tibet shall bear an even greater responsibility in the future.

Unfortunately, Tibetans living in Tibet have not shared in the democratic freedoms that we have implemented in exile. In fact, over the last several decades, our brothers and sisters in Tibet have suffered immeasurably. Through direct attacks on all things Tibetan, the very culture of Tibet has been threatened. I believe that the Tibetan people have a right to preserve their own unique and distinct cultural heritage. I also believe that they should be able to decide their future, their form of government, and their social system. No Tibetan is interested in restoring outdated political and social institutions, but we are a nation of six million people with the right to live as human beings.

As we Tibetans have begun moving toward democracy, we have learned that to empower our people we must give them a sufficient understanding of their rights and responsibilities as citizens of a democratic society. For this reason, I have focused considerable attention on education. The more the Tibetan people learn about their individual potential and their ability to play a role in their own governance, the stronger our society will become.

In some respects, I have been the unluckiest Dalai Lama, for I have spent more time as a refugee outside my country than I have spent inside Tibet. On the other hand, it has been very rewarding for me to live in a democracy and to learn about the world in a way that we Tibetans had never been able to do before. Had I continued to live in and govern Tibet, I would certainly have made efforts to bring about changes in our political system, but it is quite probable that I would still have been influenced by the conservative political environment that existed in my homeland. Living outside Tibet has given me an invaluable perspective. I know that our previous political system was outdated and ill-equipped to face the challenges of the contemporary world.

Today, the world has become increasingly interdependent. In this age of cross-border cooperation and exchange, it is very important for the United States and other democratic countries to help preserve and promote democratic trends around the world. For example, the dismantling of the Soviet Union was seen as a significant victory for democracy and human rights. In fact, many Western leaders, including those in the United States, took credit for the Soviet Union's demise. Today, however, conditions in Russia are dire and many of the former Soviet republics face the prospect of political and economic chaos. The failure of Russia's experiment in democracy would have adverse repercussions throughout the world and could give power and strength to democracy's detractors. I therefore believe it is the responsibility of the democratic free world to come to the aid of those countries who took the courageous step toward democracy and now are struggling to make it work.

I also understand that it is the right of all people to be concerned with the security of their nation. But it is surely more important to help create stability in troubled areas like the former Soviet Union, through economic and other means of support, than to invest in increasingly sophisticated weaponry and a soaring national defense budget. Furthermore, despite the fact that each nation has the right to determine its own security needs, I believe that a nonviolent approach is the most constructive path to securing peace in the long term.

In conclusion, I would like to stress once again the need for firm conviction on all our parts in acknowledging the universality of the key ethical and political values that underlie democracy. Recognition of and respect for basic human rights, freedom of speech, the equality of all human beings, and the rule of law must be seen not merely as aspirations but as necessary conditions of a civilized society.

6

BURMA'S QUEST FOR DEMOCRACY

Aung San Suu Kyi

Aung San Suu Kyi, *recipient of the 1991 Nobel Peace Prize, was also awarded the European Parliament's Sakharov Prize for Freedom of Thought in 1990. This essay appeared in* Freedom from Fear and Other Writings, Revised Ed. *by Aung San Suu Kyi, foreword by Václav Havel, translated by Michael Aris © 1991, 1995 Aung San Suu Kyi and Michael Aris. Used by permission of Viking Penguin, a division of Penguin Group (USA) Inc.*

Opponents of the movement for democracy in Burma have sought to undermine it by on the one hand casting aspersions on the competence of the people to judge what was best for the nation and on the other condemning the basic tenets of democracy as un-Burmese. There is nothing new in Third World governments seeking to justify and perpetuate authoritarian rule by denouncing liberal democratic principles as alien. By implication they claim for themselves the official and sole right to decide what does or does not conform to indigenous cultural norms. Such conventional propaganda aimed at consolidating the powers of the establishment has been studied, analyzed, and disproved by political scientists, jurists, and sociologists. But in Burma, distanced by several decades of isolationism from political and intellectual developments in the outside world, the people have had to draw on their own resources to explode the twin myths of their unfitness for political responsibility and the unsuitability of democracy for their society. As soon as the movement for democracy spread out across Burma there was a surge of intense interest in the meaning of the word "democracy," in its history and its practical implications. More than a quarter-century of narrow authoritarianism under which they had been fed a pabulum of shallow, negative dogma had not blunted the perceptiveness or political alertness of the Burmese. On the contrary, perhaps not all that surprisingly, their appetite for discussion and debate, for uncensored information and objective analysis, seemed to have been sharpened. Not only was there an eagerness to study and to absorb standard theories on modern politics

and political institutions, there was also widespread and intelligent speculation on the nature of democracy as a social system of which they had
had little experience but which appealed to their common-sense notions
of what was due to a civilized society. There was a spontaneous interpre-
tative response to such basic ideas as representative government, human
rights, and the rule of law. The privileges and freedoms which would be
guaranteed by democratic institutions were contemplated with understandable enthusiasm. But the duties of those who would bear
responsibility for the maintenance of a stable democracy also provoked
much thoughtful consideration. It was natural that a people who have
suffered much from the consequences of bad government should be preoccupied with theories of good government.

Members of the Buddhist *sangha* [monastic community] in their customary role as mentors have led the way in articulating popular
expectations by drawing on classical learning to illuminate timeless
values. But the conscious effort to make traditional knowledge relevant
to contemporary needs was not confined to any particular circle—it
went right through Burmese society from urban intellectuals and small
shopkeepers to doughty village grandmothers.

Why has Burma, with its abundant natural and human resources, failed
to live up to its early promise as one of the most energetic and fastest-
developing nations in Southeast Asia? International scholars have
provided detailed answers supported by careful analyses of historical,
cultural, political, and economic factors. The Burmese people, who have
had no access to sophisticated academic material, got to the heart of the
matter by turning to the works of the Buddha on the four causes of
decline and decay: failure to recover that which had been lost, omission
to repair that which had been damaged, disregard of the need for reasonable economy, and the elevation to leadership of men without morality
or learning. Translated into contemporary terms: when democratic rights
had been lost to military dictatorship, sufficient efforts had not been
made to regain them; moral and political values had been allowed to
deteriorate without concerted attempts to save the situation; the economy
had been badly managed; and the country had been ruled by men without integrity or wisdom. A thorough study by the cleverest scholar using
the best and latest methods could hardly have identified more correctly
or succinctly the chief causes of Burma's decline since 1962.

Under totalitarian socialism, official policies with little relevance to
actual needs had placed Burma in an economic and administrative limbo
where government bribery and evasion of regulations were the indispensable lubricant to keep the wheels of everyday life turning. But
through the years of moral decay and material decline there has survived
a vision of a society in which the people and the leadership could unite
in principled efforts to achieve prosperity and security. In 1988 the movement for democracy gave rise to the hope that the vision might become

reality. At its most basic and immediate level, liberal democracy would mean in institutional terms a representative government appointed for a constitutionally limited term through free and fair elections. By exercising responsibly their right to choose their own leaders, the Burmese hope to make an effective start at reversing the process of decline. They have countered the propagandist doctrine that democracy is unsuited to their cultural norms by examining traditional theories of government.

Buddhist Views of Government

The Buddhist view of world history tells that when society fell from its original state of purity into moral and social chaos a king was elected to restore peace and justice. The ruler was known by three titles: *Mahasammata*, "because he is named ruler by the unanimous consent of the people"; *Khattiya*, "because he has dominion over agricultural land"; and *Raja*, "because he wins the people to affection through observance of the *dhamma* (virtue, justice, the law)." The agreement by which their first monarch undertakes to rule righteously in return for a portion of the rice crop represents the Buddhist version of government by social contract. The *Mahasammata* follows the general pattern of Indic kingship in Southeast Asia. This has been criticized as antithetical to the idea of the modern state because it promotes a personalized form of monarchy lacking the continuity inherent in the Western abstraction of the king as possessed of both a body politic and body natural. However, because the *Mahasammata* was chosen by popular consent and required to govern in accordance with just laws, the concept of government elective and *sub lege* is not alien to traditional Burmese thought.

The Buddhist view of kingship does not invest the ruler with the divine right to govern the realm as he pleases. He is expected to observe the Ten Duties of Kings, the Seven Safeguards against Decline, and the Four Assistances to the People, and to be guided by numerous other codes of conduct such as the Twelve Practices of Rulers, the Six Attributes of Leaders, the Eight Virtues of Kings, and the Four Ways to Overcome Peril. There is logic to a tradition which includes the king among the five enemies or perils and which subscribes to many sets of moral instructions for the edification of those in positions of authority. The people of Burma have had much experience of despotic rule and possess a great awareness of the unhappy gap that can exist between the theory and practice of government.

The Ten Duties of Kings are widely known and generally accepted as a yardstick which could be applied just as well to modern government as to the first monarch of the world. The duties are: liberality, morality, self-sacrifice, integrity, kindness, austerity, nonanger, nonviolence, forebearance, and nonopposition (to the will of the people).

The first duty of liberality *(dana)*, which demands that a ruler should contribute generously toward the welfare of the people, makes the tacit assumption that a government should have the competence to provide adequately for its citizens. In the context of modern politics, one of the prime duties of a responsible administration would be to ensure the economic security of the state.

Morality *(sila)* in traditional Buddhist terms is based on the observance of the five precepts, which entails refraining from destruction of life, theft, adultery, falsehood, and indulgence in intoxicants. The ruler must bear a high moral character to win the respect and trust of the people, to ensure their happiness and prosperity, and to provide a proper example. When the king does not observe the *dhamma,* state functionaries become corrupt, and when state functionaries are corrupt the people are caused much suffering. It is further believed that an unrighteous king brings down calamity on the land. The root of a nation's misfortunes has to be sought in the moral failings of the government.

The third duty, *paricagga,* is sometimes translated as generosity and sometimes as self-sacrifice. The former would constitute a duplication of the first duty, *dana,* so self-sacrifice as the ultimate generosity which gives up all for the sake of the people would appear the more satisfactory interpretation. The concept of selfless public service is sometimes illustrated by the story of the hermit Sumedha who took the vow of Buddhahood. In so doing he who could have realized the supreme liberation of *nirvana* in a single lifetime committed himself to countless incarnations that he might help other beings free themselves from suffering. Equally popular is the story of the monkey king who sacrificed his life to save his subjects, including one who had always wished him harm and who was the eventual cause of his death. The good ruler sublimates his needs as an individual to the service of the nation.

Integrity *(ajjava)* implies incorruptibility in the discharge of public duties as well as honesty and sincerity in personal relations. There is a Burmese saying: "With rulers, truth, with [ordinary] men, vows." While a private individual may be bound only by the formal vows that he makes, those who govern should be wholly bound by the truth in thought, word, and deed. Truth is the very essence of the teachings of the Buddha, who referred to himself as the *Tathagata* or "one who has come to the truth." The Buddhist king must therefore live and rule by truth, which is the perfect uniformity between nomenclature and nature. To deceive or to mislead the people in any way would be an occupational failing as well as a moral offense: "As an arrow, intrinsically straight, without warp or distortion, when one word is spoken, it does not err into two."

Kindness *(maddava)* in a ruler is in a sense the courage to feel concern for the people. It is undeniably easier to ignore the hardships of those who are too weak to demand their rights than to respond sensitively to their needs. To care is to accept responsibility, to dare to act in accordance with the dictum that the ruler is the strength of the helpless.

In *Wizaya,* a well-known nineteenth-century drama based on the *Mahavamas* story of Prince Vijaya, a king sends away into exile his own son whose wild ways have caused the people much distress: "In the matter of love, to make no distinction between citizen and son, to give equally of loving kindness, that is the righteousness of kings."

The duty of austerity *(tapa)* enjoins the king to adopt simple habits, to develop self-control, and to practice spiritual discipline. The self-indulgent ruler who enjoys an extravagant lifestyle and ignores the spiritual need for austerity was no more acceptable at the time of the *Mahasammata* than he would be in Burma today.

The seventh, eighth, and ninth duties—nonanger *(akkodha),* nonviolence *(avihamsa),* and forebearance *(khanti)*—could be said to be related. Because the displeasure of the powerful could have unhappy and far-reaching consequences, kings must not allow personal feelings of enmity and ill will to erupt into destructive anger and violence. It is incumbent on a ruler to develop the true forebearance which moves him to deal wisely and generously with the shortcomings and provocations of even those whom he could crush with impunity. Violence is totally contrary to the teachings of Buddhism. The good ruler vanquishes ill will with loving kindness, wickedness with virtue, parsimony with liberality, and falsehood with truth. The Emperor Ashoka, who ruled his realm in accordance with the principles of nonviolence and compassion, is always held up as an ideal Buddhist king. A government should not attempt to enjoin submission through harshness and immoral force, but should aim at *dhamma-vijaya,* a conquest by righteousness.

The tenth duty of kings, nonopposition to the will of the people *(avirodha),* tends to be singled out as a Buddhist endorsement of democracy, supported by well-known stories from the *Jakatas.* Pawridasa, a monarch who acquired an unfortunate taste for human flesh, was forced to leave his kingdom because he would not heed the people's demand that he should abandon his cannibalistic habits. A very different kind of ruler was the Buddha's penultimate incarnation on earth, the pious King Vessantara. But he too was sent into exile when, in the course of his strivings for the perfection of liberality, he gave away the white elephant of the state without the consent of the people. The real duty of nonopposition is a reminder that the legitimacy of government is founded on the consent of the people, who may withdraw their mandate at any time if they lose confidence in the ability of the ruler to serve their best interests.

By invoking the Ten Duties of Kings, the Burmese are not so much indulging in wishful thinking as drawing on time-honored values to reinforce the validity of the political reforms they consider necessary. It is a strong argument for democracy that governments regulated by principles of accountability, respect for public opinion, and the supremacy of just laws are more likely than an all-powerful ruler or ruling class, uninhibited by the need to honor the will of the people, to observe the traditional duties of Buddhist kingship. Traditional values serve both to justify and to decipher popular expectations of democratic government.

Human Rights and Traditional Values

The people of Burma view democracy not merely as a form of government but as an integrated social and ideological system based on respect for the individual. When asked why they feel so strong a need for democracy, the least political will answer: "We just want to be able to go about our own business freely and peacefully, not doing anybody any harm, just earning a decent living without anxiety and fear." In other words, they want the basic human rights which would guarantee a tranquil, dignified existence free from want and fear. "Democracy songs" articulated such longings: "I am not among the rice-eating robots . . . Everyone but everyone should be entitled to human rights." "We are not savage beasts of the jungle, we are all men with reason; it's high time to stop the rule of armed intimidation: if every movement of dissent were settled by the gun, Burma would only be emptied of people."

It was predictable that as soon as the issue of human rights became an integral part of the movement for democracy, the official media would start ridiculing and condemning the whole concept of human rights, dubbing it a Western artifact alien to traditional values. It was also ironic. Buddhism, the foundation of traditional Burmese culture, places the greatest value on man, who alone of all beings can achieve the supreme state of Buddhahood. Each man has in him the potential to realize the truth through his own will and endeavor and to help others to realize it. Human life therefore is infinitely precious: "Easier is it for a needle dropped from the abode of Brahma to meet a needle stuck in the earth than to be born as a human being."

But despotic governments do not recognize the precious human component of the state, seeing its citizens only as a faceless, mindless (and helpless) mass to be manipulated at will. It is as though people were incidental to a nation rather than its very life-blood. Patriotism, which should be the vital love and care of a people for their land, is debased into a smokescreen of hysteria to hide the injustices of authoritarian rulers who define the interests of the state in terms of their own limited interests. The official creed is required to be accepted with an unquestioning faith more in keeping with orthodox tenets of the biblical religions which have held sway in the West than with the more liberal Buddhist attitude:

> It is proper to doubt, to be uncertain. . . . Do not go upon what has been acquired by repeated hearing. Nor upon tradition, nor upon rumors. . . . When you know for yourself that certain things are unwholesome and wrong, abandon them. . . . When you know for yourself that certain things are wholesome and good, accept them.

It is a puzzlement to the Burmese how concepts which recognize the inherent dignity and the equal and inalienable rights of human beings, which accept that all men are endowed with reason and conscience and which recommend a universal spirit of brotherhood, can be inimical to indigenous values. It is also difficult for them to understand how any of the rights contained in the thirty articles of the Universal Declaration of Human Rights can be seen as anything but wholesome and good. That the declaration was not drawn up in Burma by the Burmese seems an inadequate reason, to say the least, for rejecting it, especially as Burma was one of the nations which voted for its adoption in December 1948. If ideas and beliefs are to be denied validity outside the geographical and cultural bounds of their origin, Buddhism would be confined to north India, Christianity to a narrow tract in the Middle East, and Islam to Arabia.

The proposition that the Burmese are not fit to enjoy as many rights and privileges as the citizens of democratic countries is insulting. It also makes questionable the logic of a Burmese government considering itself fit to enjoy more rights and privileges than the governments of those same countries. The inconsistency can be explained—but not justified—only by assuming so wide a gulf between the government and the people that they have to be judged by different norms. Such an assumption in turn casts doubt on the doctrine of government as a comprehensive spirit and medium of national values.

Weak logic, inconsistencies, and alienation from the people are common features of authoritarianism. The relentless attempts of totalitarian regimes to prevent free thought and new ideas and the persistent assertion of their own rightness bring on them an intellectual stasis which they project on to the nation at large. Intimidation and propaganda work in a duet of oppression, while the people, lapped in fear and distrust, learn to dissemble and to keep silent. And all the time the desire grows for a system which will lift them from the position of "rice-eating robots" to the status of human beings who can think and speak freely and hold their heads high in the security of their rights.

From the beginning, Burma's struggle for democracy has been fraught with danger. A movement which seeks the just and equitable distribution of powers and prerogatives that have long been held by a small elite determined to preserve its privileges at all costs is likely to be prolonged and difficult. Hope and optimism are irrepressible, but there is a deep underlying premonition that the opposition to change is likely to be vicious. Often the anxious question is asked: Will such an oppressive regime *really* give us democracy? And the answer has to be: Democracy, like liberty, justice, and other social and political rights, is not "given," it is earned through courage, resolution, and sacrifice.

Law, Justice, and Peace

Revolutions generally reflect the irresistible impulse for necessary changes which have been held back by official policies or retarded by social apathy. The institutions and practices of democracy provide ways and means by which such changes could be effected without recourse to violence. But change is anathema to authoritarianism, which will tolerate no deviation from rigid policies. Democracy acknowledges the right to differ as well as the duty to settle differences peacefully. Authoritarian governments see criticism of their actions and doctrines as a challenge to combat. Opposition is equated with "confrontation," which is interpreted as violent conflict. Regimented minds cannot grasp the concept of confrontation as an open exchange of major differences with a view to settlement through genuine dialogue. The insecurity of power based on coercion translates into a need to crush all dissent. Within the framework of liberal democracy, protest and dissent can exist in healthy counterpart with orthodoxy and conservatism, contained by a general recognition of the need to balance respect for individual rights with respect for law and order.

The words "law and order" have so frequently been misused as an excuse for oppression that the very phrase has become suspect in countries which have known authoritarian rule. Some years ago a prominent Burmese author wrote an article on the notion of law and order as expressed by the official term *nyein-wut-pi-pyar*. One by one he analyzed the words, which literally mean "quiet-crouched-crushed-flattened," and concluded that the whole made for an undesirable state of affairs, one which militated against the emergence of an alert, energetic, progressive citizenry. There is no intrinsic virtue to law and order unless "law" is equated with justice and "order" with the discipline of a people satisfied that justice has been done.

Law as an instrument of state oppression is a familiar feature of totalitarianism. Without a popularly elected legislature and an independent judiciary to ensure due process, the authorities can enforce as "law" arbitrary decrees that are in fact flagrant negations of all acceptable norms of justice. There can be no security for citizens in a state where new "laws" can be made and old ones changed to suit the convenience of the powers that be. The iniquity of such practices is traditionally recognized by the precept that existing laws should not be set aside at will. The Buddhist concept of law is based on *dhamma,* righteousness or virtue, not on the power to impose harsh and inflexible rules on a defenseless people. The true measure of the justice of a system is the amount of protection it guarantees to the weakest.

Where there is no justice, there can be no secure peace. The Universal Declaration of Human Rights recognizes that "if man is not to be compelled to have recourse, as a last resort, to rebellion against tyranny and oppression," human rights should be protected by the rule of law. That just laws which uphold human rights are the necessary foundation of peace and security would be denied only by closed minds which interpret peace as the silence of all opposition, and security as the assurance of their own power. The Burmese associate peace and security with coolness and shade:

> The shade of a tree is cool indeed,
> The shade of parents is cooler,
> The shade of teachers is cooler still,
> The shade of the ruler is yet more cool,
> But coolest of all is the shade of the Buddha's teachings.

Thus to provide the people with the protective coolness of peace and security, rulers must observe the teachings of the Buddha. Central to these teachings are the concepts of truth, righteousness, and loving kindness. It is government based on these very qualities that the people of Burma are seeking in their struggle for democracy.

In a revolutionary movement there is always the danger that political exigencies might obscure, or even nullify, essential spiritual aims. A firm insistence on the inviolability and primacy of such aims is not mere idealism but a necessary safeguard against an *Animal Farm* syndrome, wherein the new order, after its first flush of enthusiastic reforms, takes on the murky colors of the very system it has replaced. The people of Burma want not just a change of government but a change in political values. The unhappy legacies of authoritarianism can be removed only if the concept of absolute power as the basis of government is replaced by the concept of confidence as the mainspring of political authority: the confidence of the people in their right and ability to decide the destiny of their nation, the mutual confidence in the principles of justice, liberty, and human rights. Of the four Buddhist virtues conducive to the happiness of laymen, *saddha,* confidence in moral, spiritual, and intellectual values, is the first. To instill such confidence, not by an appeal to the passions but through intellectual conviction, into a society which has long been wracked by distrust and uncertainty is the essence of the Burmese revolution for democracy. It is a revolution which moves for changes endorsed by universal norms of ethics.

In their quest for democracy, the people of Burma explore not only the political theories and practices of the world outside their country, but also the spiritual and intellectual values that have given shape to their own environment.

There is an instinctive understanding that the cultural, social, and political development of a nation is a dynamic process which has to be given purpose and direction by drawing on tradition as well as by experiment, innovation, and a willingness to evaluate both old and new ideas objectively. This is not to claim that all those who desire democracy in Burma are guided by an awareness of the need to balance a dispassionate, sensitive assessment of the past with an intelligent appreciation of the present. But threading through the movement is a rich vein of the liberal, integrated spirit which meets intellectual challenges with wisdom and courage. There is also a capacity for the sustained mental strife and physical endurance necessary to withstand the forces of negativism, bigotry, and hate. Most encouraging of all, the main impetus for struggle is not an appetite for power, revenge, and destruction; but a genuine respect for freedom, peace, and justice.

The quest for democracy in Burma is the struggle of a people to live whole, meaningful lives as free and equal members of the world community. It is part of the unceasing human endeavor to prove that the spirit of man can transcend the flaws of his own nature.

III

Judaism and Christianity

7

JUDAISM AND POLITICAL LIFE

Hillel Fradkin

Hillel Fradkin, *senior fellow and director of the Project on the Muslim World at the Hudson Institute, has taught at the University of Chicago, Columbia, and Yale. He served as president of the Ethics and Public Policy Center from 2001 to 2004, and has written widely on the relationship between religion and politics. This essay originally appeared in the July 2004 issue of the* Journal of Democracy.

What is the relationship between Judaism and democracy—past, present, and future? This is an extraordinarily complex question, not least because Jewish tradition and corporate existence are at least three thousand years old, traversing the Biblical, post-Biblical, rabbinic, medieval, and modern eras. Over this period, the Jewish faith and way of life have undergone many significant changes and have bequeathed a diverse legacy.

As the most sacred object for the Jewish people is a book, upon which a vast amount of interpretive labor has been expended, the sources for an answer include a large body of literature consisting of a variety of interpretations. Much of that literature is legal, and thus obviously has some implications for political questions. First laid down in the Bible and then discussed in legal works, Jewish law continues to be elaborated down to the present.

But no answer to our question could be complete if it did not go beyond the Bible and its interpretations to consider the political experience of the Jewish people. At several times, this took the form of an independent political existence, first in the Biblical period and then again during late Hellenistic times. For much of their history, however, Jews found themselves dispersed throughout the world, living in the midst of many other peoples and under a great variety of political systems. In these cases, Jews have almost always been a small minority and frequently a persecuted one. Liberal democracy appeared to offer a solution to this problem, a solution reflecting the promise of democracy generally. In fact, the situation of Jews in this or that country has often been considered a kind of touchstone for the success of democratic life. Today, by some counts, almost six million of the world's approximately thirteen million Jews reside in the United States, the world's oldest and most successful democracy. There are also significant Jewish communities in such West European democracies as France and Great Britain. Until recently, large numbers of Jews suffered under Soviet tyranny. Finally, of course, there is the experience with contemporary democratic life embodied in Israel, the sole state in which Jews (who number almost five million there) form a majority.

It is evident that the question with which we began (like analogous questions about other religious traditions) is receiving heightened attention because of two main global trends, characteristic of our era, which taken together seem to present a paradox and perhaps a problem. On the one hand, we live in a democratic era. In most of the contemporary world, the only recognized principle of political legitimacy is democratic—understood as meaning the consent of the governed. It is, of course, true that democracy often exists de jure but not de facto. This is especially true with regard to liberal democracy, which has been particularly important to Jews because it seeks to combine and thus limit majority rule with the protection of individual or human rights. Nevertheless, since the victory of the United States and its allies in the Cold War and the collapse of Soviet communism, the trend, with many false steps, has been in the direction of having political reality match democratic political principle. It represents the most advanced stage of a movement that is several hundred years old and now seems to have an inexorable momentum throughout the world—with the possible exception of the Muslim part of it, where the status of democracy is still under active debate. Adding to democracy's prestige is the prosperity that has been generally associated with it.

On the other hand, we also live in an era of rising religious sensibility, attachment, and practice after a long period in which religion seemed in serious and even terminal decline. Indeed, that too seems to be underscored by the collapse of Soviet communism, which was the first and most powerful political system in human history to have avowed atheism as one of its fundamental principles. Its demise ends the most powerful *political* support that atheism has ever had. Throughout the world, with the singular exception of Western Europe, many people are strengthening their religious attachments or "returning" to them, even in places where such attachments had seemingly lapsed altogether.

The paradox referred to above stems from the fact that liberal democracy, at least in Western Europe, where it was first proposed and founded, arose in large part as a reaction to and remedy for the role that religion had played in political life, especially the depredations brought about by the religious fanaticism and warfare that plagued the sixteenth and seventeenth centuries. It is true that the democratic movement advanced the rights of the governed against the claims of monarchs and hereditary aristocrats. But the movement was also directed against clerical rule, and, more generally, against the claims of political authority to use the power of the state to enforce religious duty. Indeed, the struggle against clerical rule or interference in politics preceded the democratic movement in the early modern era and was an important factor in the rise of the modern nation-state.

Of course, proponents of liberal democracy often argued that the true interests of religion would be served by limiting its political role. Only in that way could conscience and religious faith be established on a firm footing, for the vitality of religion depends upon its independence from political and even clerical authority. Some of these proponents were no doubt sincere, and to some extent the experience of democracy in the United States, plus the continuing vitality of religious life in that country, bears them out. But it is also fair to say that many of those who made these arguments hoped and expected that religious faith would diminish and be replaced by what is today called secularism or secular humanism. Until recently, it appeared that this expectation would be fulfilled with the spread of modernization, if not always democratization. Over the last generation, however, that expectation has begun to appear more and more doubtful.

Divine Will or Popular Consent?

Why are democracy and religion growing stronger at the same time, at least in some places? Can they comfortably coexist or will they necessarily come into conflict? More particularly, will the claims and demands of religion force the subordination of democratic principles to religious ones, leading to a radical transformation of democratic life and perhaps even its extinction?

This last concern is prompted today by the establishment of *shari'a* or divine Islamic law—a law whose provenance is, at least in principle, not the consent of the governed but rather divine will—as the law of the land in a variety of places around the world. The difficulty in this case is heightened by the fact that Islam as a religion is constituted not only by faith but by adherence to a law. The same complication would seem to be raised in the case of Judaism, since it too is (or at least was) constituted by adherence to a law that is understood to be divine in origin.

This raises the question of whether Jews can be democrats. And if they are, as I will presently make clear is the case, will they remain so? Are there circumstances under which Jews would be tempted by political arrangements that are not democratic? Might these temptations arise from or be abetted by attachment to Jewish principles and teachings? Or does Judaism itself produce a presumption on behalf of democracy?

With regard to contemporary Jews, the answer to the question of whether they are democrats is emphatically yes, and the evidence is overwhelming. It would be nearly, if not quite, impossible today to find a Jew who is not a proponent of democracy. Today the vast majority of Jews live in democratic countries and have embraced democratic ways wholeheartedly. Even in countries that are nondemocratic, Jews have tended to be in the leading ranks of democratic activists. They are known as avid voters, exercising the franchise at levels well above average for the countries in which they live. In established democracies such as the United States, Great Britain, and France, Jews serve as elected and appointed officials in numbers that exceed their share of the population. They have distinguished themselves both individually and in groups as ardent defenders of individual rights. All these characteristics are especially pronounced in the United States.

Yet the U.S. Jewish community forms only about 2 percent of the total U.S. population. Thus the democratic commitment of American Jews might be regarded as primarily a function of the larger democratic society in which they live and their assimilation to it. If Jews were somehow left to their own devices, what would be their likely perspective on democracy?

Today this question has an answer by virtue of the existence of the State of Israel, the vast majority of whose citizens are Jewish. The nature of this state confirms the democratic orientation of contemporary Jews. The State of Israel, founded on the heels of the Nazi Holocaust in 1948, was conceived of as a democracy by the modern Zionist movement that brought about its creation, and was founded as a democracy. It has always remained one, despite almost continually having to fight wars and meet violent threats of the sort that have often, in other times and places, spelled democracy's doom.

This point deserves to be emphasized, inasmuch as the Arab-Israeli conflict and the disputes surrounding it have led to much tendentious questioning of Israel's right to be called a democracy. Despite important issues that will be discussed below, the fact remains that Israel has never suspended its democratic processes, even while combating terrorism and military assaults. Equally important is the fact that all of its citizens— including its non-Jewish Arab citizens, Muslim and Christian alike—enjoy the right to vote and have exercised that right by electing representatives to the Knesset, Israel's parliament. Inevitable anxieties about their loyalty to the state have never been used as grounds to restrict the franchise. Moreover, in contrast to several neighboring countries that are still under states of emergency, Israel has become more democratic in the course of its history, having rescinded certain emergency measures enacted in the 1950s in the wake of its war of independence.

Indeed, Israel has been criticized for being overly or too purely democratic on two basic counts: The first, directly political, points to the election of the Israeli legislature under rules that are almost completely proportional. While fulfilling a certain notion of what democracy requires, this has led to a situation in which no Israeli party has ever held a simple Knesset majority. All governments have been coalitions, thereby creating liabilities from the perspective of such other political desiderata as stability and authority.

The second is the social and cultural ethos of the country, which has been emphatically egalitarian. This has been partly due to the influence of the social or socialist variety of democracy that predominated during the early decades of Israel's existence. For this and some other reasons—most notably, the existence of universal military service for both men *and* women—egalitarianism has become the social norm. The liability it brings is a certain brusqueness or even rudeness of manner for which Israelis have become notorious.

This is not to say that serious problems have not arisen from the particular form of Israeli democracy and the circumstances in which it operates. Coalition government has in some ways sharpened the perennial democratic conflict between satisfying the will of the majority and responding to minority interests. Although this kind of conflict exists in all contemporary democracies, it reaches an especially high pitch in Israel under a system that rewards small parties representing special interests and often gives them extraordinary leverage in return for the one or two votes that they may contribute to the coalition's majority.

One such interest has a special bearing on our subject—the interest of religious parties in enforcing religious law in some areas, particularly that of personal and family status. Put most simply, there is no civil marriage in Israel. The State of Israel inherited this situation from the Ottoman Empire via the British Mandate, which bequeathed the so-called *milliyet* system, under which every religious community was governed by its own religious law as administered by its own religious courts. Throughout Israeli history this arrangement has been a source of dispute and has come under attack as undemocratic.[1] It remains a matter of sociopolitical debate and legal contention today.

Some opponents of this arrangement have raised, rather hysterically in my view, the specter of full-fledged theocracy dominated by rabbinic courts. Insofar as Jewish law is comprehensive, embracing civil and criminal as well as ritual and personal law, this is a theoretical possibility. But rabbinic authority over civil and especially criminal law would be crucial, and this is, to put it mildly, highly unlikely to occur for a variety of reasons. First, rabbinic courts have not exercised such authority in any extensive sense in hundreds if not thousands of years. Second, for the full exercise of such authority, rabbinic doctrine would appear to require the reconstitution of many lapsed institutions including, a supreme religious court known in antiquity as the Sanhedrin. But according to rabbinic doctrine, reconstituting these institutions is probably today a legal impossibility. Finally, there is no reason to believe that a majority of the Israeli public would cede authority to such institutions.

But what of the Israeli-Palestinian dispute and its impact on Israeli democracy? Here it must be said that the outcome of the Six Day War of June 1967 did pose a serious difficulty for democracy, by leaving Israel in control of and with responsibility for a substantial noncitizen population of Palestinian Arabs. The cause of the war was a threat to Israel's existence from hostile (and in every case nondemocratic) Arab neighbors, some of them with Soviet arms and support. Israel defended itself successfully. Its defeat of Egypt left Israel in control of the tiny yet crowded Gaza Strip, which the Egyptians had administered since 1948. The defeat of Jordan, which Israel had tried and failed to dissuade from joining the war, left Israel in charge of the West Bank of the Jordan River, an area that Jordan had ruled since 1948.

However strong the case for the legitimacy of Israel's rule over these areas might have been in international law, Israel has ever since had to wrestle with the intensely trying challenge of dealing with the sizeable, growing, and mostly hostile noncitizen Arab populations of Gaza and the West Bank. This could not help but raise questions about the "purity" of Israeli democracy. Yet it is also a fact that a large majority of Israeli citizens have never regarded this situation as desirable or acceptable, not least from the perspective of the health and viability of Israeli democracy. Indeed, the most obvious answer to the problem, the "two-state solution" and its vision of a separate Palestinian polity, has been the official Jewish and Jewish-majority position for most of the time since the British Mandate. While there have been some in Israel who have favored ruling Palestinians indefinitely, these Israelis have never formed a majority, and do so still less today.

From Persecution or Toleration to Rights

Given that contemporary Jews, whether in Israel or elsewhere, are fully committed to democracy, the question remains how they became so and in what measure this is a result of Jewish faith and practice. Lacking political independence and even rights, Jews approached modern democracy as an edifice whose intellectual and practical foundations were the work of non-Jews.[2] The modern Jewish embrace of democracy is founded upon the belief that Jews would benefit from its blessings, as indeed they have done. Unfortunately, they have also borne a fair share of its curses.

It is more or less obvious why Jews should have welcomed modern democracy. Prior to the founding of modern democracies, there was no country in the world where Jews were permitted the status of citizens. Jews might sometimes have enjoyed the right of residence, but politically speaking they were no more than tolerated aliens, even in countries where they had lived for generations. This right could be and often was rescinded at the arbitrary will of the sovereign authority. Needless to say, lacking even the right of residence, Jews lacked other rights as well, and where rights were accorded, they often came with a specific tax attached. Jews frequently found themselves targets of other forms of discrimination as well, such as exclusion from many professions and residential segregation in special Jewish quarters (known as ghettos) in cities. Jews also suffered frequent physical assaults on their persons and property, against which they had little if any legal defense. This situation was especially true for the Jews of Europe. But in different forms it also obtained for Jews living in Muslim lands.

Strictly and appropriately speaking, this situation changed only with the founding of the United States, the world's first true modern democratic polity. Under its Federal Constitution, Jews were full citizens from the start. This was, moreover, understood to be a matter of right and not majority gift. President George Washington made this clear in his magnificent August 1790 open letter to the Hebrew Congregation of Newport, Rhode Island. Describing the "enlarged and liberal" policy of the new republic as "worthy of imitation," Washington explained:

> All possess alike liberty of conscience and immunities of citizenship. It is now no more that toleration is spoken of, as if it was by the indulgence of one class of people, that another enjoyed the exercise of their inherent natural rights. For happily the Government of the United States, which gives to bigotry no sanction, to persecution no assistance requires only that they who live under its protection should demean themselves as good citizens, in giving it on all occasions their effectual support. . . . May the Children of the Stock of Abraham, who dwell in this land, continue to merit and enjoy the good will of the other Inhabitants; while every one shall sit in safety under his own vine and fig tree, and there shall be none to make him afraid.[3]

It was certainly some time before this policy was imitated elsewhere and Jews were accorded full citizenship. Even in places such as Great Britain, where the Glorious Revolution of 1688 set in motion an increasingly democratic reorientation of politics, the principle as applied to Jews remained one of "toleration" rather than full citizenship. This was even effectively the case in the United States for some time after its founding. Several of the state constitutions retained limitations on Jewish political participation, though gradually these were removed.

Given the liabilities of their premodern circumstances as a disenfranchised and much persecuted minority, it was natural for Jews to see modern democracy as a great blessing that promised not only legal and physical security but dignity as well. For even under the best of premodern circumstances, Jews self-evidently lacked the status of free men. These blessings could only be secured under democracy. As a matter of fact, they could only be fully secured under democracy in its liberal form.

The democratic movement launched in continental Europe by the French Revolution of 1789 yielded historically ambiguous consequences for Jews. The liberation of the democratic and popular will could mean and sometimes did mean the liberation of a popular will which was anti-Semitic in tone and political program, drawing upon an ancient legacy of Christian antagonism toward Jews while adding new racialist and nationalist fuel to the fires of bias and persecution. As is well known, this was often emphatically true of the continental European Right and may be said to have culminated in the extermination of most of the European Jewish community by the German Nazi regime. The latter, after all, came to power in March 1933 after an election in which it received a large plurality of the vote (almost 44 percent). But it was also true of the continental European Left, where important socialists such as Paul de Lagarde and Karl Marx (though himself Jewish by birth) made anti-Semitic pronouncements.

The extremism of much of nineteenth-century European democratic politics created difficult political choices for Jews, where such choices were to be had at all. Throughout the century most European Jews lived under Czarist or Habsburg rule. In countries with quasidemocratic institutions such as Germany, Jews did not achieve full citizenship until after the First World War. The principal exceptions were Great Britain and the United States, countries where moderate liberalism's clear protections for individual and minority rights had considerable force. But the United States lacked anything remotely like a substantial Jewish population until shortly before the Civil War. At that time, both Jewish and non-Jewish émigrés from Germany and Central Europe came to the United States in the aftermath of the failed democratic revolutions of 1848. Even so, it was only at century's end that the U.S. Jewish population increased dramatically through massive waves of immigration from Russia and Eastern Europe.

Within the context of the typically available European choices, many Jews were drawn to movements of the Left, despite the anti-Semitism cited above. There were a number of reasons for this: As indicated before, moderate liberalism had great difficulty in establishing itself. Second, the European Right was simply not an option insofar as it had come into being as the reaction to and rejection of the French Revolution of 1789. This meant that it was constituted from the beginning by a longing for the predemocratic order in which Jews had lacked a legitimate place. Worse still, that longing was, as often as not, under the influence of Romanticism, a longing which went back beyond the era of the early modern state to the Middle Ages, an era much less benign in its treatment of Jews than the situation which obtained in the modern if predemocratic nation states of the eighteenth century.[4]

Thus Jews could find no political home to the right of center on the Continent, and were under direct threat from the rightist program. In fact, anti-Semitism in a new form seemed to be the clearest principle of the European Right. Due to the difficulties of constructing and then pursuing a political program based upon a past that had been in part swept away even before 1789, the Right focused on "the Jewish question" by claiming that the new and higher status of Jews was the new order's clearest defect, and the one that could be most readily reversed by political action. These "practical" consequences of the spirit and program of continental Europe's Right were to find their final outcome in the Nazi plan to exterminate European Jewry, a plan that preoccupied Nazi authorities even at the expense of other interests. By comparison, the Left seemed not beyond hope. Its egalitarianism offered, at least in principle, a ground upon which Jews could be admitted to society, if not as Jews then as individuals.

As is well-known, the modern Zionist movement had its origins in the failure of nineteenth-century European politics, including or perhaps especially democratic politics, to fulfill the promise that Jews had expected. It was founded by Theodor Herzl, an Austrian Jewish journalist, in reaction to his experience of the Dreyfus Affair in 1890s France. Alfred Dreyfus was a Jewish army officer who was charged with and convicted of treason. It appeared likely and was later proven that the espionage case against him was trumped up to rouse the storm of French anti-Semitic opinion. That this could occur in France, the country of 1789 and the "rights of man," led Herzl to conclude that Jews could not count on European democracy. As he put it, "Who belongs and who does not belong, is decided by the majority. It is a question of power." The only solution was for Jews to establish their own state—a democracy, to be sure, but one in which Jews would form a majority. Only then could they securely enjoy the blessings of liberty and citizenship.

Herzl died in 1904, but his fears for European Jews would be borne out not only by Nazism but by communism, which re-created the minority status of Jews and persecuted them as such. His hopes for a democratic Jewish state were realized as well. But as it also turned out, there were at least some countries, principally the United States and Great Britain, where Jews found it possible to be full citizens. As was mentioned earlier, today the vast majority of Jews are full and active members of democratic societies.

Liberty, Equality, and the Bible

What does this social and political history have to do with Jewish religious tradition? As the previous historical survey makes clear, the democratic revolution of the past two centuries was launched by forces external to Jewish life. Even the state of Israel as a strictly political undertaking was pursued along lines laid down by other democratic experiments and ventures.[5] Is there something specifically Jewish about Jewish participation in the worldwide democratic movement?

For some contemporary Jews the answer is certainly no, except in the sense that the historical experience of Jews as a persecuted minority makes them natural adherents of and advocates for democracy. For such people political life is one thing and Jewish tradition another. The latter belongs to the private sphere which democracy or liberal democracy has created. Indeed, many Jews in developed democracies have become so assimilated that they retain few if any ties to religious observance.

But many and perhaps most Jews today, including many who are not very observant, see a strong link between democracy and traditional Jewish teachings. They regard this link so seriously that they believe it may inform their own political actions and justify their own understanding of what democracy requires.

What are the elements of that bond? Put most simply, it is the honored place within Jewish tradition of two principles, liberty and equality, that are obviously central to the democratic enterprise. Moreover, these principles are not merely present in Jewish tradition but are emphatically fundamental principles central to the founding teaching of Judaism as presented in the Hebrew Bible. Enunciated first in its primary document, the Five Books of Moses or the Pentateuch, they are maintained throughout and receive even greater emphasis in later books, especially those of prophets such as Amos, Micah, and Isaiah.

While it is true, according to this view, that Judaism and Jews are not directly responsible for the original establishment of actual democratic institutions in the full sense of the term, the Jewish people and their scriptures are the source—indeed the primal source, given the antiquity of the Bible and the Jewish people—of the perspective on human affairs that makes possible or made possible in the fullness of time democratic life. It thus behooves Jews to embrace democratic teaching out of fidelity to their tradition and to apply the latter's principles in their own conduct within democratic politics. This view is so common among contemporary Jews that they often voice it ineffectively and inappropriately. Nevertheless, it rests upon undeniable and well-known facets of Biblical teaching in general and its presentation of the founding of the Jewish people in particular.

As far as liberty is concerned, the single most important thing to contemporary Jews is the fact that the founding event of the Jewish people was the liberation of the ancient Israelites from slavery in Egypt and their exodus from there. Moreover, it is an event which is and has been annually celebrated since that time in the form of the festival of Passover, which is meant as a kind of re-creation of that event. Its institution is practically speaking the first law in the Bible specifically given to the Jewish people. Its liturgy asks the celebrants to imagine themselves as part of the generation of Israelite slaves on the eve of the departure and as such is a holiday whose primary celebration is in the home. Its chief component is the retelling of the story of the Exodus. Throughout, the fundamental theme is that of former bondage and present liberty. Liberty's arrival as God's gift underscores its high value.

The festival of Passover was always very important, but in the contemporary democratic era it has become even more central for many Jews. For a number of relatively unobservant and assimilated Jews, it is often one of the few and sometimes only Jewish holidays that is observed, a tendency that is strengthened by the fact that it is primarily a family celebration. That plus its emphasis on liberty has led many Jews to see liberty as being crucial to Judaism and having a direct application to contemporary political affairs. For example, during the past generation some Jews have dedicated their celebration of the holiday, the *seder,* to contemporary political causes.

In the case of equality or what is termed today social justice, contemporary Jews similarly invoke Biblical sources, especially certain features of Biblical law and the rhetoric of Biblical prophets. The Bible urges special care for widows and orphans, as well as charitable concern for the poor generally. Biblical laws include a mandate to set aside part of one's cultivated fields to be harvested by the poor. Biblical law also required that in every seventh or sabbatical year all debts were to be canceled and all Israelites who might have indentured themselves due to debts were to receive their manumission. Even more far-reaching were the provisions for every fiftieth year or the year of Jubilee. In that year, all real property, which had originally been parceled out equally in the settling of the land of Canaan, was to revert to its original owners.

These laws, and others besides, obviously prescribed a relatively egalitarian society and are seen as the original model for and continuous with the egalitarianism associated with modern democracy. It is true that, in the Biblical period, many of these provisions were frequently honored in the breach and not the observance, but we know that from the Bible itself. Its pages are replete with prophets who thunder against the impiety of injustice and indifference. Some prophets particularly denounce ill-treatment of the poor and weak, and attack what the prophets see as a tendency by the rich and powerful to embrace outward rituals while downgrading real inner concern for God and neighbor. Many modern Jews see in such Biblical passages the warrant for their own general inclination not only to support but to emphasize social and economic equality and even to see this as the core of being Jewish. For the attitude of the prophets seemed to raise to an even higher level the status of equality and to deprecate merely ritual observance.

Biblical Monotheism and Politics

More generally and most deeply, the privileged status of liberty and equality can be traced not only to the founding of the Jewish people but to the primary Biblical teaching that there is one God who creates humans in His own image. As a result, all men are equal and share equally in the qualities, especially liberty, which relate to moral and hence political life. In this sense, for contemporary Jews, Jewish teaching may be seen to be fundamentally democratic and even the original democratic teaching. On the one hand, the Biblical teaching concerning God represented a clear break with all previous and contemporary teachings, which were polytheist. On the other hand, it marked a clear departure from the laws of other people in its democratic tendencies.

This view of the essential characteristics of Biblical teaching and its relationship to democratic principles has a considerable amount of force. To it could be added, and sometimes is, certain aspects of rabbinic teaching as it has expounded Jewish law in the post-Biblical period down to the present. Such scriptural and rabbinic teachings have certainly bolstered the historical grounds upon which Jews have embraced democracy.

But there is more to the story, for not all aspects of the Jewish tradition would appear to be so supportive of modern democracy and its liberal-egalitarian precepts. To begin with, the main object of Biblical education is not liberty or equality but rather the proper worship of God and its corollary, the eradication of idolatry. Second, Biblical teaching presupposes and focuses upon a particular people and even appears to accord them a special status as God's "chosen" people. Third, whatever the social and economic implications of its laws may be, Biblical legislation is presumed to come from God and therefore requires obedience. What is left to legislative self-governance as understood by democracy is not immediately clear. Fourth and finally, the Bible and Jewish tradition do apparently have a political teaching that is not democratic but monarchic.

While none of these considerations appears likely to undermine the contemporary and universal Jewish embrace of democracy, they might one day be relevant to intra-Jewish discussions and debates about the precise character of democracy and its authority. This might especially be so if orthodox Jews come to form an ever larger proportion of the Jewish community, as may happen if more and more nonobservant Jews fully assimilate and effectively cease to be part of it. Orthodox Jews embrace the whole of the tradition and not merely those parts that appear to be democratic.

It is therefore appropriate to close by addressing some of these issues, beginning with the monarchic aspect of the Jewish political tradition. This is most visible in the celebration of the Davidic monarchy as the highpoint of the Jewish or Israelite polity in Biblical times. So impressed was Jewish tradition by this political experience that it has looked forward to the restoration of this monarchy through a descendant of David as a definitive feature of the messianic or utopian future. For the word "messiah" means in Hebrew "the anointed one" and refers to the ancient Israelite practice of anointing new kings with oil as a sign of divine strength and blessing. Jewish tradition has elaborated many different versions of the messianic future, including some that entail miraculous events. But a purely political aspect of this vision has always been prominent, and according to some authorities—most notably Moses Maimonides, the great medieval authority on Jewish law—the rule of the Messiah would be nothing more than a purely political phenomenon.[6]

By any measure, however, this monarchic tradition raises a question about the Jewish relationship to democracy. How may one understand the apparent Biblical and Jewish endorsement of this mode of rule?

As is evident from many things, this endorsement is not unqualified. The qualifications open up a complicated political teaching. To begin with, the first institution of the monarchy through the selection of King Saul, David's predecessor, came at the request of the Israelite people rather than as an initiative of God or His then-designated representative, the judge and prophet Samuel. Indeed, Samuel was very much against the establishment of the monarchy, and before fulfilling the people's wishes he warned them against the dangers of kings.[7] This speech is so eloquent that it became a staple of rebel rhetoric against the British Crown at the time of the U.S. war of independence.

Moreover, as the context of these events makes clear, the people were moved less by a love of monarchy as such than by ancient Israel's desperate need for the honest administration of justice and a well-led war effort against deadly foreign aggressors. God's acceptance of the people's request over Samuel's objections might be understood as a recognition of its wisdom or at least the need to give the polity greater institutional strength than it had been enjoying during the time of disjointed and even chaotic rule by "the judges of Israel," as recounted in the Biblical book named for them.

Governance and Human Flaws

Such an understanding is consistent with a general Biblical tendency to regard all political arrangements as at best necessary accommodations to the failings of humans, in particular their propensity for injustice and cruelty. Indeed, the Bible at first presents political life as a human institution reflecting human evil rather than as a good in its own right. The Bible's ultimate acceptance of political life and other questionable human contrivances depends upon the Biblical acceptance of the need to work through, even while improving, such frameworks born of human weakness.[8]

This may be seen in many instances in the Bible, including the founding events of the Israelite polity. Soon after leading the Hebrews from Egypt, God adopts a definition of the Israelite nation's character—a holy nation, a nation of priests—that envisions a certain democratic equality on a noble plane. Yet as it grows clear that the Israelites are having a hard time dropping idolatrous ways, God moves to establish a separate class of priests and a ritual service over which they will preside to teach the nation true worship.[9]

It would appear, then, that from the Biblical perspective a variety of political arrangements are in principle admissible and possible. The crucial consideration is their relative contribution to remedying, if not solving, the problems of political life. Indeed, as has often been observed, Moses himself saw fit to draw upon the purely human advice of his father-in-law Jethro regarding the establishment of a system for the administration of justice which involved the devolution of some of the prophet's authority.[10]

One might even regard the basic orientation of Biblical politics to be more democratic than not in light of a certain Biblical egalitarianism mentioned on several occasions in this essay. To this may be added the fact that the establishment of the Israelite nation was dependent upon a covenant between it and God. A number of scholars, most notably the late orthodox Jewish political scientist Daniel Elazar, have argued that this was in essence an act of consent on the part of the governed and thus fits democratic criteria. Finally, it must be noted that Biblical monarchy was a limited or constitutional one—limited, that is to say, by a law to which the king would himself be subject.[11] This would bear some resemblance to other constitutional monarchies, at least some of which combine both monarchic and democratic features.

But there remain the questions of the law, its status and special purposes, and the apparently undemocratic distinction drawn between the Israelite or Jewish people and all other nations. Nothing here need be construed as irreconcilably at odds with democratic sensibilities and understandings. First, it is clear that the highest purpose of the law—the correct understanding of God and the eradication of the false belief in idolatry and multiple gods—is not intended to be the restricted patrimony of the Israelites. Rather it fulfills a need that all human beings share and upon whose proper fulfillment depends their ultimate wholeness and felicity.

Accordingly, as presented in the Bible, the so-called election of Israel as a chosen people is as much a burden as it is a privilege. Before his death, for example, Moses indicated that the Israelite nation was meant to serve as an example of justice and wisdom to underwrite both the spread of these virtues and the true understanding of God.[12] Later prophets reinforced and emphasized this view with the formula that Israel was to be a "light unto the nations."

Hence, the Bible's general political vision points to a certain ultimate equality of nations, which would resemble each other, if not be identical to one another, in their adherence to proper moral and religious principles. This is not, of course, the same as a universal democratic empire, for the nations retain their individual existence. Nor is it meant to be, since in its typically hardheaded way the Bible still finds political power suspect.

None of the preceding may be taken to prove that the Jewish understanding of politics is simply democratic. And yet, short of the Messiah's appearance, it is likely that Jews can and will draw upon this moral and intellectual heritage as they affirm their attachment to—and offer constructive criticisms of—the democratic way of conducting political life. Jewish historical experience has taught Jews the bitter lesson of just how drastically bad the alternatives to democracy can be, while Jewish religious tradition reminds Jews that all humanly devised political systems are suspect. Both the lesson and the reminder offer sound spiritual sustenance to all those who would undertake the tasks of democratic citizenship.

NOTES

1. It is worth noting that practically all the critics have been Jews. It is likely that Israel's Muslim and Christian communities would be opposed to civil marriage and to the dilution of the authority of their religious courts.

2. One possible exception to this rule is Benedict Spinoza, who was the first explicit modern proponent of liberal democracy. The difficulty is that Spinoza did not regard himself as a Jew nor was he regarded as such by contemporary Jews, who excommunicated him from the Jewish community. At a minimum, Spinoza understood himself to have rejected the Bible's teaching on politics, not to mention other important teachings. See Hillel Fradkin, "The Separation of Religion and Politics: The Paradoxes of Spinoza," *Review of Politics* 50 (Fall 1988): 603–27.

3. George Washington, "Address to the Hebrew Congregation in Newport, Rhode Island, 18 August 1790," in W.W. Abbot et al., eds., *The Papers of George Washington: Presidential Series* (Charlottesville: University Press of Virginia, 1996), 6: 284–86.

4. For an account of this development and its impact of the fate of liberalism and Jews in Germany, see the preface to Leo Strauss, *Spinoza's Critique of Religion* (Chicago: University of Chicago Press, 1997).

5. This was true even with regard to the designation of the state as Jewish. The latter was meant as a national rather than religious identity and the immediate purpose of the state was to provide safety for Jews. For the complications of this strictly political definition, see Strauss's preface, cited in note 4 above.

6. *Treatise on Resurrection,* English translation of the Arabic text by Hillel Fradkin in Ralph Lerner, *Maimonides' Empire of Light: Popular Enlightenment in an Age of Belief* (Chicago: University of Chicago Press, 2000), 154–77.

7. 1 Samuel 8.

8. Hillel Fradkin, "Poet-Kings: A Biblical Perspective on Heroes," in Thomas L. Pangle and Michael Palmer, eds., *Political Philosophy and the Human Soul: Essays in Memory of Allan Bloom* (Lanham, Md.: Rowman & Littlefield, 1995); Hillel Fradkin, "God's Politics: Lessons from the Beginning," *This World* 4 (Winter 1983): 86–104.

9. Exodus 19:4–6.

10. Exodus 18:13–27.

11. Deuteronomy 17:14–20.

12. Deuteronomy 4:5–8, Deuteronomy 9:4–6.

8

THE CATHOLIC WAVE

Daniel Philpott

Daniel Philpott *is associate professor of political science at the University of Notre Dame and faculty fellow at the Joan B. Kroc Institute for International Peace Studies. He is the author of* Revolutions in Sovereignty: How Ideas Shaped Modern International Relations *(2001). This essay originally appeared in the April 2004 issue of the* Journal of Democracy.

In his influential study of the "third wave" of democratization—that is, of the thirty countries that made the transition to democracy between 1974 and 1990—Samuel P. Huntington notes that roughly three-quarters were predominantly Catholic. It was "overwhelmingly a Catholic wave," he writes.[1] Rising in Portugal and Spain, the Catholic wave then surged across Latin America, carried democracy to the Philippines, and crested in Poland with the first of several East European revolutions against communism.

Catholicism and democracy? Historically, the two have clashed. Latter-day liberals still thrust with reminders of nineteenth-century papal condemnations of religious liberty and twentieth-century concordats between the Church and fascist dictatorships; contemporary Catholics still parry with the irony of French revolutionaries decapitating Catholic men in order to advance the rights of man. How, then, did democracy break out in Catholic-majority states the world over? The Catholic wave in fact culminated a centuries-long rapprochement by which the Church and the democratic state each slowly came to tolerate the other in doctrine and practice, eventually arriving at a mutual and reciprocal agreement upon what Alfred Stepan has termed the "twin tolerations."[2] The tolerations are essential to liberal democracy: the state respects the rights of all religious bodies to practice and express their faith and to participate in democratic politics, while religious bodies accept religious freedom for people of all faiths (and no faith) and renounce claims to special constitutional status or prerogatives.

Church and state each had to do their part. The world's states have embraced toleration in sporadic succession—in this time, in that place, in waves, spurts, reversals, and resurgences, beginning with the English, French, and American revolutions. Even today, still less than half have arrived. The Church, chary toward the anticlericalism that so many European democracies had long practiced, clutching its own conviction that the state ought to promote the faith and restrict dissent, delayed its own embrace of toleration until 1965, when it endorsed the principle of religious freedom at its Second Vatican Council. Once the Church did give its approval to toleration, however, it found itself free to become an agent of change in states, predominantly Catholic in population, where democratic toleration had not yet achieved preeminence. In such states would the Catholic wave take place.

During this wave, the Church in Rome opposed authoritarianism globally. In each country, though, the opposition of the local Church varied in form and extent. In Poland, the Philippines, Brazil, and Spain, Church leaders and members defied authoritarianism with vigor and virtuosity. Elsewhere the Church cleaved, with some of its voices oppositional, others accommodationist. In still other locales, it was united in lukewarmth or even resistance toward democracy. Why did the Church's influence vary? To identify the reasons is to discover those features and activities of the Church—nay, of any religious body—that do the most to nurture the twin tolerations which lie at the heart of liberal-democratic governance.

The Long Rapprochement

Beneath the Church's historic hostility to democracy lay an even older hostility to the sovereign state itself. Scholars trace the origins of the system of sovereign states to the Peace of Westphalia, where European powers gathered in 1648 to settle the catastrophic Thirty Years' War. Pope Innocent X declared that settlement "null, void, invalid, iniquitous, unjust, damnable, reprobate, inane, empty of meaning and effect for all time." The Church tended its enmity well into the nineteenth century, when it condemned international law as a "Protestant science" and censured the works of the Dutch philosopher Hugo Grotius, often considered the intellectual godfather of international law.[3]

Westphalia drew the Church's scorn because it inflicted a mortal wound on the *Respublica Christiania,* the vision of society that the Church carried forward from medieval Christendom. At the core of this vision was a unity rooted in Christian faith. The trustees of this unity were authorities whose prerogatives mingled the religious with the political and the temporal with the spiritual—admixtures most sharply vivified when kings and emperors brandished arms to defend Catholic Christianity against threats to its unity.

Westphalia replaced unity with segmentation. What triumphed there was a system of polities, defined by territory, within each of which a single authority—typically a monarch at the time—was supreme, or sovereign. Each sovereign could set the terms of religious practice across its realm, and some stripped ecclesiasts of their remaining temporal powers or even sought to supplant the Catholic Church altogether. To the Church, such a system was idolatrous, its authorities accountable to no larger moral order.

But the Church did not reject the state categorically. Were it ruled by a crown that upheld the Church's authority and proclaimed and enforced the faith in its realm—in effect creating a local remnant of Christendom— then it might be acceptable. Such were the Latin states of Spain and Portugal, as well as their replicas in Latin America and the Philippines.

When the doctrines of popular suffrage and the rights of man began to emerge in the eighteenth century, the Church saw in them much the same threats that it had seen in the system of sovereign states. It faced a rabid and at times violent anticlericalism in the French Revolution, in the republican movements that it inspired around Europe, in the *Kulturkampf* of Bismarck's Germany, and in socialist movements. Amid this atmosphere of assault, the Church denounced liberalism in edicts as stentorian as Innocent X's condemnation of Westphalia: In 1832, Pope Gregory XVI called freedom of conscience "an absurd and erroneous opinion."[4] Even more pointedly, Pope Pius IX's 1864 *Syllabus of Errors* condemned religious freedom, the separation of Church and state, and "progress, liberalism, and recent civilization."

The Church thus upheld its old doctrine that temporal authorities ought to promote the Church's prerogatives and permit dissenters no rights. Where circumstances prevented this ideal, the Church could compromise in practice, but not in principle. In an 1895 letter to the U.S. Church, Pope Leo XIII praised the freedom accorded to Catholicism there, but rejected this arrangement as a universal, enduring ideal.[5] Where facing far greater threats from authoritarian regimes, the Church sought concordats (agreements) for protection. It was in the spirit of this second-best strategy that the Church signed concordats with fascist regimes in Italy and Germany in the early twentieth century.

It was not until the 1930s that Catholic intellectuals began to offer more deeply principled arguments for religious freedom. What inspired them most was the United States, whose constitutional guarantee of religious freedom, they thought, merited a far stronger endorsement than Pope Leo XIII's. The most prominent of these intellectuals were Jacques Maritain and John Courtney Murray, who did the most to lay the theoretical groundwork for the Church's endorsement of liberal democracy.

Maritain excoriated the sovereign state and defended human rights and democracy via the Catholic tradition. Murray argued for the compatibility of Catholicism and the American founding. A Catholic understanding of natural law could provide the objective moral grounding that constitutional democracy needed, while the U.S. Constitution's First Amendment safeguarded the Church's right to exist and operate.

Though religious freedom was not to be thought of as an "article of faith," or theological truth, it was still morally praiseworthy as an "article of peace," that is, a law that helped the Church to flourish in a modern state.

Both Murray and Maritain would have to await the victory of their ideas. Under pressure from Rome, Murray's Jesuit superiors ordered him in 1955 to cease writing on church-state issues. The Vatican would likely have condemned Maritain's views, too, had Pope Pius XII not died in 1958.[6]

It was only four years later that Pope John XXIII convened the Second Vatican Council, where the long rapprochement between Catholicism and liberal democracy culminated. In 1963, during the Council, John XXIII wrote his encyclical letter *Pacem in Terris,* in which the Church endorsed human rights for the first time. The most important departure from the medieval model, though, came in 1965 with Pope Paul VI's encyclical *Dignitatis Humanae.* Strongly influenced by Murray, the document declared that religious liberty is a basic right rooted in the very God-given dignity of the human person. The Church had always taught that authentic faith cannot be coerced. Now it affirmed that no individual, group, or state may rightly interfere with an individual's search for truth. The first half of the document appealed to reason, arguing that true faith is explored and adopted through free communication, teaching, expression, dialogue, and assent, which require both psychological freedom and immunity from coercion. The second half argues from revelation, holding that coercion in faith is contrary to the way of Christ. The Church insisted that it was not abridging its doctrine of truth, affirming a "right to error," or endorsing a theory of liberal democracy rooted in Enlightenment individualism, skepticism, or mere proceduralism. Rather, it was forbidding coercive restriction of the pursuit of truth.

Subsequent popes taught democracy and human rights, especially religious freedom, all the more vigorously. John Paul II toted these ideas around the world, often proclaiming them in authoritarian states. He "seemed to have a way of showing up in full pontifical majesty at critical points in democratization processes," writes Huntington. As the Pope explained: "I am not the evangelizer of democracy; I am the evangelizer of the Gospel. To the Gospel message, of course, belong all the problems of human rights; and if democracy means human rights, it also belongs to the message of the Church."[7] After the Cold War, he defended liberal democracy as the form of government most conducive to justice and the mission of the Church at great length in his encyclical *Centesimus Annus* (1991). From the perspective of the long rapprochement, though, a more poignant message was his plaintive statement to the European Parliament in 1988:

> Our European history clearly shows how often the dividing line between "what is Caesar's" and "what is God's" has been crossed in both directions.

Medieval Latin Christendom to mention only one example, while theoretically elaborating the natural concept of the State . . . did not always avoid the
integralist temptation of excluding from the temporal community those who
did not profess the true faith. Religious integralism, which makes no proper
distinction between the proper spheres of faith and civil life, which is still
practiced in other parts of the world, seems to be incompatible with the very
spirit of Europe, as it has been shaped by the Christian message.[8]

The Contours of the Catholic Wave

Having come to teach liberal democracy, the Church could now act
to bring it about. But if the Church's new teachings corresponded in
timing and form to the Catholic wave, the extent of Church influence
on any of the far-flung new democracies is hard to know. In degrees
difficult to measure, this influence has had to compete with economic
advancement, changing popular attitudes, the decay of authoritarian
regimes, the role of secular actors, and the influence of powerful external democracies such the United States. More readily identifiable are
those actions through which the Church has consciously defied juntas
and communists in the name of liberties and elections. Such defiance
often corresponds to democratic transitions.

What then becomes clear is that the Church's support for democracy
has not been the same everywhere. In some places, the Church has
kindled a fire of oppositional soul force, with nuns facing down tanks,
candlelight protests winding through medieval streets, a bishop risking
his life by speaking out against a dictator, or a pope celebrating an
open-air mass for tens of thousands under the windows of a communist
commissariat. At the other extreme, Church authorities have languished
in coexistence with autocracy, their defiance tepid.

The Church's democratizing influence, then, was complex, varying in time, manner, and extent. Complexity lies first in the Church
itself. Sometimes, "the Church" is a metonymy for the pope, who
speaks in its name. Papal preferences, though, are not always mediated smoothly as they gain distance from Rome: Bishops and other
clerics often implement the Vatican's wishes with varying degrees of
enthusiasm and efficacy, depending on their own convictions, politics, and local circumstances. The Church is also the "people of God,"
as the Second Vatican Council taught, comprising a laity of voters,
parishioners, protestors, collaborators, Christian Democratic parties,
base communities that serve and mobilize the poor, and conservative
aristocrats, all of whom approach democratization differently and often separately.

Complexity also characterizes the sorts of democratic activities in
which the Church's sundry actors may engage. Some become public
protestors. Distinctively, Church leaders also celebrate masses and other
ceremonies with a partly political intent, as did Pope John Paul II in his

choreographed travels. Leaders and laypeople within nations forge links with forces foreign and domestic—unions, parties, newspapers, non-governmental organizations—that can invigorate their struggle.

Such activity threatens regimes. It can establish a condition that George Weigel aptly calls "moral extraterritoriality"—an island of free thought and speech, of truth speaking to power, in a sea of regime-controlled discourse.[9] From this island redoubt, dissenters can challenge the regime's legitimacy as well as encourage others to join them. The resulting movement may well form the seed of a new, democratic government.

A survey of the Catholic wave shows who undertook what sort of democratization, and where. Not surprisingly, the contours of the Catholic wave corresponded to the distribution of the world's Catholic population—a total of more than a billion people, with 461 million in Latin America, 286 million in Europe, and 120 million in Africa.[10]

In Europe, prior to the Catholic wave, two sorts of autocracy prevailed in Catholic countries. In Iberia there were Spain and Portugal, authoritarian Latin states that supported the Church and enjoyed the legitimacy that came from Church approval. To the east there were Poland, Czechoslovakia, Hungary, and Lithuania, all governed by communist regimes that persecuted and sought to suppress the Church.

The Church in Spain was one of the most forceful democratizers in the Catholic wave. It is also one of the churches upon which Vatican II exercised its strongest influence. Among the factors that caused the demise of Spanish authoritarianism, the Church's opposition was arguably the most formidable. Paradoxically, though, the Church did not apply this resistance through energetic popular participation, but rather through its power of withdrawal. It significantly aided democratization by deciding no longer to support the regime of Generalissimo Francisco Franco.

The efficacy of the Church's withdrawal lay in the strength of its legitimization of Franco's regime in the first place. Through most of the history of this country that remains 94 percent Catholic, the Vatican and the Crown collaborated closely, a bond that Franco fortified when he reestablished the Church's privileges, its moral authority, and its religious near-monopoly upon his triumph in the Spanish Civil War in 1939.

Following the Second Vatican Council, the Church in Rome jarringly reversed its attitude toward Franco. The Spanish Church, devoutly loyal to Rome, accepted a virtual mandate to disentangle itself from state institutions. In 1971, its bishops endorsed the separation of church and state, called prelates to resign government posts, and, by a majority vote (though still short of the two-thirds needed to pass), disavowed the Church's role in the civil war: "[W]e must humbly recognize and ask pardon for the fact that we failed to act at the opportune time as true 'ministers of reconciliation' in the midst of our people divided by a war between brothers." After Franco's death in 1975, the Church exercised its taciturn iconoclasm, withdrawing from politics and allowing proponents of democracy to establish a new constitution.[11]

In Eastern Europe, democratization meant bringing down communist regimes that sought to control Church governance and finances; suppress religious education and ban Catholic schools, presses, newspapers, and civic organizations; confiscate Church property; take control of Church hospitals, nursing homes, and orphanages; abolish monastic houses; and imprison or murder dissenting priests and prelates. Virtually every East European church—Catholic, Protestant, and Orthodox alike—suffered thus under a communist regime.

Long before it took up the cause of human rights, the Church regularly excoriated communism. Pope Pius XII showered it with his choicest invective. The next two popes, John XXIII and Paul VI, continued to oppose communist regimes, but now in the language of human rights and through a strategy of *Ostpolitik,* by which, through diplomatic dialogue, they would seek concordats with communist regimes to protect the Church. John Paul II challenged communist regimes more assertively by speaking directly to their citizens, animated by a vision of Europe as a Christian civilization united by human rights and democratic governance.[12]

Among the national churches, Poland's was a prototype of nationalist resistance to communism. In a country where more than 90 percent of the population identifies itself as Catholic, the Church has been an important symbol of the nation. In the early years of communist rule, Stefan Cardinal Wysziński spoke out against the regime, spent three years in prison, and then asserted the Church's autonomy in a nine-year "Great Novena" of pilgrimages, catechesis, and preaching. "The fulcrum of the revolution of 1989," though, was the election to the papacy of native son Karol Cardinal Wojtyła, who, as Pope John Paul II, visited Poland three times beginning in 1979, galvanized Poles to protest, and encouraged the formation of the free trade union known as Solidarity.[13]

Lithuania, like Poland, is a highly Catholic country—81 percent of the population—where religion is woven into the national identity, and where the Church sustained a strong and consistent opposition to communist rule, championing liberal constitutionalism and human rights, sustaining underground publications, and remaining the most important symbol of nationalist opposition through song, story, and traditional ritual. By contrast, no strong Catholic opposition movement emerged in Czechoslovakia, though here, too, John Paul II inspired resistance, emboldening Bohemia's František Cardinal Tomášek to speak out more strongly against the regime and mobilizing popular protest. In Hungary, apart from the lonely resistance of József Cardinal Mindszenty, the Church largely remained supine, showing little effective resistance until 1988, the year before communism collapsed.[14]

The Church in Developing Countries

Latin America is home to a larger share of Catholics—44 percent—than any other region of the world, and had the highest concentration of democratizing states in the Catholic wave. Virtually all these states, in South America and Central America alike, began as colonies, where Church and state were closely integrated partners. But in most of these states all or part of the post–Vatican II Church—sometimes the national bishops, sometimes other communities within the Church, in different patterns, to different degrees—sooner or later came to oppose authoritarianism in the name of human rights and democracy.

The Southern Cone states, Argentina, Brazil, and Chile, typify this contrast. In Brazil, home to more Catholics than any other state in the world—115 million in all—the opposition of priests and bishops was among the strongest in Latin America. Not only the teachings of Vatican II, but also liberation theology, a doctrine of social justice for the poor that had caught fire at the 1968 Latin American bishops' conference at Medellín, Colombia, inspired the clerics, who then carried these ideas to Brazil's thousands of ecclesial base communities, where they mobilized opponents of the regime.[15]

The Church in Chile also became a strong voice for human rights, creating advocacy groups to oppose the dictatorship of General Augusto Pinochet after he took power in a 1973 coup. Relative to Brazil and Chile, the Church in Argentina was passive, stuck in a long history of close association with the state and economic elites. During the dictatorship and the dirty wars of 1976 to 1983, only a few Church leaders denounced human rights violations or criticized the military (two of the exceptional bishops were murdered), while the official Church did not advocate democracy until 1981.

In three Central American lands, the Church ceased being the partner of an authoritarian state and became either one of its foes or else a body divided in its loyalties, in each case in an atmosphere of brutal civil war. In Guatemala, a traditionally anticommunist Catholic Church began to speak out against human rights violations and to call for peace, especially in the late 1970s, when the dictatorship there stepped up its violence. A traditional Church-state alliance in El Salvador also began to break down in the early 1970s, when Archbishop Luis Chávez y González adopted Medellín and Vatican II. His successor was Óscar Romero, whom the regime assassinated in 1980 because he spoke out on behalf of the poor and their rights. Opposition was strong, too, among the poor in the ecclesial base communities, many members of which took up arms, though usually not with the encouragement of Church activists. In the Nicaraguan Church, the grassroots supported the revolution of the communist Sandinistas in 1979 against the rightist Somoza dictatorship, while the hierarchy opposed both the Somoza family and the Sandinista revolution.

Elsewhere in Latin America, the Church had broken its ties with the state many years before democratization. The Mexican Church, suppressed by an anticlerical government for most of the twentieth century, arose in the 1980s to challenge electoral fraud and became a force for democratization in the 1990s. The Peruvian Church, long a progressive force, helped democracy in the 1980s by developing ties of solidarity with the urban and rural poor, thus making them more likely to reject the Shining Path terrorist movement. In two other states—Uruguay and Paraguay—the Church hierarchy remained largely passive while grassroots Catholic organizations mounted modest opposition.[16]

It was not in Latin America proper, however, but in a former Spanish colony far across the Pacific that Catholics would marshal their most redoubtable effort against an authoritarian Latin state. In the Philippines (84 percent Catholic) as elsewhere in the Latin world, the Church had long been tied to the state and the landed aristocracy. Vatican II and Medellín then recast the Church's stance even more thoroughly than elsewhere, inspiring numerous groups to proclaim and live a mission to the poor, including the national bishops' conference, several social-justice groups, and two-thousand base communities. After President Ferdinand Marcos declared martial law in 1972, the Church gradually grew more unified in its stance against him. Following the assassination of opposition politician Benigno Aquino in 1983, Manila's Jaime Cardinal Sin and his fellow bishops cited the Gospel in leading a sustained nonviolent movement for democracy, culminating in two-million–strong "people power" protests that forced Marcos out in February 1986.[17]

In two other East Asian states, the Church also impressively resisted authoritarian regimes. In South Korea, groups of Catholics joined Protestant counterparts in advocating human rights, democracy, and economic justice in the wake of Vatican II and Medellín. Increasingly during the 1970s and 1980s, Catholic students followed the call of Seoul's cardinal-archbishop Stephen Kim Su-hwan to take to the streets in peaceful protest against the dictatorship of President Park Chung Hee.[18]

In East Timor, the Church's historic relationship to the state followed the colonial model. When Portugal granted independence in 1975, Indonesia promptly invaded, touching off a bloody conflict that lasted until 1999, when a new Indonesian president at last allowed East Timor to vote on independence. During the war, Bishop Carlos Ximenes Belo led the Catholic Church and the people of East Timor in resisting occupation.[19]

Finally, in several African countries, Catholic opposition helped to bring about democratization. Most striking was Malawi, where the national bishops' pastoral letter of 1992, "Living Our Faith," distributed to parishes across the country, was the first public criticism leveled against the one-party rule of Hastings Kamuzu Banda, and a turning point in bringing him down. In Kenya, Zambia, and Ghana, the Church led popular opposition movements against authoritarianism as well. In other African states, though—Uganda, Cameroon, and Rwanda—Catholics proved ineffective as brokers of democracy and, in the case of Rwanda, were sometimes even implicated in atrocities.[20]

All along the general sweep of the global Catholic wave, the Church coaxed and goaded the state to take up democracy, but not everywhere or to the same extent. Catholic opposition could be high-profile enough to win the Nobel Peace Prize—Lech Wałęsa and Bishop Belo were both so honored—and yet could also be moderate, lukewarm, or even feeble.

What Makes the Churches Effective

Why these differences? What features and activities have led some national Catholic churches to help democracy, and others to hinder it or do nothing? What sort of church can best avoid being coopted by caudillos or crushed by communists? This is indeed to ask: What sort of church flourishes most robustly in the modern political world, so far removed from anything like Christendom?

Surely it is the one that takes up the Catholic magisterium's teachings on justice in the modern political world. Promulgated from Rome to the entire Church, these teachings again and again changed the political posture of national churches. Spain is the strongest example. But again, some churches have imbibed these teachings more deeply and spread them more widely than others. Why? The answer leads back to the twin tolerations.

In a democracy, church and state are differentiated. Churches eschew constitutional privileges, their clerics forgo temporal powers, and state officials in turn refrain from trying to govern the Church. Differentiation of Church and other social spheres was an important concept among sociologists of religion in the 1950s and 1960s, who considered it a sign of religious decline that accompanied enlightenment, reason, and scientific progress.[21] What has become apparent over the decades since, though, is that differentiation may well foster the health of religion, giving it the very autonomy by which it flourishes. This is what the French Catholic intellectual Alexis de Tocqueville observed in America in the 1830s and what Murray and Maritain observed a century later—religion thriving in a liberal-democratic state. Not only might a differentiated Church flourish, but its very distance from the state might allow it to influence politics more powerfully—and democratically, through persuasion, protest, and appeals to legitimacy. Even in the modern world, the church can remain robustly public, as sociologist José Casanova has argued.[22]

If the Catholic Church may flourish through the differentiation that democracy entails, then might it not also be true that those churches which best bring about democracy are the ones that, even while living under authoritarianism, already embody—albeit in a limited, beleaguered way, to be sure—the differentiation that they will enjoy far more fully once a democratic constitution has been realized? From their differentiated position, they can engage in the protodemocratic politics of contesting the regime's legitimacy. From its differentiated nook, the Church can wield the tools of democracy to bring about a democratic regime.

Differentiation is in fact a conglomerate of factors that embody and strengthen the Church's separation from the state. The strength of each factor varies from state to state, of course. One of the most important is governance: Does the Church enjoy autonomy from the state in its finances, appointments, doctrine, and practice? The most effective democratizers were churches that maintained some autonomy under authoritarianism, even in the face of duress and persecution. The Polish Church doggedly guarded its prerogatives right up through the 1980s, drawing on a degree of popular prestige that made government attempts at suppression costly indeed. The Church and Catholic organizations in the Philippines, though hardly free from suppression, remained able to govern their internal ranks and thus lead their flock in mass protest when the time came. Churches in Brazil, Lithuania, Peru, South Korea, East Timor, Malawi, Kenya, Ghana, and elsewhere also enjoyed substantial autonomy and were a democratizing influence. By contrast, in countries such as Argentina, where Church and state remained interlocked, the Church was a weak democratizer.

Often, the churches that preserved relative autonomy were inheritors of a legacy of autonomy that long predated modern authoritarianism. The Polish Church had established a fierce tradition of resistance to encroachment during Poland's triple occupation by neighboring great powers from 1795 to 1918. Three decades later, the tradition was available to be resumed. By contrast, the Catholic Church in Bohemia, which was weakly resistant to communism, had cooperated with the Habsburg monarchy in forming a Counter-Reformation state in the seventeenth century and continued to remain cozy with it into the twentieth century. In South Korea the Church had remained distant from the state since the arrival of missionaries in the late eighteenth century.

Transnational ties with allied outsiders are another way in which the Church remains differentiated from the state. For the Catholic Church, such ties are built into its very structure. More than any other Christian church or world religion, the Catholic Church teaches that its unity is a visible one, sustained by a network of bishops that teaches faith and morals commonly and obligingly to all and links distant Catholics together in solidarity. Such a network was a formidable asset against authoritarian regimes. The teachings of Vatican II could be transmitted easily and authoritatively across borders. A peripatetic pope could travel to a country and speak to ready crowds of Catholics, sometimes numbering in the millions.

The strength of transnationalism also varied. Some national churches were more receptive than others to Vatican II teachings. The Spanish Church's strong respect for the authority of Rome allowed it to be transformed from the outside, even though it ranked low on other dimensions of differentiation. Other churches, such as Argentina's, were less receptive to the new teachings. Popes differed, too, in their transnational strategies. Pope Paul VI's caution toward communist regimes contrasted with John Paul II's far more aggressive approach of traveling to Poland, Czechoslovakia, the Philippines, Nicaragua and other sites of autocracy. In many of the Latin American countries that democratized, the papal nuncio played an influential role.

Links to movements and organizations outside the Church but within the same state can provide another ally against undemocratic regimes—also a mode of differentiation. In Poland, the Church and Solidarity fortified one another. In Brazil, the oppositional Church allied closely with labor unions and social movements for the poor. In other settings—Chile, Ghana, Kenya, Malawi, the Philippines, South Korea, Zambia, and elsewhere—Catholics forged ecumenical contacts with prodemocratic Protestants to create a unified movement.

A final mode of Church differentiation from the state was an alliance with national identity that fostered an antiregime solidarity with citizens at large. Poland, again, is the quintessential case. During long years of occupation, the Church had become a symbol of the Polish nation's ability to survive despite hardship. Under communism, the Church drew upon this same bond to great effect. In Lithuania, the Church's identification with the nation was also exceptionally strong, and a source of solidarity against communist rule. In Brazil, the Philippines, and Spain, the Church also symbolized national identity to great effect.

In all of these ways, differentiation fortified the Catholic Church even in locales where secularism was gaining ground, as evidenced, say, by declining rates of religious observance. In Europe, for instance, even as the Church was exercising democratizing power, religious attendance was sliding. The nature of the Church's relationship to the state, then, is more important for democracy than a country's level of religious belief or practice. Of course, high levels of Catholic devotion can certainly strengthen an oppositional Church, as they did in Poland and the Philippines. But the example of the Orthodox Church in Greece shows that a high level of religiosity measured in belief and practice is perfectly compatible with a church that remains passively on the sidelines of democratization.

The Church and Democracy Today

Today it is difficult to think of an influential Catholic sector in any state that actively opposes liberal democracy. That is the significant result of the revolution in the Church's approach to politics of the past generation. Far more common are Catholics who are persecuted for their faith, as many of the estimated 7.5 million Catholics are in China. If one day these Catholics help to overthrow their oppressors, then they will become the last bursts of energy in the Catholic wave.

The far more prevalent challenge for the Catholic Church is to navigate its way through democratic politics, finding the proper contours of the twin tolerations, the appropriate limits of differentiation. Within democracy, as outside of it, the Church is advantaged by differentiation. Lacking temporal powers, it need not amend its message or activities in order to safeguard them. The state reciprocally grants the Church freedom to govern itself. From this healthy distance, the Church may then promote human flourishing through characteristic democratic activities such as persuading, lobbying, preaching, and advising voters. The dilemma of democracy for the Church is that in comparison with the pre–Vatican II ideal state, it enjoys far less certainty that its teachings will be promoted actively in the political order; electoral politics, in fact, may well yield antithetical policies. The Church then faces a choice. It can accept temporary defeat and continue to play the democratic game; it can withdraw from the game; or it can challenge the very terms of the democratic association, risking a loss of support among those who perceive it as overstepping its bounds.

Poland and the Philippines exemplify these dilemmas. In both cases, the Church plays a strong role in democratic politics, as it did in making such politics possible. In both cases, critics charge it with violating democratic boundaries. In Poland, the Church sought to shape the new constitution so that it would make Christian values the foundation of law, to secure passage of laws to uphold marriage and the protection of life from the moment of conception, and to secure a concordat between Poland and Rome that guarantees substantial rights to the Polish Catholic Church. The Church gingerly declares that it will support no ticket in an election but urges Catholics to vote for tickets that uphold Catholic commitments.[23] In the Philippines, Cardinal Sin again exercised the "power of the people" by calling for mass prayer vigils and demonstrations to oust the corrupt government of President Joseph Estrada in 2001.

It is not clear that a Church which seeks to shape its state's laws on marriage and life or even its constitution or its concordat is acting illiberally or undemocratically. The United Kingdom and all of the Scandinavian countries retain established churches, while states such as Germany recognize and support official religions, even while guaranteeing religious freedom. Still, the calumnious rhetoric of some Polish prelates violates the democratic virtue of civility and risks alienating the Church from mainstream Polish opinion. In the Philippines, though Cardinal Sin's religious leadership in bringing democracy in 1986 continues to inspire, his continued use of mass popular pressure to force out leaders, albeit unsavory ones, raises questions about the viability of the rule of law.

Such dilemmas of democracy are variations of a much older dilemma for the Church: discovering how to advance its timeless truths in the political order. A new development in the Church's understanding of this dilemma brought it not only to favor, but to help create, a new sort of regime—one that safeguards human rights, especially religious freedom. In modernity, the Church has committed itself to conduct politics from a distance. Modernity's surprise is that this commitment turned out not to be a retreat from politics, but rather an effective strategy for speaking the Church's timeless truths authentically in the public realm. Partisans of these truths will celebrate this strategy's victories, but in witnessing liberal democracies' own injustices, will soberly remember, too, its limits and its setbacks, its retreats and its dilemmas.

NOTES

The research for this article was completed through support provided by a grant for a project on "Religion in Global Politics" sponsored by the Weatherhead Center for International Affairs at Harvard University and the Smith Richardson Foundation. For helpful research reports, I thank Edgar Chen, Robert Portada, Robert Dowd, Laurie Johnston, Katherine Diaz, and Colleen Gilg. I also thank Kevin McCormick and Erin Urquhart for their research assistance. For helpful comments on the manuscript, I thank Scott Mainwaring and James McAdams.

1. Samuel P. Huntington, *The Third Wave: Democratization in the Late Twentieth Century* (Norman: University of Oklahoma Press, 1991), 76.

2. Alfred Stepan, "Religion, Democracy, and the 'Twin Tolerations,'" *Journal of Democracy* 11 (October 2000): 37–57. See also Alfred Stepan, *Arguing Comparative Politics* (Oxford: Oxford University Press, 2001), 213–53.

3. Quoted in Daniel Philpott, *Revolutions in Sovereignty: How Ideas Shaped Modern International Relations* (Princeton: Princeton University Press, 2001), 87, 261–62.

4. Quoted in John T. McGreevy, *Catholicism and American Freedom: A History* (New York: W.W. Norton, 2003), 241.

5. Pope Leo XIII, "Longinqua Oceani," in John Tracy Ellis, ed., *Documents of American Catholic History* (Milwaukee, Wis.: Bruce, 1956), 517–18.

6. John T. McGreevy, *Catholicism and American Freedom*, 201–8.

7. Samuel P. Huntington, *The Third Wave*, 83–84.

8. Quoted in Luigi Accattoli, *When a Pope Asks for Forgiveness* (Boston: Pauline Books & Media, 1998), 178.

9. George Weigel, *The Final Revolution: The Resistance Church and the Collapse of Communism* (Oxford: Oxford University Press, 1992), 151.

10. Figures are for the year 2000 and are drawn from David B. Barrett, George T. Kurian, and Todd M. Johnson, eds., *World Christian Encyclopedia,* 2nd ed. (Oxford: Oxford University Press, 2001), 1:12.

11. Stanley G. Payne, *Spanish Catholicism: A Historical Overview* (Madison: University of Wisconsin Press, 1984), 194, 201, 213; and Raymond Carr and Juan Pablo Fusi Aizpurua, *From Dictatorship to Democracy* (London: George Allen & Unwin, 1979).

12. J. Bryan Hehir, "Papal Foreign Policy," *Foreign Policy* 78 (Spring 1990): 26–48; Michael Sutton, "John Paul II's Idea of Europe," *Religion, State, and Society* 25 (March 1997): 17–30; and John Paul II, "Ecclesia in Europe," Post-Synodal Apostolic Exhortation delivered on 28 June 2003.

13. George Weigel, *Final Revolution,* 129–37.

14. Kestutis Girnius, "Nationalism and the Catholic Church in Lithuania," in Sabrina P. Ramet, ed., *Religion and Nationalism in Soviet and East European Politics* (Durham, N.C.: Duke University Press, 1989); Paul Mojzes, *Religious Liberty in Eastern Europe and the USSR: Before and After the Great Transformation* (Boulder, Colo.: East European Monographs, 1992), 182, 246–56.

15. Edward L. Cleary, "The Brazilian Catholic Church and Church-State Relations: Nation-Building," *Journal of Church and State* 39 (Spring 1997): 235–72.

16. On events in Latin America, see Emilio Mignone, *Witness to the Truth: The Complicity of Church and Dictatorship in Argentina* (Maryknoll, N.Y.: Orbis, 1986), 366; Jeffrey Klaiber, *The Church, Dictatorship, and Democracy in Latin America* (Maryknoll, N.Y.: Orbis, 1998), 66–91.

17. Robert L. Youngblood, *Marcos Against the Church* (Ithaca, N.Y.: Cornell University Press, 1990).

18. Yun-Shik Chang, "The Progressive Christian Church and Democracy in South Korea," *Journal of Church and State* 40 (Spring 1998): 437–66.

19. Robert Archer, "The Catholic Church in East Timor," in Peter Carey and G. Carter Bentley, eds., *East Timor at the Crossroads: The Forging of a Nation* (Honolulu: University of Hawaii Press, 1995), 120–33.

20. An excellent comparative study of the role of the Church in African democratization is Paul Gifford, *The Christian Churches and the Democratisation of Africa* (Leiden: E.J. Brill, 1995).

21. On differentiation and secularization, see David Martin, *A General Theory of Secularization* (New York: Harper & Row, 1978).

22. José Casanova, *Public Religions in the Modern World* (Chicago: University of Chicago Press, 1994).

23. Timothy Byrnes, "The Challenge of Pluralism: The Catholic Church in Democratic Poland," in Ted Gerard Jelen and Clyde Wilcox, eds., *Religion and Politics in Comparative Perspective: The One, the Few, and the Many* (Cambridge: Cambridge University Press, 2002), 27–46.

9

THE PIONEERING PROTESTANTS

Robert D. Woodberry and Timothy S. Shah

Robert D. Woodberry *is assistant professor of sociology at the University of Texas–Austin. Much of the research supporting this essay is available from him through* bobwood@mail.la.utexas.edu. ***Timothy S. Shah** is Senior Fellow in Religion and International Affairs at the Pew Forum on Religion & Public Life and editor of a forthcoming Oxford University Press series on evangelical Protestantism and democracy in the global South. This essay originally appeared in the April 2004 issue of the* Journal of Democracy.

"The authority of Christ," wrote the Scots Calvinist divine William Graham in 1768, "removes all civil distinctions, and all superiority founded upon such distinctions, in his kingdom. All are upon a level equally, as they shall soon be before the awful tribunal of the great Judge."[1] This stirring fusion of theology, eschatology, and politics not only characterizes Scottish Calvinism but also says much about the relationship between Protestantism and democracy. As an egalitarian religion profoundly opposed to hierarchy, Protestant Christianity would seem to enjoy a powerful affinity with democracy.

If the affinity between Protestantism and democracy is powerful, however, it is not automatic or uncomplicated. History and social science show that Protestantism has contributed to the development of democracy, yet they also show that the connections are often far from straightforward. After all, Protestantism has at times countenanced the establishment of brutal regimes and antidemocratic movements: The "righteous" dictatorship of Oliver Cromwell enjoyed the overwhelming support of English Puritans; the Dutch Reformed Church of South Africa theologized in defense of apartheid; and while some German Protestants (especially in the Confessing Church) fought Nazism, many others gave Hitler their warm backing. Recently, Protestant evangelicals in the Third World have lent their support to "godly" authoritarians such as former Zambian president Frederick Chiluba.

In other words, opposing hierarchy and liberating individual consciences in religion does not automatically make one a foe of authoritarianism and a friend of liberty in politics. In fact, some Protestants, including founding figures such as Martin Luther and John Calvin, favored authoritarian politics as a means of defending or extending the purity of Reformed doctrines and practices. As Michael Walzer argues, it was precisely a zeal for the comprehensive spiritual purification of society that led some Protestants—particularly Calvinists—to pursue a militant and authoritarian politics in seventeenth-century England, ending in Cromwell's Protectorate.[2] By the same token, hierarchical and communal religions—such as Roman Catholicism—do not automatically support a hierarchical or authoritarian politics.[3]

We argue that there is nonetheless compelling cross-national evidence of a causal association between Protestantism and democracy. At the same time, we emphasize that the association is not direct or automatic but mediated and contingent. Among the major mediating influences or mechanisms, we number: 1) the rise of religious pluralism and what Alfred Stepan terms the "twin tolerations"[4] or the mutual independence of church and state; 2) the development of democratic theory and practice; 3) civil society and independent associational life; 4) mass education; 5) printing and the origins of a public sphere; 6) economic development; and 7) the reduction of corruption. These mechanisms help to explain how and why Protestantism tends, on balance, to promote democracy and democratization over time.

Protestantism's contribution to democracy via such mediating mechanisms explains both the strength and the contingency of the relationship. These mechanisms *often* directly result from Protestant influences, and when present, *often* directly foster democratization. Yet "often" is different from "always." Various factors, including not only changing material conditions but also the complex interests and motives of Protestant actors themselves, may disrupt the positive relationship and cause Protestantism to have neutral or even negative effects on democracy.

When Luther in 1521 defied an imperial order to recant by insisting that "my conscience is captive to the Word of God," he stopped being the reformer of an old order and instead became the founder of a new stream of Christianity. He could flout the commands of popes, church councils, and emperors, but not those of his own individual conscience. Most Protestants follow his lead in a few large, defining ways. First, Protestants are Christians not in communion with Roman Catholicism or Orthodoxy. Second, they tend to believe that people can acquire saving faith only as they personally and individually appropriate God's Word. They thus tend to make the Bible (and particularly Paul's message of salvation by grace alone) the touchstone of faith and life, reject the independent salvific significance of most (if not all) sacraments, deny the necessary mediation of priests, and insist on the priesthood of all believers. Third, they tend toward separation and independence from ancient church structures and traditions as well as political authorities. The main reason for this is the important role of individual conscience. Because saving faith must be uncoerced and individual, it requires in practice a diversity of independent churches to satisfy the inevitable diversity of individual consciences.

The importance of Luther's latter-day descendants to democracy becomes clear from demography. Not only do Protestants presently constitute 13 percent of the world's population—about 800 million people—but since 1900 Protestantism has spread rapidly in Africa, Asia, and Latin America. According to the most extensive survey of religious demographics available, in 1900 about 2 percent of Africans were Protestant; by 2000 more than 27 percent were. In Latin America, the figures for those dates are 2.5 and 17 percent, while in Asia they are 0.5 and 5.5 percent.[5] Taking these three continents together, then, Protestants went from an average population share of just 1.66 percent in 1900 to a share of 16.5 percent in 2000—a stunning increase of almost 1,000 percent in just a hundred years. Much of the growth, moreover, has occurred quite recently, meaning since post–World War II decolonization across Africa and Asia, and since the historically Catholic countries of Latin America lifted restrictions on Protestant activities a few decades ago.[6]

To the extent that Protestantism facilitates democratic transitions, its recent and dramatic expansion may have important implications for many societies in the global South. Also of significance may be the reality that much of this intense recent growth has not been among older Protestant denominations, but rather among groups that are charismatic or Pentecostal in nature, and which may now be able to count as many as 400 million adherents across the whole of Asia, Africa, and Latin America. The full array of social and political effects that will flow from this remains a matter of disagreement and speculation even among experts.

Yet cross-national statistical research suggests a strong and consistent association between a society's proportion of Protestants and its level of political democracy. This association is consistent over time and across regions, and does not change with the application either of various statistical controls or of various ways to define and measure political democracy. Furthermore, Protestantism has a strong statistical association with the durability of democratic transitions. Neither the proportion of "nonreligious" people in the population nor the proportion of adherents of any other religious tradition seems to have a similar association with democracy.[7]

Some scholars, however, argue that the association between Protestantism and democracy is merely an association between European influence and democracy and, furthermore, that the original association between Protestantism and democracy in Europe is spurious. Perhaps preexisting social or economic conditions determined where Protestantism would emerge in Europe, and perhaps they—and not Protestantism—facilitated the later spread of democracy.

But the association between Protestantism and democracy is also found where Protestantism spread through later settlement or missionary activity. For example, a comparison across former colonies whose populations are mostly of European-settler stock reveals that democracy has fared better in historically Protestant-settler societies such as Canada, Australia, New Zealand, and the United States than it has in Catholic-settler societies such as Argentina, Chile, Costa Rica, and Uruguay. British colonialism may be a factor in these cases, but the pattern extends beyond European-settler colonies. Protestantism is associated with democracy outside of Europe and its daughter countries, so whatever causes the association must be portable.

Moreover, religious tradition remains a statistically significant predictor of democracy even when one controls for the identity of the former colonial power, the number of years when that power was in control, the number of years (if any) when that power was a democracy, the penetration of the English language, and the percentage of European descendants in the population. Thus, whatever causes the association seems to be distinct from European influence, British influence, or indirect exposure to democracy. Given the variety of regions in which the association between religious tradition and democracy can be observed, and the broad range of statistical controls used in previous analyses, an alternative explanation is more difficult to imagine.

Religious Pluralism and Democratic Theory

In identifying the mechanisms that explain why Protestantism has contributed to democracy, we begin with religious pluralism. Pluralism was built into the nature of Protestantism. From the beginning of the Reformation, the Protestant movement kept dividing in an endless ecclesial mitosis because it lacked a clear mechanism for settling doctrinal disagreement.[8] This pluralism fostered the "twin tolerations" that Alfred Stepan argues are essential to democracy—that is, the independence of the state from religious control and the independence of religion from state control.

First, as G.W.F. Hegel pointed out in 1821, the end of Catholic hegemony and the rise of religious pluralism facilitated state autonomy.[9] In societies with a significant Protestant presence, religious pluralism both made it harder for any single religious body to control state and society and gave the state a sharper incentive to exert its own autonomous control over the potentially destabilizing realm of religion. Eventually this made the rise of free government more feasible because states enjoyed an exclusive jurisdictional sway over their territories, a sway that could later be distributed democratically. The contrasting situation in predominantly Catholic societies underscores the importance of religious pluralism: In such societies, the state and the Catholic Church either combined to enforce repressive religiopolitical unity, or else fell into power struggles that reduced state autonomy and undermined the stability and liberality of democratic transitions.[10]

Second, Protestant pluralism helped to foster the other of Stepan's "twin tolerations," religious liberty. While Calvinists often took Old Testament Israel as the model for the ideal state and thus sometimes established theocracies, they also emphasized that true saving faith cannot be compelled by any earthly authority. So although a Calvinist such as Cromwell did not allow religious liberty in anything like the modern sense, he allowed more religious liberty than most of his secular, Catholic, or Anglican contemporaries. This relative freedom increased religious pluralism, as people formed new sects, and this increased pluralism in turn created greater pressure for religious liberty. For example, by the time Parliament restored the monarchy in 1660, Nonconformist sects had become too numerous to crush—a fact which impressed the young John Locke, causing him to revise his early absolutist views in favor of religious toleration. Eventually the sects forced the Crown to issue the Act of Toleration (1689). When transplanted to the New World, such sects (especially Baptists and Quakers) became major advocates of religious liberty in the colonies and the early American republic.

Beyond the Anglo-American world, the Protestant missionary movement played an important role in spreading religious liberty. Originally, the British banned missions in many colonial territories because officials feared that missionary activities would create turmoil and interfere with profits. But in 1813, Protestant missionary supporters forced the government to allow free access to all religious groups. The Protestant missions lobby also pressed for religious liberty in colonies of historically Catholic powers, but less successfully. Mission organizations collected international data on religious liberty and lobbied governments to insert religious-liberty clauses in international treaties, including the charter of the United Nations. This Protestant lobbying increased religious liberty in former British colonies and helped to spread it to other societies.

Moreover, Protestantism constituted one important source for early democratic theory. Robert A. Dahl rightly suggests that the antimonarchical and prorepublican thought of the English Puritans and Levellers arose from their understanding of Christianity.[11] Later, Calvinist families or schools produced many prominent democratic thinkers, including John Locke, James Madison, Alexander Hamilton, John Jay, and John Adams. Among other things, scholars argue that the Calvinist "societal covenant" inspired the "social contract"; that the doctrine of original sin helped to motivate the concern for checks and balances in the U.S. Constitution; and that belief in the inviolability of the individual conscience fueled the urge to limit state power. Even the Presbyterian form of church governance—in which ministers are subject to elders elected by congregations—influenced the organizational form of modern representative democracy.

The New Testament and the example of the early church also eased Protestant experimentation with democracy. Jesus said "my Kingdom is not of this world," and set up no political or legal system. The Apostle Paul declared that much of Jewish law does not apply to Christians. The lack of a mandatory political or legal model in the Bible permitted Protestants to develop their own. When Protestant beliefs in freedom and equality demanded a democratic politics, the Bible did not seem to stand in the way.

Civil Society and Mass Education

According to many scholars, a robust civil society is crucial for democracy. Here too, Protestants played a central role. As already noted, Protestant groups kept dividing, and not every denomination could be the state church. Governments generally discriminated against nonstate churches, which in turn drove such churches to fight for their own rights. This activism helped to establish the principle that organizations could exist outside state control—a principle that developed only later in societies with thinner nonstate religious sectors.

Moreover, because nonestablished churches received no money from the state, they needed to instill habits of voluntarism and giving in their congregants. The laypeople who ran religious organizations affiliated with these churches learned leadership skills, built wide geographical networks, and accumulated other resources helpful in organizing nongovernmental organizations and social movements. Nonstate churches were especially prominent in training women, then commonly excluded from much of life outside the home. In the early nineteenth century, Protestants from nonestablished churches were central to founding and supporting a plethora of voluntary organizations and social movements for causes such as combating slavery or alcohol use.

Michael Young has argued that modern social-movement organizations and tactics developed in the United States when the lay-focused revival movements of upstart sects such as the Methodists and the Baptists linked up with transnational organizations developed by Calvinists to promote missions and orthodoxy.[12] However, the 1820s and 1830s saw parallel social movements flower in England, the United States, and India—a phenomenon for which traditional state- or economy-centered explanations of the rise of such movements cannot account. What these politically and economically diverse areas had most saliently in common was the presence of activist Protestants from outside any state-sponsored church.

In fact, Protestant missions have been central to the development of organized civil society across much of the non-Western world. For instance, there is a clear link between Protestant missionary activity and the appearance of indigenous NGOs in India. Protestant missionaries tried to convert Hindus and to promulgate controversial social reforms such as outlawing widow-burning and improving the treatment of "untouchables." Both sorts of activity spurred Hindu groups to form in response. Such organizations were new in Indian history and later facilitated the development of the Indian National Congress and other anticolonialist, prodemocratic groups (as well as groups that advocate more problematic ideologies such as Hindu nationalism).

A similar pattern—Protestant activism followed by a local reaction imitating Protestant organizational forms in order to counter Protestant aims—can be traced throughout the histories of places as diverse as China, Egypt, Japan, Korea, Palestine, and Sri Lanka, to give a partial list. Protestant missionaries came to win souls and reform social customs, and both Christians and non-Christians organized in response. Religious competition among Christians, Muslims, Hindus, Jains, Sikhs, and Buddhists had gone on for centuries or even millennia across India, the Middle East, China, Japan, and elsewhere, yet no widespread budding of voluntary organizations happened in these lands until Protestant missionaries from nonestablished churches appeared on the scene.

Research also shows a consistent association between mass education and democracy. Mass education fosters democracy by increasing exposure to democratic ideals, promoting economic growth and the rise of a middle class, and dispersing influence beyond a small elite. Both historical and quantitative evidence suggests a close association between Protestantism and the spread of mass education, not least because of the Protestant emphasis on the need for all believers to read the Bible in their own languages. Calvinists especially made massive investments in education, building what today are many of the elite universities of the North Atlantic world. Lutheran Pietists first promulgated the ideal of universal literacy, and literacy campaigns spread rapidly through the Protestant world. Protestants started Sunday schools to teach reading to the poor, founded Bible and tract societies, and pressed governments to fund mass education.

Protestant missions were also central to expanding mass education outside the West, despite the resistance of local colonialists who feared the effects of widespread literacy among subject peoples. Other religious groups typically invested in mass education only when they had to compete with Protestants. Protestant missionaries lobbied so effectively that, for instance, British-run India had government-funded schools by 1813, twenty years before England did. Moreover, because the souls of all humans had equal value in the spiritual economy of the missionaries, they often provided the only formal education open to women and marginalized groups such as slaves, blacks in South Africa, or members of "untouchable" castes in India.

Areas of the non-Western world where Protestant missionaries had their strongest influence continue to have higher education rates. This is true both between countries and within countries. After statistical controls are applied to account for "Protestant missionaries per capita in 1925" and "percentage of the population evangelized by 1900," the impact of Gross Domestic Product on primary-education rates in non-Western societies disappears. To the extent that education fosters democracy, then, we would expect higher levels of democracy in areas with more Protestants and where Protestant missionaries had more influence.

Printing, Economic Development, and Corruption

While democratic theorists such as Jürgen Habermas and David Zaret emphasize the importance of printing for the development of a democratic public sphere, they underestimate or ignore the role of religion in facilitating this process.[13] Printing technology appeared in the West in the late 1400s. But the public debates that fostered a democratic public sphere in England did not develop until the mid-1600s—during the religious controversies surrounding the English Revolution. Similarly, in Germany religious controversies between Pietists and other Protestant groups spurred printing and lively public discourse before the coffee houses and salons of Habermas's account.

Because of the divisions within Protestantism and also because no one person or group had clear authority to decide theological questions, Protestantism spurred public religious debate and widespread printing more than other religious traditions. Protestants also believed that God's Word was uniquely available in the Bible, and that the Bible was translatable into vernacular languages without losing its core meaning. The mass literacy that Protestants promoted made widespread reading of petitions and newspapers possible and mass printing economically viable. While printing may have made possible the development of a public sphere, Protestantism not only promoted the early development and diffusion of such printing technologies as the steam press but also fostered the public theological debates that resulted in the emergence of a public sphere in Europe and North American.

Outside Western Europe and North America, the impact of Protestantism in spreading mass printing is especially clear. Protestant missionaries emphasized vernacular printing so that people could read the Bible in their own language. Wherever Protestant missionaries went, they rapidly gave local tongues a written form, translated the Bible into them, brought in printing presses, designed vernacular fonts, and began printing Bibles, tracts, textbooks, and even newspapers. Protestant missionaries often viewed newspapers as encouraging literacy, creating good will, and providing opportunities to discuss social reforms and religious issues. No other sizeable religious group placed comparable emphasis on literacy and the mass availability of religious texts. The Muslims of the Ottoman Empire, for example, had access to printing from 1493 onward, but made little use of it until spurred by Protestant missionary printing in the nineteenth century.

Like a vibrant public sphere, economic development and a large middle class are robust predictors of the level of political democracy and the durability of democratic transition, and Protestantism may have helped to promote both these predictors. Max Weber famously argues that Protestantism (particularly Calvinism) spurred the rise of modern capitalism. Others counter that this causal claim is spurious, and that both Protestantism and economic growth grew out of the same set of conditions in early-modern northwestern Europe. If this is so, however, one would not expect to see a robust association between Protestantism and economic development in non-European countries, where Protestantism is a transplant. Yet such an association exists.

Statistical research suggests that both in Africa and in other former colonies, areas with more Protestants have greater postcolonial economic-growth rates.[14] Ethnographic and statistical evidence also confirmed the association between Protestantism (or sometimes Christianity in general) and intergenerational improvements in the economic status of individuals—for example, in Latin America, New Guinea, Nigeria, Indonesia, and India. In Latin America, Protestantism has spread disproportionately among poor and marginalized people, yet Protestantism seems to foster moderate improvements in their incomes. Although Protestantism may not remove people's marginalized status, the children of Protestants tend to do better economically than other children in their original community. Protestantism may foster prosperity by reducing drinking and drug-taking, extramarital sex and child-bearing, and spending on communal festivals, while promoting education and a male sense of commitment to stable family life.

Protestantism seems to have fostered economic development even in societies where few people actually converted to Protestantism. This is because of the massive transfer of resources that accompanied the missionary movement, the impact that missionaries free of state affiliation had on moderating colonial abuses, and the changes that Protestant missionary presence induced in the behavior of other religious communities. Of course, Catholics also made major missionary efforts and transferred resources to colonies. But in historically Catholic countries and their colonies, Church-state pacts to bar religious competition also boosted state control and limited both resource transfers and the ability of Catholic missionaries to fight colonialist abuses.

Nonstate missionaries' reform campaigns also indirectly promoted economic development. Missionaries and their supporters were the main lobbyists for the immediate abolition of slavery and other forms of forced labor in the colonies, and were also often in the front rank of opposition to the officially sanctioned opium trade, the violent excesses of some colonial officials, and the tendency of European settlers to expropriate native lands. Because missionaries in historically Protestant colonies usually enjoyed more independence than their Catholic counterparts, the former could fight abuses more effectively. The British Empire banned slavery and forced labor earlier, punished abusive colonial officials more regularly, and on the whole managed to arrange more peaceful decolonization processes than did other European colonial powers— even when these were relatively democratic states such as France and Belgium. Historical evidence suggests that Protestant missionaries and their backers initiated these British reforms, which were not only generally humane but aided prosperity.

More than sheer altruism, of course, lay behind these efforts. Colonial abuses sowed anti-Western and hence anti-Christian resentment, as missionaries well knew. Other Europeans on the scene might know of abuses, but often benefited from them and had little incentive to expose them. Indigenous peoples had scant power to defend their own interests in the colonizing state. Missionaries—especially if they had political influence back home—were the main group with the means, motive, and opportunity to advance reform.

Moreover, Protestant competition seems to have spurred other religious groups to make "human-capital" investments in mass education and social services for the poor. Once Protestant groups initiated these services, other religious groups had to follow suit or risk losing congregants. This probably explains why former colonies of Catholic powers (which typically restricted Protestant activity) display historically lower levels of investment in schooling and social services, while non–Catholic-majority lands with histories of free religious competition usually feature Protestant and Catholic populations that boast similar levels of educational and economic attainment: In the latter type of society the Catholic Church had to invest while in the former it did not, and that has made a difference.

One way in which Protestantism contributes to both a vibrant public sphere and economic development is by reducing corruption. Scholarly research suggests that political corruption inhibits the emergence and survival of democracy by hampering social organization, undermining trust, and undercutting support for the political system. Corruption also indirectly hampers democracy by stifling economic development, increasing economic inequality, and restricting education. These findings hold for countries with different growth experiences, at different states of development, and using various indices of corruption.

Published statistical analyses universally find that societies with more Protestants are less corrupt and have more efficient governments. These results remain strong when scholars control for multiple factors, including economic development and democratic experience. They also hold for different regions of the world and for all societal subgroups scholars have tested so far: corruption by judges, policemen, politicians, and bureaucrats; elite corruption and street-level corruption. Even in the few cases where corruption data exist for the city or province level, areas with fewer Protestants per capita tend to be more corrupt. Other religious traditions do not seem to similarly reduce corruption or increase the efficiency of government.

Seymour Martin Lipset and Gabriel Lenz suggest that Protestantism minimizes corruption through an ethical mechanism. Other possible mechanisms include the reduction of resources controlled by church leaders (meaning less scope for clerical corruption), the creation of small face-to-face accountability groups that monitor individual behavior, and an organizational civil society that monitors government elites.[15]

Other Traditions and Newer Protestantisms

Our analysis suggests both that religion plays an important role in determining the political character of societies, and that religions other than Protestantism play a weaker role in promoting democracy—or may foster a different politics altogether. While the "democracy gap" between Protestantism and Catholicism is closing, this does not seem to be true of all other religious traditions. For example, quantitative research shows that predominantly Muslim societies are less democratic and have less durable democratic transitions. This is true across multiple regions and with multiple statistical controls. Claims that oil wealth allows elites to dodge democratization do not suffice, for majority-Muslim societies both with and without oil are consistently less democratic than their non-Muslim neighbors. Moreover, although the average Freedom House democracy score of non-Muslim societies has increased since the 1980s, the average democracy score of majority-Muslim societies has not.[16]

Yet just as the positive association between Protestantism and democracy is far from inevitable, so too is the observed negative association between Islam and that form of government. Religious traditions are multivocal; different groups and thinkers can and do interpret them differently in varying situations. Both Protestantism and Catholicism have shifted toward a stronger rapport with democracy over time, and other traditions—Islam included—may do so as well. To the extent that a religious tradition fosters the types of mediating mechanisms discussed above, it will be more likely to foster democracy. This is not to say that all the causal mechanisms enumerated above are prerequisites for democracy—a religious tradition that does not foster each and every one of them may still be compatible with liberal democracy. No religious tradition is either a necessary or sufficient cause of democratization, or an insuperable barrier to it.

Currently, newer strains of Protestantism—most often charismatic, evangelical, or Pentecostal—are growing rapidly across the global South. Will they, like older forms of Protestantism, exert a democratizing effect? Our analysis suggests the answer may depend on whether they foster the democracy-friendly mediating conditions enumerated above.

The ongoing paucity of democracy in Africa suggests at the very least that the impact of Protestantism is not immediate. Prior to 1900 there were very few Protestants and Catholics in Africa, but now many sub-Saharan African countries have Christian majorities. Although Catholic and Protestant leaders have condemned abuses by African governments and pressed for democracy, most African societies have poor democratic records. This also suggests that religious tradition is not the only factor that influences democracy; extreme poverty, a legacy of colonialist abuses, ethnic conflict, and other factors influence it as well. Moreover, religion may take generations to make its impact felt. The adoption of a new religious tradition does not instantly and completely transform all beliefs, practices, and social institutions. Change also takes resources. Protestants in poor countries may want universal literacy, but that will not pay for schools.

Nor is time the only issue. Some of Protestantism's contributions may be losing their distinctiveness as other religious traditions copy previously "Protestant" characteristics and as new forms of Protestantism—particularly Pentecostalism—develop and proliferate.

Over the past century, belief in mass education has spread well beyond Protestants. Increasingly, governments and other religious groups are willing to invest in it. Newer Protestant groups still advocate basic instruction, but the intensity of their stress on education does not match that of classical Calvinists. In many Pentecostal congregations, authority comes from spiritual gifts rather than higher study, making advanced schooling less important. Printing has also become widespread and commercially viable, so a distinction in print cultures between Protestant societies and others may disappear over time.

Some newer Protestant groups aggressively seek to insert religious symbols into the public sphere—such as declaring Zambia a "Christian nation" or organizing Christian prayers at government functions. This type of activity is of course not new and not unique to the global South. Moreover, such efforts are often designed more to serve evangelistic purposes than to restrict the religious liberty of others or to alter the character of the state. While Pentecostals and other evangelical Protestants may support particular policies or candidates based on their religious beliefs or even on putative special revelations, they lack an evangelical equivalent of Islamic *shari'a* to impose on society. The conviction that saving faith must come from within and cannot be compelled by the state is held firmly by both the newer and the older Protestantisms. Structurally, the conditions for Protestants to impose a new "Christendom" do not exist, because the religious diversity that prevents them from forming new state churches remains. As other religious traditions permit religious liberty, Protestant distinctiveness on this question may erode. But it does not appear that the newer Protestants pose a threat to religious liberty.

Newer Protestant groups are still lay-supported voluntary organizations with weekly face-to-face meetings. They are likely to develop and promote organizations, skills, and resources among nonelite citizens and thus to foster civil society. In the long run, this should promote transitions to stable democratic government across the global South.

Where the newer Protestants may not be able to match their older counterparts or the Catholic Church is in the area of "speaking truth to power" and spurring rapid and overt regime change. The Catholic and Anglican churches, along with certain historic Protestant denominations, have a transnational presence and strong ties to Western societies that can offer resources, protection, and an identity that transcends sundry particularisms. Pastors of localized religious denominations are more vulnerable to both raw persecution and subtler pressures to make them trim religious principles with an eye to nearby realities. In addition, interviews with West African church leaders suggest that older denominations may be more adept "change agents" than their newer counterparts because the old-line groups have informational advantages—their church schools often count among their alumni many top government officials—that help church leaders know when to press an authoritarian regime and when to hold back.

Despite the consistent association between Protestantism and lower levels of corruption in cross-national statistical analysis, evidence from Africa and Latin America suggests that Protestantism is not a panacea. Over the past 75 years, Protestantism has spread rapidly—often among marginalized groups—in areas long troubled by high levels of corruption. Under these circumstances, some Protestants have arguably imitated more than firmly opposed dominant patterns of clientelist behavior. Concerns about corruption have regularly mobilized Protestants into politics and some Protestant politicians have vigorously fought corruption, but many vocally Protestant leaders (such as former president Kim Young-Sam of Korea) have fallen from grace precisely because of corruption in their administrations. While Protestants claim that such fallen politicians merely touted Protestant credentials to troll for votes, many new Protestant (and particularly Pentecostal) churches reproduce patron-client structures. Some also proclaim that God will materially bless those who give money to the church—a pattern that has often led to corruption.

Substantial evidence suggests that Protestantism still moderately increases the wealth of people who convert. The scale of change remains modest, however, and it may take considerable time before the changes are large enough to substantially alter a country's democratic potential.

Protestantism has played an important role in fostering and diffusing democracy. Over time the special association between Protestantism and democracy seems to be waning because other religious traditions are fostering many of the democracy-friendly, Protestant-aided social processes noted above. In addition, many new varieties of Protestantism have developed in the twentieth century. In particular, Pentecostal varieties have spread in Africa, Asia, and Latin America. Available evidence suggests that these new Protestant communities will on balance continue to foster democracy—although perhaps not as distinctively and dramatically as in previous generations.[17]

NOTES

Robert D. Woodberry thanks the Louisville Institute General Grant, Lilly Endowment, for financial support. Both authors gratefully acknowledge the support of the Harvard Academy for International and Area Studies' "Religion in Global Politics" project, funded by the Smith Richardson Foundation and the Weatherhead Center for International Affairs.

1. Quoted in James E. Bradley, "The Religious Origins of Radical Politics in England, Scotland, and Ireland, 1662–1800," in James E. Bradley and D.K. Van Kley, eds., *Religion and Politics in Enlightenment Europe* (Notre Dame, Ind.: University of Notre Dame Press, 2001), 215.

2. Michael Walzer, *The Revolution of the Saints: A Study in the Origins of Radical Politics* (Cambridge: Harvard University Press, 1965).

3. Samuel P. Huntington, *The Third Wave: Democratization in the Late Twentieth Century* (Norman: University of Oklahoma Press, 1991), 72–85.

4. Alfred Stepan, "Religion, Democracy, and the 'Twin Tolerations,'" *Journal of Democracy* 11 (October 2000): 37–57.

5. Figures are for the year 2000. We drew them from David B. Barrett, George T. Kurian, and Todd M. Johnson, eds., *World Christian Encyclopedia*, 2nd ed. (Oxford: Oxford University Press, 2001). To arrive at our figures, we combine the *Encyclopedia*'s "Anglican," "historic European Protestant," and "independent" categories.

6. Paul E. Sigmund, ed., *Religious Freedom and Evangelization in Latin America: The Challenge of Religious Pluralism* (Maryknoll, N.Y.: Orbis, 1999). For global Protestant and particularly evangelical growth, see Donald Lewis, ed., *Christianity Re-Born: Evangelicalism's Global Expansion in the Twentieth Century* (Grand Rapids, Mich.: Eerdman's, 2004).

7. Most of the arguments and citations for this and subsequent sections come from Robert D. Woodberry, "The Shadow of Empire: Christian Missions, Colonial Policy, and Democracy in Postcolonial Societies" (Ph.D. dissertation, University of North Carolina–Chapel Hill, 2004); and Robert D. Woodberry, "Religion and Democratization: Explaining a Robust Empirical Relationship," paper presented at the annual meeting of the Religious Research Association, Boston, 5–7 November 1999.

8. Daniel Philpott, *Revolutions in Sovereignty: How Ideas Shaped Modern International Relations* (Princeton: Princeton University Press, 2001), 105.

9. G.W.F. Hegel, *Elements of the Philosophy of Right,* trans. Allen W. Wood (Cambridge: Cambridge University Press, 1991), 301–2.

10. For a discussion of the historically Catholic dynamic, see David Martin, *A General Theory of Secularization* (Oxford: Blackwell, 1978), 15–27, 36–54.

11. Robert A. Dahl, *Democracy and Its Critics* (New Haven: Yale University Press, 1989), 32.

12. Michael Young, "Confessional Protest: The Religious Birth of U.S. Social Movements," *American Sociological Review* 67 (October 2002): 660–88.

13. David Zaret, "Petitions and the 'Invention' of Public Opinion in the English Revolution," *American Journal of Sociology* 101 (May 1996): 1497–1555. Jürgen Habermas, *The Structural Transformation of the Public Sphere* (Cambridge: MIT Press, 1991). For religious printing's impact on newspapers and secular printing, see David Paul Nord, *Faith in Reading: Religious Publishing and the Birth of Mass Media in America* (New York: Oxford University Press, 2004).

14. Robin Grier, "The Effect of Religion on Economic Development: A Cross-National Study of 63 Former Colonies," *Kyklos* 50 (February 1997): 47–62.

15. Daniel Treisman, "The Causes of Corruption: A Cross-National Study," *Journal of Public Economics* 76 (June 2000): 399–457; and Seymour Martin Lipset and Gabriel S. Lenz, "Corruption, Culture, and Markets," in Lawrence E. Harrison and Samuel P. Huntington, eds., *Culture Matters: How Values Shape Human Progress* (New York: Basic, 2000), 112–24.

16. Christopher Clague, Suzanne Gleason, and Stephen Knack, "Determinants of Lasting Democracy in Poor Countries: Culture, Development, and Institutions," *Annals of the American Academy of Political and Social Science* 573 (January 2001): 16–41.

17. On the newer Protestant forms and democracy in the global South, see Paul Freston, *Evangelicals and Politics in Asia, Africa and Latin America* (Cambridge: Cambridge University Press, 2001) and Timothy S. Shah, "Evangelical Politics in the Third World: What's Next for the 'Next Christendom'?" *Brandywine Review of Faith and International Affairs* 1 (Fall 2003): 21–30.

10

THE AMBIVALENT ORTHODOX

Elizabeth Prodromou

Elizabeth Prodromou *is assistant professor of international relations and associate director of the Institute on Culture, Religion, and World Affairs at Boston University. This essay originally appeared in the April 2004 issue of the* Journal of Democracy.

As the twenty-first century dawns, religion remains politically salient around the globe to a degree that has surprised many observers. Among other things, religious institutions, personalities, and ideas have become forces for democratization across a wide variety of traditions and societies—and in ways that should spur a reconceptualization of what we mean by the terms "modern," "secular," and "democratic," as well as the relations among them. Are these terms, for instance, as fully interchangeable as many seem to assume? Today, most social scientists who have studied the topic share a consensus that Christianity in its Catholic and Protestant forms is compatible with the institutional and cultural dimensions of democracy. But what of that other grand stream of Christianity, the Orthodox tradition? To date, scholars of democracy have tended either to ignore Orthodoxy or to dismiss it—citing both history and contemporary experience—as incompatible with democracy and hostile to secularity and modernity as well.[1]

In fact, there is ample empirical evidence to suggest that Orthodox Christianity and democracy are generally compatible, in theory as well as in practice. Yet there is no denying that Orthodox churches often display a certain ambivalence about key elements of the pluralism that characterizes democratic regimes. Whether, how, and when Orthodoxy addresses this ambivalence toward pluralism will go far toward determining how effectively Orthodox churches and believers will be able to contribute to democratization in semi-authoritarian and newly democratic countries, and engage confidently and creatively in the political lives of countries where democracy is more fully and solidly established.

Focusing on pluralism may help us to clarify the ways in which Orthodox ideas and practices can contribute to at least basic democratization. Such a focus may also suggest ways in which Orthodox concerns about pluralism—and particularly its characteristic features of competition and difference—offer insights about how to avoid some of the self-destructive tendencies that democracy, whether new or established, can sometimes manifest. Such a focus is far more likely to be fruitful, in both intellectual and practical terms, than accounts of Orthodoxy's relationship to democracy that simplistically portray the former as antiliberal or antimodern.

To see why this is so, it is helpful to begin with a glance at the history and geography of the Orthodox Christian world. Sometimes called "Eastern" Orthodoxy to distinguish it from the Western (or Latin) Christian tradition to which both Roman Catholicism and most forms of Protestantism belong, Orthodoxy is, in effect, one side of the first major division between East and West in Christian history. This Great Schism formally occurred with an exchange of condemnations between Pope Leo IX in Rome and Patriarch Michael Cerularius in Constantinople during 1053–54, though its roots run back much farther.[2] The proximate cause of the Great Schism lay in theological controversies of a doctrinal nature, but the split was actually the product of a long, complicated process that was political and economic as well as cultural and religious. The clash split Christendom into antagonistic theological and institutional entities whose territorial-ecclesiastical jurisdictions more or less corresponded to the eastern (mostly Greek-speaking) and western (mostly Latin-speaking) halves of the old Roman Empire, which had been divided administratively into eastern and western segments as early as 284 C.E.[3]

Orthodox Christians or their descendants predominate or form substantial minorities in what are today the countries of southeastern Europe and the eastern Mediterranean as well as Russia, Ukraine, and the Baltic states. As with the movement of Protestantism's and Catholicism's geographic-cum-demographic centers of gravity from their onetime European core to the global South,[4] Orthodoxy has become globalized over the last century or so via emigration from the Orthodox "heartland" (mainly the former Byzantine, Ottoman, and Russian imperial lands, as well as parts of northeast and west-central Africa) to the United States, Canada, Australia, and certain countries in western Europe. More recently, missionary activity has bolstered Orthodoxy's presence in East Asia.

With about 300 million members worldwide (estimates vary), the Orthodox Church is the third-largest Christian communion, and contains roughly 15 percent of all Christians. A hundred million or more Orthodox Christians live in the countries that once formed the Soviet Union. The next-largest concentration is located in such historically Orthodox southeastern European states as Greece, Romania, Bulgaria, Serbia-Montenegro, and Cyprus (other parts of Europe have significant Orthodox minorities). Orthodox Christians are the majority of all Christians in

Israel and Palestine, Jordan, Syria, Lebanon, and Egypt. Important Orthodox communities may also be found in Africa, Australia, Canada, and the United States. Finally, non-Chalcedonian[5] Christians, or Oriental Orthodox Christians, constitute a majority in Armenia as well as numerically, economically, or politically significant minorities in Ethiopia and Somalia as well as Egypt (where they are known as Copts). Although these communities have been exploring the possibility of reconciliation with the Eastern Orthodox Church since the end of the Cold War, for purposes of this essay I judge it best to set them aside while pausing to note that they share ecclesiastical structures, liturgical practices, and historical experiences which resemble those of Eastern Orthodoxy, and tend to harbor comparable reservations toward pluralism.

Viewed as a whole, Orthodox Christianity today is the product of a process of global diffusion. An institutional chart of worldwide Orthodoxy resembles a wheel. At the hub sit the ancient Patriarchates of Constantinople (as Istanbul is identified in Christian ecclesiastical terminology), Antioch, Alexandria, and Jerusalem. Radiating out like a set of spokes from this center is a far-flung network of churches designated as either autocephalous or autonomous in order to identify their degrees of independence from their respective historic Patriarchates, or "mother churches." This network administers regional or local clusters of Orthodox church communities that are defined in territorial terms, usually with the name of the country or continent that they call home.

The reality of global diffusion has begun to generate an internal dynamic of pluralization that is transforming Orthodoxy's ecclesiastical and jurisdictional contours. Most importantly for the purposes of this essay, the dynamics of pluralization are also reshaping Orthodoxy's engagement with democracy. To date, however, Orthodoxy has not joined Catholicism and Protestantism in laying out a theological framework to explain and justify its global political engagements. This "theory gap" is among the reasons why Orthodoxy's approach to engagement in democratization around the world has had a largely ad hoc quality, and likewise, why the links between Orthodoxy and democracy have remained largely outside the scope of comparative analysis, whether by scholars or democratic practitioners.[6]

Foundational Resources

The most powerful internal influences on Orthodoxy's engagement with democracy and democratization are the basic theological doctrines, as well as associated institutional structures and organizational behaviors, that define this tradition within Christianity. The key doctrinal resources are the theology of creation, the anthropology of personhood, and Orthodoxy's Trinitarian concept of God (the first two resources also reflect the influence of this last teaching, of course).

The Eastern Orthodox Church claims to be the bearer and embodiment of the correct beliefs (literally, "orthodoxies") and practices of the "One, Holy, Catholic (universal), and Apostolic Church" of Christ as laid down in the Nicene Creed of 325 C.E. As such, Orthodoxy considers itself a vital and unbroken tradition that is "inwardly changeless, [but] . . . constantly assuming new forms, which supplement the old without superseding them."[7]

The truth claims of Orthodoxy derive from the doctrine of God as Trinity. Orthodox theology uses the Trinitarian concept to posit that the inherent character of all creation lies in its original and potential integrity. Orthodoxy's understanding of what it means to be human expresses itself through an anthropology of personhood, which is linked directly to creation theology, since movement toward the reintegration of created (but fallen) reality and the communion of humanity with God is possible only if human persons use their free will responsibly, "to participate intentionally in [bringing about] creation's fulfillment . . . [by being] . . . 'co-creators'. . . with the Creator."[8] Thus Orthodoxy, like other Christian traditions, affirms both freedom and responsibility.

The Trinitarian construct of God also informs Orthodox ecclesiology. The Church is one, yet admits a plurality of orders (bishops, clerics, and lay believers) that play vital roles in its mission. Similarly, the Trinitarian notion of unity in diversity informs the way in which the Church is organized. It is unified at the global level by common beliefs, practices, and institutions, but also allows for a measure of diversity and distinctiveness through the practice of decentralization, which spreads authority out to the regional, national, and local levels. Hence the Patriarch of Constantinople bears the unique title of "Ecumenical," but his position vis-à-vis the Patriarchs of Jerusalem, Antioch, and Alexandria is that of an honorary "first among equals" rather than that of a superior. Moving out from the Patriarchal center, the administrative flexibility of the autocephalous and autonomous churches, as well as the daily operational freedom of the regional (diocesan) networks and local parishes, is designed to encourage the diversity and dynamism that are the hallmarks of Trinitarian personhood. In this respect, the realities of cultural specificity and historical experience are meant to be acknowledged and reflected in the unity in diversity of the institutional order of global Orthodoxy.

To judge by Orthodox theology, whose reflections on the triune God lead it to put a strong emphasis on freedom and equality, Orthodoxy and democracy should be intrinsically compatible. The Orthodox tradition believes that freedom, choice, and human agency are the prerequisites for all forms of social change: Surely there is a strong affinity for basic democratic principles and values here. Furthermore, the Orthodox Church's emphasis on integration as a principle of both organization and action is another example of affinity with democracy, understood as a system of peaceful conflict regulation.[9]

Having said all this, one must also note that Orthodoxy's foundational resources implicitly endorse a concept of pluralism that comes with qualifications attached. Theology may privilege diversity and choice, but many in the Orthodox world see competition and difference as problematic phenomena that must be managed according to national particularities rooted in historical experience and contemporary confining conditions.[10] Because the Trinitarian emphasis on the unity in diversity of persons necessarily leads to a rejection of material and symbolic imbalances of power, pluralism's emphasis on difference (versus distinctiveness, in the Orthodox formulation) is viewed as an acceptance of boundaries and demarcations that can generate social division and fragmentation born of power differentials.

Equally important, Orthodoxy's emphasis on love and harmony leads to skepticism about pluralism as the protection of difference and the primacy of unfettered competition. Playing fields are seldom really level, as the actual conditions of competition frequently fall short of providing all players with full information, free access, and equal resources. Similarly, the formalistic commitment to difference often creates conditions in which proceduralism camouflages asymmetries of power that may lead to social disintegration and even violence. Finally, Orthodoxy—like other forms of revealed religion—makes truth claims upon which personal salvation is thought to depend, and offers moral teachings that are not up for a vote. How far such religions can or should go in accommodating pluralism is a profound and difficult question in the Orthodox community as elsewhere.

History has hardened Orthodoxy's ambivalence toward competition and difference as features of pluralism. The historic Orthodox heartlands of the Byzantine Empire and Russia were subject to conquest by non-Christians (Seljuk and Ottoman Turks in the former case, Mongols in the latter). Difference meant subordination and oppression, or even extermination. More recently, Orthodoxy's experience of difference has been dominated by the struggle for survival under powerful secularist and totalitarian regimes intent on either coopting or eliminating Orthodoxy in its historic homelands, or by efforts to survive as an insecure minority religion under authoritarian Middle Eastern or African regimes with records of repressing or abusing communal minorities.[11] These negative experiences of what it can mean to be different have done little to foster enthusiasm for the idea of competition as a process of engagement on a level playing field, with transparent rules and neutral authorities extending equal protection to all. On the contrary, maltreatment and exclusion bred attitudes of cynicism and suspicion toward the very notions of impartiality and a fair struggle for advantage within the bounds of consensual rules.

In contrast to the centuries during which it lived under conquest or was forced to endure vulnerable minority status, Orthodoxy has had relatively little experience with life amid democratic pluralism. Until the end of the Cold War, democracy was largely unknown to Orthodox populations outside Greece or the Orthodox diasporas of North America, Australia, and Western Europe. The collapse of communism across Eastern Europe and the USSR was a watershed moment in the Orthodox encounter with democracy. Yet memories of state-imposed difference and uneven playing fields remain vivid, and painful deficits linger in the institutional capital needed to compete in a relatively open religious and cultural climate. This has produced a situation in which Orthodox authorities have tended to endorse freedom, democracy, and pluralism in principle, while in practice remaining wary of the open competitiveness and embrace of difference that democracy promotes.

The belatedness of Orthodoxy's engagement with consolidated democracy and robust pluralism has put churches in places such as the United States, Canada, and Australia—where Orthodox believers have lived for generations as full and active citizens—at the forefront of activity and discussion regarding Orthodoxy's role in democratization and response to pluralism. Studies of income, education, and political participation in these democratic countries make clear that Orthodox Christians know how to make good use of the opportunities that pluralism offers. At the same time, the Orthodox have shown that they are not uncritical celebrators of pluralism, but instead are aware of the ways in which competition can be rendered less than fair and difference turned into a pretext for injustice.[12] Moreover, the growing sense of agency among Orthodox populations in the diaspora is now changing their relationships with the "old countries" in general, and the "mother churches" of those countries in particular. Thus Orthodoxy is not only coming to grips with pluralism in the outside world, but is also feeling pressure for greater internal pluralism from influential quarters within its own ranks.

The advance of globalization and democratization is sparking new questions about pluralism in the global Orthodox space. How should pluralism be understood? What are its proper limits? What type and degree of pluralism best sustain a democratic regime? How tightly should pluralism be identified with democracy? What role do—and should—history, tradition, and culture play in shaping a society's reception of pluralism? How should pluralism be managed?

The reservations that Orthodox Christians and other religious believers harbor toward pluralism suggest that it is unwise to argue that democracy must depend upon an unexamined embrace of pluralism. Can there be an elastic definition of pluralism, and if so, what would that mean for democracy? In country after country around the globe—particularly in the former Soviet lands and in Muslim societies, but increasingly in European and North American societies as well—there is evidence that sustainable democratization demands serious consideration of the relationship between democracy and pluralism.

The loose consensus among scholars of democratizaion that the minimalist focus on procedure identifies a necessary, but not sufficient, set of conditions for democracy has led many of these scholars to admit that it is time to do more than just focus on such formalistic aspects of democracy as elections. At the same time, the turn toward maximalist models of democracy has been tempered by an awareness that privileging rule by the majority in the name of the common good can pose a risk to minorities. The question of pluralism, therefore, is central to the questions of democratic authenticity and durability, both of which are highly salient inquiries in a world where the "third wave" of clear-cut transitions from nondemocratic to democratic rule has passed its peak, and is now giving way to a vast "gray zone" of countries where powerholders conceal various forms of authoritarianism behind a façade of democratic rhetoric, institutions, and procedures.[13]

Democracy Yes, Pluralism Maybe?

Comparative evidence can help to put flesh on the bones of what might otherwise appear to be a rather abstract account of Orthodoxy's attitudes toward democracy and pluralism. A review of one particularly critical case will be helpful, especially given that findings from this case resonate with comparative evidence from other lands.

In Greece, relations between the state and the Orthodox Church tell a fascinating tale about the interaction of Orthodoxy with democratization and the management of pluralism. Like other countries in the European Union—which hold to varying models of religion's legal status and public role, yet which tend to share a common sense that the combined effects of EU enlargement, immigration, and demographic shifts since the Cold War's end call for a considered response—Greece has been grappling with the question of how to reinforce its model of national identity in a way that balances its historical majority religious tradition with a commitment to basic democratic rights and freedoms for all citizens.

Several factors have come together to intensify Orthodoxy's encounter with pluralism in Greece. Since the democratic transition began in the mid-1970s, the country's public space has become wider, deeper, and more heterogeneous. The arrival of substantial numbers of immigrants, voluntary as well as forced, from troubled regions of the former Yugoslavia in the last decade or so has accelerated the diversification of public life in Greece, as have the effects of EU membership (Greece was admitted in 1981) and the country's consequent integration into globalized processes of socioeconomic, political, and cultural change. The Orthodox Church remains the constitutionally established church of Greece (according to the "prevailing religion" formula common in the EU), and now finds itself required to participate in a public sphere

whose pluralization is accelerating under the influence of potent domestic, regional, and systemic forces.

The Church's responses to pluralism show that the Church grasps
both its need and its ability to engage other religious and secular actors
in civil society, and to take part in EU-level discussions and activities
that touch on matters of religion and culture in an expanding Europe.
Pluralism in its interactive or relational aspect has evoked an active and
largely positive Church response. Greek Orthodox leaders both lay and
clerical have seen democratization as offering a challenge and an opportunity to redefine the Church's public role in Greek society—in part
by revitalizing the conciliar, participatory features of key Church institutions, but above all by raising prospects for renegotiating the Church's
relations with the state in ways that can enhance Orthodoxy's capacity
to contribute to Greek democracy. When pluralism as competition or
pluralism as ethnic or religious difference has come to the fore, however, the Church's response has been deeply ambivalent. How, Orthodox
leaders have seemed to ask, can they act under democratic conditions to
preserve Orthodoxy's vital place in any understanding of what it means
to be Greek and, more generally, manage the overall scope and potentially divisive socioeconomic and security effects of pluralism?

Church-state relations have been consistently on the Greek public
agenda for the last three decades. The record reveals Orthodoxy's capacity to play within the democratic rules of the game while
simultaneously tending to endorse limits on types of difference that
the Church views as a threat to Orthodox Christianity's unique position in Greek national culture. For example, the consolidation of
democracy in the 1980s involved a move by the Panhellenic Socialist
Party (PASOK) government to implement a long-discussed but politically loaded proposal to disestablish the Orthodox Church. Following
a series of social reforms related to family law and abortion rights, the
PASOK government proposed a bill to disestablish the Orthodox
Church, arguing that this was a necessary step in the qualitative en-
hancement of liberal democracy.

Worried by the possible electoral effects of the highly publicized opposition campaign waged by key Orthodox hierarchs and many laypersons,
PASOK backed down. Discussions of disestablishment since then have
tended to simplify the issue by construing it as a question of endorsing or
rejecting liberal democracy. Supporters of disestablishment argue that full
acknowledgement of the right to religious freedom must mean the end of
the "prevailing religion" formula—notwithstanding the use of this formula
in many other EU member states. Similarly, the PASOK government's spring
2001 announcement that Greek national-identity cards would no longer
have to list the bearer's religion was explained not only as necessary for
compliance with EU mandates, but also as a move beyond merely formalistic support for the political and civil equality of all citizens.

On the other side of the identity-card fracas, many Church hierarchs have grounded their opposition to disestablishment on what they have called the indissoluble links between Orthodoxy and the nation (98 percent of Greeks are Orthodox). These bishops and their lay supporters have stressed the historical centrality of Orthodoxy to the defense of Greek national awareness, first under direct Ottoman rule and later under real or perceived threats from the Ottomans' successors in the modern-day Republic of Turkey. The Church's media-savvy campaign included a well-organized national petition drive that gathered more than three million signatures (Greece has a total population of about 10.7 million) in favor of a referendum to resolve the identity-card issue. Speaking more broadly, Archbishop Christodoulos of Athens had warned in 1999 about the EU melting pot and the "tragic [cultural and security] consequences for Hellenism and Orthodoxy"[14] that EU rules might bring.

The identification of Orthodoxy with national cohesion, and implicitly with the territorial integrity of the nation-state, compellingly illustrates Orthodoxy's ambivalence toward pluralism as an organizing logic based on difference and competition. And yet it bears emphasizing that the Church's response was not univocal. Indeed, the disestablishment proposals that PASOK had first put forward in the 1980s were crafted with the input of key hierarchs, clerics, and lay theologians. They argued that Orthodoxy's legitimacy as a promoter of social justice demanded that the Church display tolerance of religious and social diversity in Greece. Moreover, these figures maintained that the Church had allowed its relationship with the state to sap the transformative potential of Orthodoxy's evangelical message. Orthodox Christian advocates of disestablishment hoped that the competitive demands set loose by the Church's loss of constitutional primacy would help spur Orthodoxy to play a public role compatible with democratic principles of freedom and equality, precisely because of the intrinsic Orthodox theological affinity for these values. Similarly, hierarchs and clerics adopted competing public positions on the identity-card issue, with some hierarchs (joined by certain lay intellectuals) maintaining that the archbishop's identification of Orthodoxy and nationalism was theologically incorrect.

The Greek case, then, lays bare the ambivalent posture that many influential people in Orthodox ranks take regarding the competitive pressures and sources of difference that inevitably flourish under pluralist conditions. Reactions against those elements of pluralism raise questions concerning Orthodoxy's level of commitment to other core elements of pluralism, such as tolerance, choice, and diversity. Does Orthodoxy's call to set limits on the former dimensions of pluralism impede respect for the latter aspects of it? By the same token, does Orthodoxy's apparent endorsement of the management of pluralism, simultaneous with a commitment to democracy, point to similar tendencies around the world and, therefore, merit further inquiry?

Some Tentative Conclusions

The multivocal interpretations and responses that pluralism has sparked among Orthodox actors in Greece indeed point to several preliminary conclusions that deserve further investigation. Determining whether or not these conclusions hold up could improve our understanding of what types of democracy can best cope with the economic and social pressures exerted by globalization. Moreover, we might also learn how to help policy makers leverage those Orthodox institutions and actors that hold a stake in democratization efforts in various countries and under differing types of conditions.

First and foremost, the Greek case underscores an apparent paradox worthy of clarification—namely, that when Orthodox figures express ambivalence toward pluralism, they frequently do so by relying on democratic premises, processes, and practices. As the identity-cards petition drive illustrates, official representatives of the Church, as well as believers acting on their own, demonstrated their agreement that the legal, institutional, and normative foundations of democracy deserve Orthodox Christianity's unequivocal support.

The most recent Freedom House findings bespeak Orthodoxy's capacity to thrive under full or partial democracy, as well as to contribute to democratization. These annual cross-national rankings of political rights and civil liberties within all the countries (and certain not fully sovereign territories) of the world serve as the leading index of democracy around the globe and enjoy wide currency among scholars and commentators. The latest Freedom House report ranks the twenty countries that can be included within the Orthodox well within the range of those it defines as Free or Partly Free.[15] (All the Free countries in the world are unambiguously democratic. The Partly Free countries are often "electoral democracies," where some consent-based institutions exist, but where large gaps remain in the protection accorded citizens' civil liberties and rights to a say in their own government.) These findings reinforce the need to make analytical and practical distinctions between democracy and pluralism and to recognize that varying ways of managing the issues that pluralism raises can deeply affect the vitality and quality of democracy.

Looking beyond Greece to a case such as Russia, the same phenomenon is observable. Many officials of the Orthodox Church of Russia have explained their support for legal restrictions on proselytizing by non-Orthodox religions in terms of the Orthodox Church's lack of capacity, given the residual effects of the Soviet experience, to match the transnational resources that Catholic and Protestant groups can bring to bear on Russian soil. Similarly, many Russian Orthodox Christians point to public statements in which Pentecostal and evangelical Protestants call their activities in Russia efforts at "Christianization"—and also to the Vatican's creation of new Catholic dioceses in former Soviet republics whose Christian minorities are overwhelmingly Orthodox—as evidence that appeals to competition and difference, under the rubric of pluralism, can camouflage an actual lack of tolerance for diversity within Christianity.

Second, Orthodox actors are using the opportunities that democracy creates for the interpretation of pluralism's sources and implications in a manner that is pluralizing Orthodoxy from within. This dynamic of internal pluralization highlights not only diversity and tolerance, but also competition and difference as sources for explaining and pursuing institutional transformation. A case in point is the movement now underway among many Orthodox jurisdictions in the United States to consolidate their array of overlapping, ethnically based churches (currently qualified with adjectives such as "Greek," "Russian," "Ukrainian," "Romanian," "Serbian," and so on) into a single Orthodox Church of America. Advocates of change argue not only that the application of such democratic principles as self-government, equality, and participation to the official workings of Orthodoxy in the United States makes sense given the competitive U.S. religious "marketplace," but also that sound theology supports such a move. Opponents object to the marketplace metaphor and complain that its use, especially by laypeople, runs the risk of reducing Orthodoxy to a producer-consumer model that eradicates the mystical and transcendent elements of faith. The recent resort to the U.S. courts by a lay movement contesting changes in the governance charter of the Greek Orthodox Archdiocese of America, say these critics, is evidence of the divisive potential of market ideology when applied to questions of faith.

Regardless of the outcome of the dialogue and institutional moves that surround the question of pan-Orthodox unity in the United States, there can be no doubt that Orthodoxy's encounter with U.S. democratic pluralism has been the catalyst for this highly significant debate, with its global implications for Orthodoxy. Pluralism's effects have been complex, tending both toward tighter faith-based cohesion that is beginning to supersede old ethnolinguistic differences among Orthodox churches on the American scene, and toward the renegotiation of ties between U.S. Orthodox churches and their respective "mother churches" abroad. It is significant that the Ecumenical Patriarchate of Constantinople has recently announced a pluralization of its Holy Synod, which will begin to operate with hierarchical participation from the various jurisdictions around the world that remain under the Ecumenical Patriarchate's administrative aegis. This institutional adaptation points to the Patriarchate's efforts to manage the competitive, differentiating effects of pluralism on Constantinople's global network of Orthodox jurisdictions.

Given the strains that the economic demands and social heterogeneities of a globalized world can impose on democratizing countries, Orthodoxy's tendency to try and manage the limits and consequences of pluralism in diverse environments bears consideration by all who want to see democratic transitions succeed and become irreversible. Both the recent French law banning certain kinds of religious clothing and symbols from public schools and the 1998 U.S. International Religious Freedom Act—which makes the promotion of religious liberty a core goal of U.S. foreign policy—represent the application of particular national understandings of and preferences for the operation of pluralism at home and abroad. In these and other cases, what we are seeing amounts to the customizing of democracy according to historically grounded, nationally specific conceptions of pluralism, as well as an effort to buttress democracy in the face of competitive challenges and power dynamics aggravated by globalization.

In short, policy makers should realize that Orthodoxy's engagement with democracy or democratization in diverse contexts comes at a time when questions about the effects and limits of pluralism are pressing not only for the Orthodox, but for just about everyone else as well. Consequently, international agencies and states invested in sustaining the democratization processes underway in postcommunist European states with significant Orthodox populations should find ways to help those states mitigate the real and perceived threats of pluralism. Economic-development initiatives that promote social justice and wealth distribution across communal lines are especially critical, as are efforts to encourage transnational economic investment by Orthodox-diaspora groups with successful track records in market economies and competitive democracies.

Equally important, efforts to press for the restructuring of legal-constitutional relations between Orthodox churches and states according to a putative Western model of unlimited pluralism should not be seen as the only method for promoting sustainable democracies that protect religious freedom and other civil liberties. Instead, the cause of democratization may be better served through the use of economic and security incentives to encourage political leaders and Orthodox churches to back constitutional arrangements and judicial systems that safeguard political and civil rights on the basis of citizenship. An emphasis on citizenship—as opposed to an aggressive-seeming commitment to religious pluralism—could offer a means for democracy-building that is sensitive to national particularities that are rooted in both history and present-day economic and security concerns.

Public-diplomacy efforts that use international educational and interfaith exchanges built on principles of tolerance and equality should

consider the benefits that could accrue to democratization if more Orthodox intellectuals and activists from around the world are included.
In various lands, Orthodox Christian minorities are now enduring life in
conflict zones and under semi-authoritarian regimes. These communities need broader contacts to help them cope with the threats that they
face in ways that will not only help them survive, but that will help
make Orthodox churches and believers more effective forces for and
stakeholders in the processes of democratization and peace-building.
Policy makers need to consider creative ways to give traction to the
ideational and practical affinities that link Orthodox Christianity to
democracy, while recognizing that Orthodoxy's methods of understanding, navigating, and negotiating pluralism will add to the battery of
modifiers and prefixes that already attach to democracy in a world that
is globalized, yet remains diverse.

NOTES

The ideas in this article emerged in the context of a project on "Orthodox Chris-
tianity in American Public Life: The Challenges and Opportunities of Religious
Pluralism in the 21st Century," organized at Boston University. I am grateful for
helpful comments from Nancy Ammerman, Kyriacos Markides, Aristotle
Papanikolaou, Andrew Walsh, and R. Stephen Warner, as well as from participants
in a conference on "Orthodox Churches in a Pluralistic World" at Holy Cross Greek
Orthodox School of Theology in Brookline, Massachusetts. Above all, I thank
Alexandros K. Kyrou for his insights on various versions of this article.

1. The best-known argument that Orthodoxy sits poorly with democracy may
be found in Samuel P. Huntington, "The Clash of Civilizations?" *Foreign Affairs*
72 (Summer 1993): 22–49. For representative, yet diverse, discussions that posit
Orthodoxy as hostile to and an impediment to modernity, see Victoria Clark, *Why
Angels Fall: A Journey Through Orthodox Europe from Byzantium to Kosovo* (New
York: St. Martin's, 2000); Daniel Clendenin, *Eastern Orthodox Christianity: A
Western Perspective* (Grand Rapids, Mich.: Baker, 1994); and Adamantia Pollis,
"Greece: A Problematic Secular State," in William Safran, ed., *The Secular and the
Sacred: Nation, Religion, and Politics* (London: Frank Cass, 2003).

2. On the Great Schism, see Timothy Kallistos Ware, *The Orthodox Church*
(Middlesex, England: Penguin, 1983), 51–95.

3. The fragmentation in Christendom had begun well before the eleventh century; theological controversies had led to the formal separation of the Eastern or
Nestorian churches by the middle of the fifth century, followed by the formal
break with the non-Chalcedonian (Oriental Orthodox) churches a little more than
a century later. For a clear and concise account of these divisions, see Mircea
Eliade, ed., "Eastern Christianity," *Encyclopedia of Religion* (New York: Macmillan,
1987): 4:558–63.

4. Philip Jenkins, *The Next Christendom: The Coming of Global Christianity*
(New York: Oxford University Press, 2002).

5. The non-Chalcedonian or Oriental Orthodox churches are also sometimes
called the Monophysite churches because they never accepted the doctrine—promulgated by the Fourth Ecumenical (General) Council, held at Chalcedon (near
Constantinople) in 451 C.E.—that Jesus has two natures (one fully human, one

fully divine) in one person, but continued to hold that as the Second Person of the Holy Trinity, Jesus has one nature (in Greek, *monophysis*), a divine one. The Eastern Orthodox Church of today, like the Roman Catholic Church and most Protestant denominations, affirms the teachings of each of the first seven Ecumenical Councils (held between 325 and 787 C.E.), including Chalcedon.

6. For an argument in favor of a Protestant theological framework to support democratization in global terms, see Mark T. Mitchell, "A Theology of Global Engagement for the 'Newest Internationalists,'" *Brandywine Review of Faith and International Affairs* 1 (Spring 2003): 11–19.

7. Timothy Kallistos Ware, *The Orthodox Church,* 2nd ed. (New York: Penguin, 2003), 206.

8. Gennadios Limouris, "Introduction," in Gennadios Limouris, ed., *Justice, Peace and the Integrity of Creation: Insights from Orthodoxy* (Geneva: World Council of Churches, 1990), ix–x.

9. Alfred Stepan, "Religion, Democracy, and the 'Twin Tolerations,'" *Journal of Democracy* 11 (October 2000): 39.

10. Most relevantly, the Merriam-Webster Online Dictionary defines "pluralism" as "a state of society in which members of diverse ethnic, racial, religious, or social groups maintain an autonomous participation in and development of their traditional culture or special interest within the confines of a common civilization," and "a concept, doctrine, or policy advocating this state." See *www.m-w.com/cgi-bin/dictionary.*

11. This experience has been especially dominant for non-Chalcedonian (Oriental Orthodox) churches, which have made moves toward full theological communion in the face of the survival challenges that they have had to meet under authoritarian and semi-authoritarian regimes in the Middle East and Africa.

12. For representative treatments of the emerging debate on pluralism versus democracy in Orthodoxy, see Harley Balzer, "Managed Pluralism: Vladimir Putin's Emerging Regime," *www.sais-jhu.edu*; Emmanuel Clapsis, ed., *Orthodoxy and Pluralism: An Ecumenical Conversation* (Geneva: World Council of Churches, 2004); and Nikolas K. Gvosdev, "'Managed Pluralism' and Civil Religion in Post-Soviet Russia," in Christopher Marsh and Nikolas K. Gvosdev, eds., *Civil Society and the Search for Justice in Russia* (Lanham, Md.: Lexington Books, 2002).

13. Thomas Carothers, "The End of the Transition Paradigm," *Journal of Democracy* 13 (January 2002): 5–21.

14. Christodoulos, Archbishop of Athens and All Greece, *From Earth and Water* (Athens: Kastaniotis Press, 1999), 15. Author's translation.

15. The twenty countries that can be logically placed under the umbrella of "the Orthodox world" are Albania, Armenia, Belarus, Bosnia and Herzegovina, Bulgaria, Cyprus, Eritrea, Estonia, Ethiopia, Finland, Georgia, Greece, Lebanon, Macedonia, Moldova, Romania, Russia, Serbia-Montenegro, Syria, and Ukraine. A country can be said to fit into the "Orthodox" grouping if one or more of the following criteria obtain: Orthodox Christians form a majority of the population; Orthodoxy is legally identified as the state religion; Orthodoxy has had a formative impact on the political and cultural development of the country; Orthodox Christians play key roles in social and governmental affairs. For a ranking of countries that situates Orthodox countries according to the index of freedom, see *www.freedomhouse.org/research/freeworld/2003/averages.pdf.*

11

CHRISTIANITY: THE GLOBAL PICTURE

Peter L. Berger

Peter L. Berger *is professor of sociology and theology, and director of the Institute on Culture, Religion, and World Affairs, at Boston University. He is the author of more than twenty books, including* Questions of Faith: A Skeptical Affirmation of Christianity *(2003),* The Desecularization of the World: Resurgent Religion and World Politics *(1999), and* The Sacred Canopy: Elements of a Sociological Theory of Religion *(1967). This essay originally appeared in the April 2004 issue of the* Journal of Democracy.

Modern democracy originated in one part of the world—Western Europe—and there only, though of course it has more recently spread around the globe. In religious terms, it originated in the part of the world crucially shaped by Christianity, and by Western Christianity at that. In all likelihood this was not an accident. Modern democracy presupposes two basic assumptions, one anthropological and one sociological. Anthropologically, it presupposes that every individual, regardless of birth, must confront God by himself ("there is neither Jew nor Greek, there is neither bond nor free, there is neither male nor female; for ye are all one in Christ Jesus"[1]). This has often, and correctly, been identified as a key source of what later came to be understood as universal human rights. Sociologically, it presupposes that the church must be differentiated from the state. This idea was present from the beginning ("render therefore unto Caesar the things which are Caesar's; and unto God the things that are God's"[2]), but it was sharpened in Western Christendom by the struggle between the Holy Roman Empire and the papacy. The outcome of this struggle, which was pretty much a victory of popes over emperors, laid the groundwork of institutional pluralism and of what later developed into civil society.

Let me now offer some comments on the three preceding essays, which explore the relationship to democracy of each of the three major Christian traditions—Catholicism, Protestantism, and Orthodoxy, respectively.

Daniel Philpott provides a clear picture of the development of the Roman Catholic attitude toward democracy, from sharp opposition through reluctant accommodation to a theologically justified embrace. The big turn, of course, came with the Second Vatican Council, and once again it was no accident that a pivotal figure in that event was an American Jesuit, John Courtney Murray, who provided a distinctively Catholic legitimation of religious liberty and democracy. Of the three major branches of Christianity, Roman Catholicism is the only one with a central authority exercising global jurisdiction (indeed, one might argue that the Church of Rome was the first truly global institution). Philpott is undoubtedly correct in seeing this fact as crucial in the Church's rapid shift from opposing democracy to promoting it: Once Rome had decided that democracy was a good thing, bishops from Peru to the Philippines became ardent advocates of democratization. Thus Samuel P. Huntington was correct in identifying the Roman church as a key factor in the "third wave" of democratization in the 1970s and 1980s.

Yet one must also ask how this Church-endorsed democratization relates to the economic development of the societies in question. There are sound empirical grounds for understanding democracy and a market economy as linked phenomena. Historically, Rome had been as opposed to the market economy as it was to democracy. Vatican II did nothing to change the former attitude, and the council was followed by a flowering of various forms of Christian socialism, most powerfully expressed in "liberation theology." This changed somewhat under the pontificate of John Paul II, notably with his encyclical *Centesimus Annus* (1991), which cautiously endorsed the market economy (though the encyclical sought to differentiate it from what the pope called "capitalism"). The resurgence of an anticapitalist discourse reminiscent of liberation theology in the current antiglobalization movement reopens the question of how far Rome is prepared to legitimate the global capitalist economy. A replay of liberation theology, this time with papal blessing, cannot be ruled out.

Democracy poses a persistent problem for any religious tradition committed to a set of binding moral principles, regardless of whether these are understood to be grounded in revealed scriptures or in a putative natural law: How can such principles be held hostage to the vicissitudes of the popular will? After all, the Christian doctrine of original sin necessarily leads to the expectation that majorities will vote for laws that are morally unacceptable. This is by no means only a Catholic problem; it is shared by Orthodox Christians and conservative Protestants. It is particularly acute for Catholics, however, because of the claim of the Roman *magisterium* to make authoritative statements on specific moral issues. The vigorous stance (aptly called "countercultural" by some observers) that the Catholic Church has taken on questions involving abortion and homosexuality clearly illustrates this problem. One might say, then, that the acceptance of democracy by any religious authority with such claims will have certain limits—that is, the outcomes of the democratic process will be accepted only if they do not violate certain nonnegotiable moral principles. (Interestingly, this is also a central issue in current debates over the relationship of Islam to democracy.) Put differently, Roman Catholicism, like any other religious tradition claiming the authority to legislate moral principles, will be able to accept popular sovereignty only within certain limits.

Protestantism and Orthodoxy

Robert D. Woodberry and Timothy S. Shah persuasively describe an inherent affinity between Protestantism and democracy, but they are also careful to point out that this affinity does not mechanically lead to democratic outcomes. These outcomes, they argue, depend on "mediating mechanisms," notably the development of civil society institutions and church-state relations. The Protestant Reformers of the sixteenth century were certainly not interested in political democracy. Yet certain key features of Protestantism inadvertently laid the cultural foundations for what, under favorable conditions, could become democracy. These features were: 1) the emphasis on individual conscience guided by the scriptures (classically expressed by the image of Luther refusing to recant before the Imperial Diet); 2) the doctrine of the universal priesthood of all believers (which, as Max Weber showed, led to a secular concept of vocation); and 3) the importance ascribed to literacy and lay education, which naturally followed from the other two.

David Martin, the British sociologist of religion, has recently discussed a trilogy of types of state-church relations in Western Christianity.[3] First, there was the "Counter-Reformation baroque," characteristic of Catholic southern Europe and Latin America, in which state and Church collaborated in maintaining an overarching ideological "dome." Under this model, the coming of democracy required that the Church be dislodged from this dome and replaced by the republic, most dramatically in the French Revolution and its offshoots. Second, there was "Enlightened absolutism," characteristic of Lutheran Germany and Scandinavia, with an increasingly relaxed established church permitting a widening religious pluralism, followed by democratization (especially in Scandinavia), and eventually an all-embracing welfare state. And third, there was what Martin calls the "bourgeois Protestant axis"—Amsterdam-London-Boston—which was pluralist and democratizing almost from the beginning. Again, one should note the Weberian irony that this was mostly an unintended outcome: Neither the Church of England nor the various Calvinist polities were happy with this development, but social and political realities forced them to accept it, at first reluctantly, but then with varying degrees of enthusiasm. The basic sociological reality underpinning this model is the church as a voluntary association—in Dutch sectarianism,

English Nonconformity, and, most dramatically, in American "denominationalism." And, of course, it is the principle of voluntary association that is the foundation of both civil society and political democracy.

In considering the relationship of Protestantism to democracy, then, one must ask *what kind* of Protestantism one is looking at. This will lead to the conclusion that Protestantism has the most fertile relationship with democracy where the church is most clearly a voluntary association. To the extent that other religious traditions come to accept pluralism and democracy, it is quite appropriate that this process be perceived as a sort of "Protestantization"—not, of course, in terms of theology or piety, but in terms of the social forms of religion. This is precisely how conservative Catholics and Orthodox Christians have (pejoratively) perceived the process; from their vantage point, they have been quite right.

In recent cases of democratization, both Catholicism and Protestantism have made important contributions. Thus the role of the Catholic Church in the collapse of Poland's communist regime is mirrored by that of the Lutheran Church in the final days of the German Democratic Republic. Similarly, one can compare the role of the Catholic Church in the peaceful overthrow of the Marcos regime in the Philippines with that of the English-speaking Protestant churches in the ending of apartheid in South Africa. (One may add that, in the latter case, an important factor was the shift by the Afrikaans-speaking Dutch Reformed Church from a proponent to a critic of apartheid.) There continues to be a very significant difference between the two traditions, however, in their relation to capitalism. While only a few Protestant churches have come out as overt advocates of capitalism, the virtues and habits that Protestantism fosters continue to facilitate the development of market economies, especially in their early stages.

Max Weber's famous "Protestant ethic" is as relevant today in many parts of the developing world as it once was in Europe and North America. This is especially clear in the case of Pentecostalism, which has undergone an astonishingly massive explosion over the past half-century in Latin America, sub-Saharan Africa, and parts of Asia. Thus in Latin America, where there are now tens of millions of Pentecostals, one can observe a cultural revolution that is changing the values and behavior of these new Protestants—all in the direction of that "inner-worldly asceticism" which Weber analyzed as helping to engender the "spirit of capitalism." One might say that Max Weber is alive and well, and living in Guatemala (which happens to be the Latin American country with the highest percentage of Protestants). Once again, to the extent that democracy and market economies are linked phenomena, this is an important matter to consider when looking at the relation of Protestantism and democracy.

Elizabeth Prodromou's essay draws our attention to the very different history of the Orthodox tradition. In terms of Martin's trilogy, Orthodoxy fits, if at all, into the category of the baroque "dome" (one may think here of Constantinople's Hagia Sophia), but it was constructed quite differently from the Roman Catholic one. In the East there was no struggle between papacy and empire, and of course there has been neither a Reformation nor a Counter-Reformation, let alone a Vatican II. Yet the Byzantine "dome" has persisted as an ideal, resurrected after the fall of Constantinople in the "caesaropapism" of Holy Russia, and continuing to haunt the Orthodox imagination in the diaspora as well as in countries that were or are under Muslim rule (such as, for example, the former Ottoman lands of Southeastern Europe).

Prodromou focuses on pluralism, as both an antecedent and concomitant of democracy. She argues that Orthodox theology provides resources for an acceptance of pluralism through the theological concept of "unity in diversity." But so far there have been only sporadic attempts to deploy these resources for a theological legitimation of democracy. Orthodoxy still awaits its John Courtney Murray. Pluralism and democracy have been realities imposed on Orthdoxy from the outside, to be either resisted or reluctantly accommodated.

The three cases discussed by Prodromou vividly illustrate this situation. Developments in Russia (undoubtedly the most important case) indicate an incipient attempt, by both the Russian Orthodox Church and the Putin government, to restore a somewhat refurbished "dome." Russia's 1997 law on religion tried to balance a commitment to democratic liberties with a visceral animus against non-Orthodox groups (especially evangelical Protestants) seeking adherents in "Orthodox" territory. The debate in Greece over the listing of religious affiliation on national-identity cards, while seemingly a trivial issue, touches on a much more basic question: Can one be Greek without being Orthodox? And, most recently, the lawsuit of a group of Orthodox laypeople in America against the Greek hierarchy presents what, from a traditionalist point of view, must appear as an alarming signal of "Protestantization." The Orthodox situation is now very much in flux, in Russia and elsewhere, and it is premature to predict its future development. It is safe to say, though, that any attempt to restore a quasi-Byzantine unity of church, state, and society will face very serious difficulties in the contemporary world.

Does Christianity *today* relate positively to democracy? In the cases of Catholicism and Protestantism, the answer is pretty definitely yes. In the case of Orthodoxy, it is maybe. On the whole, this is a far from depressing picture.

NOTES

1. Galatians 3:28. See also Colossians 3:11.

2. Matthew 22:21. See also Mark 12:17 and Luke 20:25.

3. David Martin, "Integration und Fragmentierung: Religionsmuster in Europa," *Transit* 26 (Winter 2003–2004): 120–43.

IV

Islam

12

MUSLIMS AND DEMOCRACY

Abdou Filali-Ansary

*Abdou Filali-Ansary is cofounder and former editor of the Moroccan
quarterly* Prologues: revue maghrébine du livre, *a French-Arabic journal of philosophy, literature, and the social sciences based in
Casablanca. He is the author of* Réformer l'Islam? Une introduction
aux débats contemporains *(2003). The present essay originally appeared
in the July 1999 issue of the* Journal of Democracy.

The past is often held to weigh especially heavily on Muslim countries, particularly as regards their present-day receptivity to democracy.
I do not dispute that past history has had an overwhelming and decisive
influence in shaping the contemporary features and attitudes of Muslim
societies. But the past that is most relevant today is not, as is commonly
thought, the early centuries of Islamic history, but rather the nineteenth-
century encounter of Muslims with the modernizing West.

It is widely believed that the key to understanding contemporary
Muslim societies is to be found in a structure of beliefs and traditions
that was devised and implemented at (or shortly after) the moment at
which they adopted Islam. This view, often labeled as "Muslim
exceptionalism," holds that these societies are, as Ernest Gellner has
elegantly put it, permeated by an "implicit constitution" providing a
"blueprint" of the social order.[1] This view has been subjected to intense
criticism by a number of scholars, but it still influences dominant attitudes in academia and, with much more devastating effects, in the media.

This theory rests on two assumptions: first, that the past is ever-present
and is much more determining than present-day conditions; and second, that the character of Muslim societies has been determined by a
specific and remote period in their past during which the social and
political order that continues to guide them was established. This past
has allegedly acquired such a strong grip that it can—and does—channel, limit, or even block the effects of technological, economic, or social
change. In other words, for Muslims alone a remote past has defined,

forever and without any possibility of evolution, the ways in which fundamental issues are perceived and addressed. The ultimate conclusion lurking behind these considerations is that, due to the overwhelming presence and influence of that particular part of their past, the societies in question are incapable of democratization. In other societies history may take the form of continual change, but in Muslim ones history is bound to repeat itself.

Apart from the many other criticisms that have been directed against this set of views, it should be emphasized that it is not based on any solid historical knowledge about the way in which this "implicit constitution" was shaped and implemented or imposed. Some of its proponents refer to a normative system that was never really enacted: They invoke the model of the "rightly guided" caliphate, which lasted, at most, for about three decades after the death of the Prophet. Many others cite instead the social order that prevailed during the Middle Ages in societies where Muslims were a majority or where political regimes were established in the name of Islam. In both of these versions, however, the power of this past to determine the present remains, by and large, mysterious. It is simply taken for granted, with no explanation given about why the past has had such a far-reaching and pervasive effect in these societies. To understand how the belief in these misconceptions was born and came to influence contemporary attitudes so powerfully, we must turn to a particular moment in modern times—the beginning and middle of the nineteenth century.

A Tenacious Misunderstanding

The earliest intellectual encounters between Muslims and Europeans in modern times took the form of sharp confrontations. Jamal-Eddin Al-Afghani (1838–97), one of the first and most prominent Muslim thinkers and activists in the struggle against despotism, became famous for engaging in a controversy against European secularists. He acquired a high reputation, especially for his efforts to refute European critics of religion in general and of Islam in particular. An essay that he wrote in reply to Ernest Renan bore the title *"Ar-Rad 'ala ad-Dahriyin"* ("The Answer to Temporalists"). He used the term *Dahriyin,* which literally means "temporalists," to refer to secularists. The word itself, which is of Koranic origin, had originally been applied to atheists. Al-Afghani attacked the positivist ideologues of his century, who were deeply convinced that religion was responsible for social backwardness and stagnation and that scientific progress would soon lead to its disappearance. Through his choice of terminology, Al-Afghani implicitly equated these nineteenth-century positivists with the seventh-century opponents of the Prophet. For Muslim readers, this formulation defined the terms of a large and enduring misunderstanding. From then on, secularism was seen as being intimately related to, if not simply the same thing as, atheism. The confusion was taken a step further when, some decades later, other Muslim authors wishing to coin a term for secularism, and either ignoring Al-Afghani's choice of the term *Dahriyin* or feeling that it was inappropriate, chose *ladini,* which literally means "nonreligious" or "areligious."

These initial choices of terminology gave birth to the opposition in the mind of Muslims between, on the one hand, the system of belief and the social order that they inherited and lived in, and on the other, the alternative adopted by the Europeans. Although the term *ladini* was replaced later by another, *'ilmani* ("this-worldly"), the bipolar opposition between the two views was already deeply entrenched. The feeling that has prevailed since then among Muslims is that there is a strict and irreducible opposition between two systems—Islam and non-Islam. To be a secularist has meant to abandon Islam, to reject altogether not only the religious faith but also its attendant morality and the traditions and rules that operate within Muslim societies. It therefore has been understood as a total alienation from the constituent elements of the Islamic personality and as a complete surrender to unbelief, immorality, and self-hatred, leading to a disavowal of the historic identity and civilization inherited from illustrious ancestors. It is worth noting that the vast majority of Muslims in the nineteenth century, even those who were part of the educated elite, lived in total ignorance both of the debates going on in Europe about religion and its role in the social order and of the historical changes reshaping European societies. They were not aware of the distinction between atheism and secularism. The consequences of this misunderstanding still profoundly shape the attitudes of Muslims today.

Thus secularism became known to Muslims for the first time through a controversy against those who were supposed to be their "hereditary enemies." The original distinction within Christianity between "regular" and "secular" members of the clergy,[2] which was the initial step in the long evolution toward the establishment of a separate secular sphere, had no equivalent in the Muslim context. Hence the choice of a term for the concept of secularism was decisive. In the latter part of the nineteenth century and early in the twentieth, the confrontation with the colonial powers, thought to be the carriers and defenders of a mixture of aggressive Christian proselytism and of the new secularism, played an important role in strengthening this dualism. In the diverse conflicts that local populations waged to defend their independence, identity and religion became intimately fused. The oppositions between local and intruder, between Muslim and European, between believer and secularist were, in one way or another, conflated. The resulting polarization came to dominate all attitudes and approaches to questions related to religion, politics, and the social order.

One of the most striking consequences of this evolution is that Islam now appears to be the religion that is most hostile to secularization and to modernity in general. Yet intrinsically, Islam would seem to be the religion closest to modern views and ideals, and thus the one that would most easily accommodate secularization. "The high culture form of Islam," writes Ernest Gellner, "is endowed with a number of features—unitarianism, a rule-ethic, individualism, scripturalism, puritanism, an egalitarian aversion to mediation and hierarchy, a fairly small load of magic—that are congruent, presumably, with requirements of modernity or modernisation."[3] In a similar vein, Mohamed Charfi observes that, on the level of principles, Islam should favor individual freedoms and the capacity for religious choice. The historical developments noted above, however, caused Muslim societies to evolve in the opposite direction—toward the loss of individual autonomy and total submission to the community and the state.[4]

This evolution gave birth at later stages to such dichotomies as "Islam and the West," "Islam and modernity," "Islam and human rights," "Islam and democracy," and others of the sort, which set the framework within which critical issues are addressed, whether in popular, journalistic, or even academic circles. This framework has imposed a particular way of raising questions and building conceptions, imprisoning attitudes in predefined and static formulas.[5] Muslim exceptionalism seems, therefore, to reside in the ways we raise questions about these matters. Although many studies on religion and its influence in the social and political spheres are undertaken in what were formerly referred to as Christian societies, nobody today poses the issue of "Christianity and democracy" in the same way that this question is formulated with respect to Islam. The fact that we still ask questions such as "Is Islam compatible with democracy?" shows how strong this polarization has become. It also shows that a dynamic was established, enabling the polarization that emerged in the nineteenth century to replicate itself as it extends to new fields or expresses itself in new terms.

From Settlement to System

This polarization, which still determines the type of questions that can be asked, rests on two main prejudices: The first is that Islam is a "system," and should be treated as a structure of rules. The dubious character of this assumption has been clearly pointed out by the eminent scholar of comparative religion Wilfred Cantwell Smith: "[T]he term *nizam* [or] 'system,' is commonplace in the twentieth century in relation to Islam. This term, however, does not occur in the Koran, nor indeed does any word from this root; and there is some reason for wondering whether any Muslim ever used this concept religiously before modern times. The explicit notion that life should be or can be ordered according to a system, even an ideal one, and that it is the business of Islam to provide such a system, seems to be a modern idea (and perhaps a rather questionable one)."[6] Once Islam has been defined in this way, it can be used to assess whether other new or alien concepts can be accommodated within it and to decide the degree of their compatibility with its presumed and predefined content. This stance, however, reflects a particular attitude toward religion, not a particular feature of Islam. In fact, as Leonard Binder has observed, any of the monotheistic religions, if adopted in this manner, can lead to similar conclusions: "In the light of modern liberal democratic thought, Islam is no more, nor any less democratic than Christianity or Judaism. All three monotheistic religions, if proposed as constitutional foundations of the state, and if understood as providing an ineluctable authority for the guidance of all significant human choice, are undemocratic or non-democratic."[7]

The second prejudice is more insidious. It is based on the confusion of Islam as a religion with Islam as a civilization. This confusion is deeply entrenched, again because of prevailing linguistic usages both in Arabic and in European languages. For Islam, no distinction has been drawn comparable to that between "Christianity" and "Christendom." The same word was, and still is, used to refer both to a set of beliefs and rituals and to the life of the community of believers through time and space. Only recently, thanks to the work of historian Marshall G.S. Hodgson, has the necessity of drawing a sharp line between Islam and "Islamdom" been recognized as essential for explaining key phenomena in the history of Muslims.[8] Islamdom, in its golden age, was a social and political order built on norms adopted from Islamic sources but specifically adapted to the conditions of the time. (Only at a later stage were these formulated as explicit rules.) This enabled Muslims in the Middle Ages to create and maintain a world civilization attuned to the circumstances of the era.

Muslims at that time lived within polities bound by *shari'a,* yet did not consider the political regimes to which they were subjected to be in conformity with Islamic principles. The rulers were considered to be legal but not really legitimate. Even though they were not fully legitimate, they had to be obeyed, but only to avoid a greater evil, the *fitna* (the great rebellion or anarchy). For premodern societies of Muslims, the political model remained the early caliphate, which was not bound by *shari'a,* since *shari'a* had not yet been devised. The ideal was a kind of "republican" regime, where caliphs are chosen by members of the community rather than imposed by force, and where the behavior of rulers is clearly dedicated to serving the community instead of satisfying their personal ambitions. Nonetheless, Muslims came to understand that it was no longer possible to implement the fully legitimate system of *Khilafa rachida,* the virtuous or rightly guided caliphate, that the republican ideal was out of reach, and that they had to accept the rule of despots. They could, however, limit the extent of the power accorded to autocratic rulers by invoking *shari'a,* to which a sacred character had come to be attributed. In this way, at least some degree of autonomy from the political authorities, and minimal protection against arbitrariness, could be attained. This is what one may label the "medieval compromise" or "medieval settlement." The sacralization of *shari'a* achieved through this process led to another far-reaching consequence: Ever since, Islam has been seen as a set of eternal rules, standing over society and history, to be used as a standard for judging reality and behavior.

In fact, *shari'a* was never a system of law in the sense in which it is understood nowadays. As was noted by Fazlur Rahman:

> Islamic law . . . is not strictly speaking law, since much of it embodies moral and quasi-moral precepts not enforceable in any court. Further, Islamic law, though a certain part of it came to be enforced almost uniformly throughout the Muslim world (and it is primarily this that bestowed homogeneity upon the entire Muslim world), is on closer examination a body of legal opinion or, as Santillana put it, "an endless discussion on the duties of a Muslim" rather than a neatly formulated code or codes.[9]

What happened in the nineteenth century was the transformation of the medieval settlement into a system in the modern sense of the word. The duality of fact and norm was inverted, as *shari'a*-bound societies were confused with fully legitimate Muslim communities and deemed to be fully realizable through voluntary political action, whether of a peaceful or violent character. We see therefore how the confusion between a "model" and a historical system could arise and spread among Muslims at a time when they were confronted by the challenge of modern ideas. The typical attitudes of premodern Muslims had been based on a sharp distinction between the norm (of the virtuous or rightly guided caliphate) and the actual conditions (including the implementation of the *shari'a*) under which they lived. In the face of this duality, people adopted an attitude of resignation, accepting that the norm was, at least temporarily, out of reach. By contrast, some modern Muslims have elevated the actual conditions and rules under which their medieval forefathers lived to the status of a norm, and decided that they too have to live by these rules if they are to be true Muslims.

This has led to the contradictions of the present day: Secularization has been taking place for decades in Muslim societies, yet prevailing opinion opposes the concept of secularism and everything that comes with it (like modernity and democracy). As a historical process, secularization has so transformed life in Muslim societies that religion, or rather traditions built on religion, no longer supplies the norms and rules that govern the social and political order. In almost all countries with substantial communities of Muslims, positive law has replaced *shari'a* (except with regard to matters of "personal status," and more specifically the status of women, where the traditional rules generally continue to be maintained). Modern institutions—nation-states, modern bureaucracies, political parties, labor unions, corporations, associations, educational systems—have been adopted everywhere, while traditional institutions are, at best, relegated to symbolic roles. Similarly, prevailing conceptions and attitudes of everyday life are founded on modern rationality and on doctrines influenced by science and philosophy rather than on traditional or premodern worldviews. Most Muslims now have come to accept the "disenchantment of the world," and this has profoundly transformed expectations and models of behavior within their societies. The evolution from the premodern attitude, combining resignation toward despotism with millennial hopes, to the typically modern combination of sharp political determination and desire for this-worldly progress, is clearly a visible consequence of these very changes, that is, of the secularization that has actually been going on in Muslim societies.

Secularism, however, continues to be rejected as an alien doctrine, allegedly imposed by the traditional enemies of Muslims and their indigenous accomplices. Islam is seen as an eternal and immutable system, encompassing every aspect of social organization and personal morality, and unalterably opposed to all conceptions and systems associated with modernity. This creates an artificial debate and an almost surrealist situation. The changes that are evident in the actual lives of individuals and groups are ignored, while ideological stances are maintained with great determination. Secularists and, more generally, social scientists are often pushed into adopting defensive positions or withdrawing altogether from public debates. Frequently they feel obliged to prove that they are not guilty of hostility toward religious belief, morality, and the achievements of Islamic civilization.

As Mohamed Charfi has pointed out, the policies adopted by some modern states under the influence of nationalist ideologies are partly responsible for this state of affairs. The education systems in many Muslim countries have taught Islam not as a religion, but as an identity and a legal and political system. The consequence is that Islam is presented both as irreducibly opposed to other kinds of self-identification or of social and political organization and as commanding certain specific attitudes regarding political and social matters.[10]

Attitudes Toward Democracy

We saw that, as a consequence of the inversion of norms that occurred in Muslim societies during the nineteenth century, the traditional rules and usages grouped under the emblem of *shari'a* were transformed into a system and elevated into norms that define the "essence" of being Muslim—that is, simultaneously the ideal status and the specific identity of Muslims. Thus *shari'a*-bound societies are now equated with "truly" Islamic societies. Implementing the *shari'a* has become the slogan for those who seek a "return" to Islam in its original and pure form, which is held to embody the eternal truth and ultimate pattern for Muslims.

What could the status of democracy be in societies that have evolved in this manner? One first must perceive the difference between a question posed in this way, which attempts to interpret the actual evolution of particular societies and their prevailing conceptions, and the kinds of questions frequently asked by fundamentalists and by some scholars, such as "What is the status of democracy with regard to Islam?" This latter formulation posits Islam as a system that one can use to evaluate everything else.

One can discern two possible answers to the question of democracy as I have posed it. The first accepts the strict identification between Islam and *shari'a*-bound systems, and thus rules out any possible future for democracy in this particular environment. The second identifies democracy itself with a kind of religious faith or "mystical ideal." As Tim Niblock has noted: "The Middle East related literature purveys a romanticized conception of the nature and characteristics of liberal democracy. This occurs not through any explicit description of liberal democracy, but precisely through the absence of any analysis of the concept and its practical application. The concept hovers, like a mystical symbol, in the background of the discussion on democratization in the Middle East, with an implied assumption that liberal democracy constitutes an ideal polity where the common good is realized by means of the population deciding issues through the election of individuals who carry out the people's will."[11]

There even appears to be a certain trend toward adopting this second attitude. More and more fundamentalists accept the idea that Islam is not opposed to democracy; some argue that by embracing the principle of *shura* (or "consultation"), for example, Islam has always favored the kind of relationship between rulers and ruled that democracy entails. Democracy may even end up being described as a Western adaptation of an originally Islamic principle. Many fundamentalists are prepared to go as far as possible to support democracy—with the notable reservation that it should be maintained only within the limits set by *shari'a*. A "guided democracy" is the system envisioned by many fundamentalists and traditionalists of different sorts. Iran may be considered as a case where this kind of doctrine has been implemented. In addition to institutions common in all democracies, like elected parliaments and executives, it also has a high council of experts and a religious guide who are entrusted with ensuring that the laws and decisions made by democratically elected bodies are in conformity with religious principles and rules.

This shows how much popularity, or rather prestige, democracy enjoys within contemporary Muslim societies. The renowned contemporary philosopher Mohamed Abed Jabri has said that democracy is the only principle of political legitimacy which is acceptable nowadays in Muslim societies, whatever their religious beliefs and attitudes may be. "Revolutionary" alternatives that postpone the implementation of democracy until other conditions are realized no longer seem to be acceptable to the masses.[12] This support for democracy reflects in some cases a realistic recognition that it responds to the needs of contemporary societies, that it is indeed the only alternative that really works and makes possible the peaceful and rational management of public affairs. In many other cases, however, this newly favorable reception of democracy arises from its being viewed as another utopia.[13] While this may have certain immediate advantages, especially in contexts where democratic systems are in place or where democratization is under way, it may also encourage attitudes that are harmful to the longer-range prospects for democratization. For it may lead to democracy's being seen as an alien or unattainable ideal, and thus strengthen the idea that the Islamic alternative is more workable and better adapted to the conditions of Muslim societies. In other words, democracy may be treated in the same way as other modern ideologies, such as nationalism and socialism, that recently enjoyed a brief ascendancy in some Muslim countries. Both nationalism and socialism were indeed endowed with a quasi-religious aura; they were adopted as ultimate worldviews and total beliefs, and considered as magical remedies to all the ills and problems of society. This kind of approach would only deepen the initial misunderstanding on the part of Muslims of both secularization and democracy. The result would be to strengthen the view that Islam and democracy represent two irreducibly separate and opposing outlooks, even if some mixture of Islam and democracy were to be envisaged and tentatively implemented.

Replacing Democracy with Its "Building Blocks"

What might be an appropriate strategy for democrats in this situation? For those who are convinced that democracy is not a new religion for humanity, but that it provides the most efficient means to limit abuses of power and protect individual freedoms, enabling individuals to seek their own path to personal accomplishment, there can be a variety of approaches. The most effective ones avoid the reified and "utopianized" version of democracy, either by highlighting such concepts as "good governance" or by supporting some of the "building blocks of democracy," that is, conceptions and systems that are linked to or part of democracy.

Replacing highly prestigious and, at the same time, highly contentious notions with terms that refer to easily understood facts and ideas is neither a retreat from conceptual clarity nor a defeatist position. A few years ago Mohamed Abed Jabri was bitterly attacked by a large number of Arab intellectuals for proposing to replace the slogan of secularization with such notions as rationality and democratization. Secularization, he contended, had become a charged issue for Arab public opinion because it was understood as being more or less equivalent to Westernization; its actual contents, however, such as rational management of collective affairs and democracy, could hardly be rejected once they were understood and accepted in their true meaning. In a similar vein, Niblock has observed: "Focusing on the 'big' issue of democratisation has detracted from the attention which can be given to a range of more specific issues which affect populations critically. Among these are the level of corruption, the effectiveness of bureaucratic organisation, the independence of the judiciary, the existence of well-conceived and clearly-articulated laws, freedom of expression, the respect given to minorities, attitudes to human rights issues, and the extent of inequalities which may create social disorder."[14]

In order to avoid a new and devastating misunderstanding that would present democracy as an alternative to religion and make its adoption appear to be a deviation from religious rectitude, it is essential to renounce quixotic confrontations and to accept some "tactical" concessions—especially when the use of appropriate terminology can bring greater clarification without sacrificing substance. Niblock's suggestion, stressing the importance of specific issues relevant to democracy, is one possible strategy, and it is certainly of real usefulness for the cases at hand. Yet it represents an external point of view, one that seems to be directed primarily at politicians and decision makers who attempt to influence political change in Muslim countries from the outside. It does not take into account the attitudes of Muslims themselves, and especially the need to foster their real acceptance and support of democracy. For this purpose, a more "conceptual" approach is required, one that would help present democracy in terms understandable and acceptable to Muslim publics, and thus bridge the gap between a "mystical" representation and a more realistic comprehension. It would answer the need for analytical terms that can clarify the conceptions and adjust the expectations of Muslims regarding democracy, and that can encourage the kind of *political* support that is equally distant from mythical or ideological fervor on the one hand, and egotistical or individualist attitudes on the other.

This approach, which should be understood not as an alternative but rather as a complement to the one proposed by Niblock, aims at clarifying the issue for a specific public that is influenced by particular worldviews and has expectations of its own. Finding the right terms is not easy. Interpretations of democracy and democratization are so rich and diverse that it may be difficult to reach a consensual view on the subject. All such interpretations, however, seem to point to some basic features as being essential conditions for achieving real democracy. It is possible to underscore at least three such conditions that seem to be required for the particular case of contemporary Muslim societies: 1) the updating of religious conceptions; 2) the rule of law; and 3) economic growth.

1) The *updating of religious conceptions* should be understood not in terms of the Reformation that occurred in sixteenth-century Christian Europe, but rather as the general evolution of religious attitudes that has affected Christians and Jews (except within limited circles of fundamentalists) since the seventeenth or eighteenth centuries and achieved its full effects only in the early decades of this century. The Reformation is a singular event in history, linked to a particular environment and to specific conditions. It cannot, as some observers are suggesting nowadays, be "replicated" in the context of another religion and under twentieth-century conditions.

There is, however, another process of change in religious attitudes that, although it first occurred in one particular environment, is of more universal scope and significance and seems to be related to modernization in general. This process leads the majority of the population to give religious dogmas a symbolic truth-value, and to consider religious narratives as contingent, historical manifestations or expressions of the sacred that are amenable to rational understanding and scientific scrutiny. Religious dogmas and narratives no longer define, in a monolithic way, people's ideas about the world and society, nor do they determine the views that believers are supposed to be guided by in their social and political interactions. This kind of "disenchantment" may discard the literal meaning of sacred words and rituals, but it maintains (and probably reinforces) the overall ethical and moral teachings. Religious attitudes are no longer defined in terms of a combination of strict observance of rituals and the adoption of premodern views, but rather as an informal but deeply felt adherence to principles of morality and a commitment to universal values. Faith becomes a matter of individual choice and commitment, not an obligation imposed upon all members of the community.

An evolution in this direction has proceeded quite far among Christians and Jews, but has made only limited headway among Muslims. The reification of Islam that began in the nineteenth century is the most important obstacle to such progress. Thus it is significant that a number of contemporary Muslim thinkers agree that new attitudes toward religion are now required both by a scrupulous interpretation of sacred sources and by modern conditions. Their teachings imply a strict separation between the sacred message of Islam and Muslim attempts to implement it in the course of history, including the political systems and legislation created in the "golden age." The Egyptian theologian Ali Abderraziq, for example, proposed to consider the early caliphate created by companions of the Prophet not as a religious institution but as a political one, amenable to critical scrutiny in the same way as any normal human institution.[15] Fazlur Rahman and Mohamed Mahmoud

Taha suggested a tempered and modernized attitude toward revelation.[16] Mohamed Talbi and Mohamed Charfi introduced and defended a clear distinction between religious principles and the legal prescriptions devised in order to implement them.[17] This trend (if one can so label a collection of otherwise unrelated thinkers who come to similar conclusions) has received little coverage in the media. Its influence has also been restricted by the educational policies of modern states and by intimidation on the part of the fundamentalists.

2) The *rule of law* is a notion that expresses something that Muslims have longed for since the early phases of their history, and have felt to be part of the message of Islam. Muslim travelers to Europe in the nineteenth century were struck by Europeans' adhesion to rules and rule-bound behavior. This made some of them think that these societies were "Muslim" without being aware of it, as Islam was clearly identified with law-abiding attitudes. Fundamentalists claim that the only way of satisfying this aspiration for lawfulness is by implementing *shari'a,* which they present as the sole remedy for the arbitrariness and abuse of power common in most "Muslim" states. This argument can be countered by showing that the modern concept of "rule of law" is clearer, more operational, and easier to monitor, and thus that the dichotomy of "Islam (or rather *shari'a*) versus despotism" trumpeted by fundamentalist propaganda is not the whole story. Experience has revealed that law-abidingness is rather a feature of truly modernized societies, where individuals feel that they have a voice in the making of public decisions.

3) *Economic growth* here refers to the idea of continuous progress, which is a basic component of modernity, replacing the messianic hopes and political resignation dominant in premodern societies with the voluntarism and this-worldly resourcefulness of modern times. Democracy, as an expression of the free will of the citizens, cannot thrive if no collective will is allowed to surface or to have a say about the changes that society is compelled to undergo. It is the direct and visible expression of what Alain Touraine called modernization (in contrast with modernity)—that is, the process through which societies take control of their own affairs, mobilize their forces and their resources, and seek to determine the course of their destiny.[18] Economic growth offers the prospect of an improvement in the conditions of life, which seems to be required in every modern society, and all the more so in "developing" ones. No prospect of democratization can be envisaged if no economic growth is actually taking place.

Toward a Universal Rule of Law

It seems obvious that democracy cannot be exported, much less imposed on peoples who are not prepared to accept it and to mobilize themselves to implement it. If great numbers of Muslims today invoke religion rather than democracy as the alternative to despotism, and others consider democracy itself (at least implicitly) as a kind of new religious belief, this is not because of some special characteristics either of Islam or of Muslims. It is rather because of the particular historical circumstances that I have tried to explain. Muslim confrontations with European colonial powers in the nineteenth century gave birth to some great and lasting misunderstandings, as a result of which Muslims have rejected key aspects of modernity (secularization and, to some degree, democratization) as an alienation and a surrender of the historical self to the "Other."

For those who believe that "civilizations" are hard-core realities that last throughout history and that have distinctive and irreducible features, such polarization is understandable, being the "normal" course of history. It should therefore be treated as such, and the appropriate behavior would be to prepare to defend one's own civilization against alien ones in the unavoidable confrontations of the future.

For those, however, who believe that modern history has, for better or worse, put an end to the separate life of different cultures, there can be convergent paths to establishing social and political systems that promote individual freedoms, human rights, and social justice. These convergent paths point to the crucial importance of the international context and especially of the ongoing relationships between established and would-be democracies.

The fact that democracy has been adopted only in some countries (where it defines the ways their interests are promoted) and not in others creates an asymmetry. The collective interests of some communities, and not of others, find a channel for their expression, and therefore for the promotion of their particular national interests. The moral values that prevail within these communities will not prevail in their relationships with others. This asymmetry will fuel deeper antagonism between nations and greater resentment from those who are weaker. It is therefore time to call for a universal rule of law, where law is not considered only as a means for defending selfish national interests, but is respected for its own sake in a "Kantian" way.

We are living, much more than did our ancestors of the nineteenth and early twentieth centuries, in a deeply integrated world. Some form of a "universal rule of law," creating a new balance between the selfish interests of nations and universal principles, would ease the evolution we are seeking. It would help to define a framework—political, cultural, and economic—that is truly compatible with democratic ideals on the scale of humanity, and favorable to their wider acceptance.

NOTES

1. "Islam is the blueprint of a social order. It holds that a set of rules exists, eternal, divinely ordained, and independent of the will of men, which defines the

proper ordering of society. . . . In traditional Islam, no distinction is made between lawyer and common lawyer, and the roles of theologian and lawyer are conflated. Expertise on proper social arrangements, and on matters pertaining to God, are one and the same thing." Ernest Gellner, *Muslim Society* (Cambridge: Cambridge University Press, 1981), 1.

2. Those priests who belong to monastic order and live according to its rules are considered "regular" clergy, while those priests living in the world and not bound by monastic vows or rules are considered "secular" clergy.

3. Quoted by Samuel Huntington, "Democracy's Third Wave," in Marc F. Plattner and Larry Diamond, eds., *The Global Resurgence of Democracy* (Baltimore: Johns Hopkins University Press, 1993), 19.

4. Mohamed Charfi, *Islam et liberté: Le malentendu historique* (Paris: Albin Michel, 1998), 191.

5. Richard K. Khuri gives a very comprehensive description of the way this build-up was achieved. See Richard K. Khuri, *Freedom, Modernity and Islam: Toward a Creative Synthesis* (Syracuse, N.Y.: Syracuse University Press), 1998.

6. Wilfred Cantwell Smith, *The Meaning and End of Religion: A New Approach to the Religious Traditions of Mankind* (New York, 1962), 117.

7. Leonard Binder, "Exceptionalism and Authenticity: The Question of Islam and Democracy," *Arab Studies Journal* 6 (Spring 1998): 33–59.

8. Marshall G.S. Hodgson's main work is *The Venture of Islam,* 3 vols. (Chicago: University of Chicago Press, 1974). A summary of his conclusions appeared in a collection of articles published posthumously under the title *Rethinking World History: Essays on Europe, Islam and World History,* edited, with an introduction and a conclusion, by Edmund Burke, III (Cambridge: Cambridge University Press, 1993).

9. Fazlur Rahman, *Islam and Modernity: Transformation of an Intellectual Tradition* (Chicago: University of Chicago Press, 1982), 32.

10. Mohamed Charfi, *Islam et liberté,* 228.

11. Tim Niblock, "Democratisation: A Theoretical and Practical Debate," *British Journal of Middle Eastern Studies* 25 (November 1998): 221–34.

12. Mohamed Abed Jabri, *Ad-Dimuqratiya wa Huquq al-Insan* (Democracy and human rights) (Beirut: Center for Arab Unity Studies, 1994).

13. Tim Niblock, "Democratisation," 226.

14. Tim Niblock, "Democratisation," 229.

15. Ali Abderraziq (1888–1966) attempted, in a famous and much-debated essay published in 1925, to dispel the misunderstanding and confusions surrounding religion and politics in Islam. His demonstration—for it was intended to be a rigorous demonstration—aimed at showing the strict separation between, on the one hand, religious principles and rules relating to social and political matters and, on the other, the laws and regulations made by theologians and political leaders to implement the faith in the temporal life of their community. He rejected the view, widely held among Sunni Muslims, that the end of the 'rightly guided' caliphate (approximately three decades after the death of the Prophet), which allegedly saw the replacement of the initially religious community by a regular polity and of a religious order by a secular or temporal order, constituted a really basic turn in the history of Muslims. The initiative of Ali Abderraziq was a founding moment in contemporary Muslim thought and politics. It did not suc-

ceed in dispelling the "big misunderstanding"; it is, however, the most radical attempt to show that a "new beginning" is possible for Muslims regarding such basic issues as the overall relation between faith and the social and political order. Ali Abderraziq, *L'Islam et les fondements du pouvoir* (Paris: La Découverte, 1994).

16. Fazlur Rahman did so in scholarly and measured terms, while Mohamed Mahmoud Taha wrote a kind of manifesto calling for a reversal of the order of prominence that Muslims give to Koranic verses: Mohamed Mahmoud Taha, *The Second Message of Islam,* Abdullahi Ahmed An-Na'im, trans. (Syracuse, N.Y.: Syracuse University Press, 1987).

17. For Mohamed Talbi, see *Plaidoyer pour un Islam moderne* (Casablanca: Le Fennec, 1996). For Mohamed Charfi, see *Islam et liberté.*

18. Alain Touraine, "Modernité et spécificités culturelles," in *Revue Internationale des Sciences Sociales* 118 (November 1988): 497–512.

13

A HISTORICAL OVERVIEW

Bernard Lewis

Bernard Lewis *is Cleveland E. Dodge Professor (emeritus) of Near Eastern Studies at Princeton University. Formerly professor of history at the University of London, he is the author of many books including* The Crisis of Islam: Holy War and Unholy Terror *(2003) and* From Babel to Dragomans: Interpreting the Middle East *(2004). This essay originally appeared in the April 1996 issue of the* Journal of Democracy. *Copyright © Bernard Lewis, 1996.*

In a necessarily brief discussion of major issues, it is fatally easy to go astray by misuse or misinterpretation of some of the words that one uses. Therefore, I ought to say first what I mean by the terms "Islam" and "liberal democracy."

Democracy nowadays is a word much used and even more misused. It has many meanings and has turned up in surprising places—the Spain of General Franco, the Greece of the colonels, the Pakistan of the generals, the Eastern Europe of the commissars—usually prefaced by some qualifying adjective such as "guided," "basic," "organic," "popular," or the like, which serves to dilute, deflect, or even to reverse the meaning of the word.

Another definition of democracy is embraced by those who claim that Islam itself is the only authentic democracy. This statement is perfectly true, *if* one accepts the notion of democracy presupposed by those who advance this view. Since it does not coincide with the definition of democracy that I take as the basis of this discussion, I will leave it aside as irrelevant for present purposes.

The kind of democracy I am talking about is none of these. By liberal democracy, I mean primarily the general method of choosing or removing governments that developed in England and then spread among English-speaking peoples and beyond.

In 1945, the victors of the Second World War imposed parliamentary democracy on the three major Axis powers. It survives in all three, precariously, perhaps, in one. In none of them has it yet confronted any crisis of truly major proportions. Among the Allies, Britain and France bequeathed their own brands of democracy—with varying success—to their former colonies during the postwar retreat from empire.

Perhaps the best rule of thumb by which one can judge the presence of the kind of democracy I mean is Samuel P. Huntington's dictum that you can call a country a democracy when it has made two consecutive, peaceful changes of government via free elections. By specifying *two* elections, Huntington rules out regimes that follow the procedure that one acute observer has called "one man, one vote, once." So I take democracy to mean a polity where the government can be changed by elections as opposed to one where elections are changed by the government.

Americans tend to see democracy and monarchy as antithetical terms. In Europe, however, democracy has fared better in constitutional monarchies than in republics. It is instructive to make a list of those countries in Europe where democracy has developed steadily and without interruption over a long period, and where there is every prospect that it will continue to do so in the foreseeable future. The list of such countries is short and all but one of them are monarchies. The one exception, Switzerland, is like the United States in that it is a special case due to special circumstances. In the French Republic, established by revolution more than two centuries ago, the march of democracy has been punctuated by interruptions, reverses, and digressions. In most of the other republics of Europe, and, for that matter, in the rest of the world, the record is incomparably worse.

In all this, there may be some lesson for the Middle East, where the dynastic principle is still remarkably strong. The most purely Arab and Muslim of Middle Eastern states, Saudi Arabia, derives its name and its identity from its founding and ruling dynasty. So, too, did the Ottoman Empire—the most recent and by far the most enduring of all the Islamic empires. Even such radical revolutionary leaders as Hafiz al-Assad in Syria and Saddam Hussein in Iraq endeavor to secure the succession of their sons. In a political culture where the strain of dynastic legitimacy is so strong, democracy might in some places fare better by going with it rather than against it.

What of our other term, "Islam"? It too has multiple meanings. In one sense, it denotes a religion—a system of belief, worship, doctrine, ideals, and ideas—that belongs to the family of monotheistic, scriptural religions that includes Judaism and Christianity. In another sense, it means the whole civilization that has grown up under the aegis of that religion: something like what is meant by the once-common term "Christendom."

When we in the West today talk of Christian art, we mean votive art, religious art. If we talk of Islamic art, however, we mean any art produced by Muslims or even by non-Muslims within Islamic civilization.

Indeed, one can still speak of Islamic astronomy and Islamic chemistry and Islamic mathematics, meaning astronomy, chemistry, and mathematics produced under the aegis of Islamic civilization. There is no corresponding "Christian" astronomy or chemistry or mathematics.

Each of these terms, Islam in the sense of a religion and Islam in the sense of a civilization, is itself subject to many variations. If we talk about Islam as a historical phenomenon, we are speaking of a community that now numbers more than a billion people, most of whom are spread along a vast arc stretching almost 10,000 miles from Morocco to Mindanao; that has a 14-century-long history; and that is the defining characteristic of the 53 sovereign states that currently belong to the Organization of the Islamic Conference (OIC). For obvious reasons, it is extremely difficult (though not impossible) to make any kind of valid generalization about a reality of such age, size, and complexity.

Even if we confine ourselves to speaking of Islam as a religion, significant distinctions must be drawn. First, there is what Muslims themselves would call the original, pristine, pure Islam of the Koran and the *hadith* (the traditions of the Prophet Mohammad) before it became corrupted by the backsliding of later generations. Second, there is the Islam of the doctors of the holy law, of the magnificent intellectual structure of classical Islamic jurisprudence and theology. Most recently, there is the neo-Islam of the so-called fundamentalists who introduce ideas unknown alike to the Koran, the *hadith*, or the classical doctrines of the faith.

Clearly this last version of Islam is incompatible with liberal democracy, as the fundamentalists themselves would be the first to say: they regard liberal democracy with contempt as a corrupt and corrupting form of government. They are willing to see it, at best, as an avenue to power, but an avenue that runs one way only.

History and Tradition

What then of the two others—historic Islam and Islam as a system of ideas, practices, and cultural traits?

A first look at the historical record is not encouraging. Predominantly Muslim regions show very few functioning democracies. Indeed, of the 53 OIC states, only Turkey can pass Huntington's test of democracy, and it is in many ways a troubled democracy. Among the others, one can find democratic movements and in some cases even promising democratic developments, but one cannot really say that they are democracies even to the extent that the Turkish Republic is a democracy at the present time.

Throughout history, the overwhelmingly most common type of regime in the Islamic world has been autocracy—which is not to be confused with despotism. The dominant political tradition has long been that of command and obedience, and far from weakening it, modern times have actually witnessed its intensification. With traditional restraints on autocracy attenuated, and with new means of surveillance, repression, and wealth-extraction made available to rulers by modern technologies and methods, governments have become less dependent than ever on popular goodwill. This is particularly true of those governments that are enriched by revenues from oil. With no need for taxation, there is no pressure for representation.

Another noteworthy historical and cultural fact is the absence of the notion of citizenship. There is no word in Arabic, Persian, or Turkish for "citizen." The cognate term used in each language means only "compatriot" or "countryman." It has none of the connotations of the English word "citizen," which comes from the Latin *civis* and has the content of the Greek *politēs*, meaning one who participates in the affairs of the *polis*. The word is absent in Arabic and the other languages because the idea— of the citizen as participant, of citizenship as participation—is not there.

At the same time, however, we can discern elements in Islamic law and tradition that could assist the development of one or another form of democracy. Islam boasts a rich political literature. From the earliest times, doctors of the holy law, philosophers, jurists, and others have reflected carefully on the nature of political power, the ways in which political power ought to be acquired and used and may be forfeited, and the duties and responsibilities as well as the rights and privileges of those who hold it.

Islamic tradition strongly disapproves of arbitrary rule. The central institution of sovereignty in the traditional Islamic world, the caliphate, is defined by the Sunni jurists to have contractual and consensual features that distinguish caliphs from despots. The exercise of political power is conceived and presented as a contract, creating bonds of mutual obligation between the ruler and the ruled. Subjects are duty-bound to obey the ruler and carry out his orders, but the ruler also has duties toward the subject, similar to those set forth in most cultures.

The contract can be dissolved if the ruler fails to fulfill or ceases to be capable of fulfilling his obligations. Although rare, there have been instances when such dissolutions took place. There is, therefore, also an element of consent in the traditional Islamic view of government.

Many *hadith* prescribe obedience as an obligation of a subject, but some indicate exceptions. One, for example, says, "Do not obey a creature against his creator"—in other words, do not obey a human command to violate divine law. Another says, similarly, "There is no duty of obedience in sin." That is to say, if the sovereign commands something that is sinful, the duty of obedience lapses. It is worth noting that Prophetic utterances like these point not merely to a *right* of disobedience (such as would be familiar from Western political thought), but to a divinely ordained *duty* of disobedience.

When we descend from the level of principle to the realm of what has actually happened, the story is of course checkered. Still, the central point remains: There are elements in Islamic culture that could favor the development of democratic institutions.

One of the sayings traditionally ascribed to the Prophet is the remark, "Difference of opinion within my community is a sign of God's mercy." In other words, diversity is something to be welcomed, not something to be suppressed. This attitude is typified by the acceptance by Sunni Muslims, even today, of four different schools of Islamic jurisprudence. Muslims believe the holy law to be divinely inspired and guided, yet there are four significantly different schools of thought regarding this law. The idea that it is possible to be orthodox even while differing creates a principle of the acceptance of diversity and of mutual tolerance of differences of opinion that surely cannot be bad for parliamentary government.

The final point worth mentioning in this inventory is Islam's emphasis on the twin qualities of dignity and humility. Subjects—even the humblest subjects—have personal dignity in the traditional Islamic view, and rulers must avoid arrogance. By Ottoman custom, when the sultan received the chief dignitaries of the state on holy days, he stood up to receive them as a sign of his respect for the law. When a new sultan was enthroned, he was greeted with cries of "Sultan, be not proud! God is greater than you!"

The Influence of the West

For the first thousand years of its history, Islamic civilization's relationship to Christendom was one of dominance. The loss of Spain and Portugal on the remote western periphery had little impact in the heartlands of Islam, and was more than compensated by the advance toward the heart of continental Europe. As late as 1683, an Ottoman army was encamped before the very gates of Vienna. Earlier in the seventeenth century, North African corsairs were raiding as far north as the British Isles. By the early nineteenth century, however, Islamic power was clearly in retreat as European power grew. Finding themselves the targets of conquest and colonization, Muslims naturally began to wonder what had gone wrong. Islam had always been generally "successful" in worldly terms. Unlike the founder of Christianity, who was crucified and whose followers saw their religion made the official faith of the Roman Empire only after centuries as a persecuted minority, Mohammad founded a state during his lifetime, and as ruler he collected taxes, dispensed justice, promulgated laws, commanded armies, and made war and peace.

Educated Muslims, chagrined by the newfound potency of their European rivals, asked: What are they doing right and what are we doing wrong, or not doing at all? Representative, constitutional government was high on the list. The nineteenth century saw the rise of elected assemblies in a number of Western countries, and democracy in our current sense was beginning to take hold. Many Muslims suspected that here—in this most exotic and alien of Western practices—lay the secret to the West's wealth and power, and hoped that the adoption of constitutions and the creation of elected legislatures in the Islamic world would redress the civilizational balance.

Getting used to the idea was not easy; the first Muslim visitors to the West disliked much of what they saw. The earliest detailed description of England by a Muslim traveler is a fascinating account by Mirza Abu Talib Khan, a Turko-Persian resident of Lucknow who was in England between 1798 and 1803. He watched the House of Commons in action, and his comments are enlightening. The government and opposition MPs sitting on their benches facing each other across the chamber reminded him of trees full of parrots squawking at each other, a common sight back home in India. When he learned that the purpose of the noisy assemblage was to make laws, he was shocked. The English, he explained to his readers, had not accepted a divine law and so were reduced to the expedient of making their own laws, in accordance with the experience of their judges and the requirements of their time.

Later accounts were more positive. The first Egyptian student mission went to France in 1826. Their chaplain, a sheikh from al-Azhar, learned a great deal (probably more than his student wards) and wrote a remarkable book about Paris. In it he discusses the National Assembly and the freedom of the press, among other things, and makes the very astute observation that the French, when they speak of freedom, mean roughly what Muslims are getting at when they talk of justice. With this insight, he cuts right to the heart of a key difference between European political culture and its Islamic counterpart.

To Muslims, the use of "freedom" as a political term was an imported novelty, dating only from the time of the French Revolution and General Napoleon Bonaparte's arrival in Egypt in 1798. Before that, it had only legal and social connotations, and meant simply the condition of not being a slave. For Muslim thinkers, as the sheikh from al-Azhar implied, justice is the ideal, the touchstone by which one distinguishes good governments from bad.

By the latter part of the nineteenth century, Islamic rulers were coming to think of a constitution as something that no well-dressed nation could afford to be without. Just as gentlemen were abandoning traditional garb in favor of Western-style frock coats, neckties, and trousers, so the state would sport a constitution and an elected legislature as essential accoutrements.

Yet the idea of freedom—understood as the ability to participate in the formation, the conduct, and even the lawful removal and replacement of government—remained alien. This notion, which belongs to the inner logic of constitutionalism and parliamentarism, is obviously a troublesome one for dynastic autocracies, which can hardly accept it and remain what they are. The real question, then, was whether constitutions, elections, and parliaments—the institutional trappings of democracy—would be only that, or would actually become means that the governed could use to gain some say in their government.

The first serious elections in the Islamic world were held to choose the parliament called for by the Ottoman Constitution of 1876. This parliament was no doubt meant to be a tame body that would supply the ceremonial ratification of the sultan's authority. But the Chamber of Deputies soon developed a mind of its own. On 13 February 1878, the deputies went so far as to demand that three ministers, against whom specific charges had been brought, should appear in the Chamber to defend themselves. The next day, in response, the sultan dissolved the parliament and sent its members home. It did not meet again until the year after the Young Turk Revolution of 1908. That phase, too, was of brief duration, and a military coup ended the stormy interval of parliamentary rule.

Since then, parliamentarism has not fared especially well in the Islamic world. All too often, elections are less a way of choosing a government than a ritual designed to ratify and symbolize a choice that has already been made by other means—something like a presidential inauguration in the United States or a coronation in Britain. This is not always so—there are intervals and cases where elections mean something, and they become more common in the record as one goes from the nineteenth into the twentieth century, in spite of (or perhaps because of) a number of dramatic moves in the opposite direction.

A Rough Classification of Regimes

Another complication surrounding the term "freedom" is a legacy of imperialism. When outsiders ruled much, though not all, of the Islamic world, freedom came also, or even primarily, to mean communal or national independence, with no reference to the individual's status within the body politic.

Most of the countries in the Islamic world today are free from external domination, but not free internally: they have sovereignty, but lack democracy. This shared lack, however, does not preclude the existence of very great differences among them. Predominantly Muslim societies (Turkey, as we saw earlier, being the great exception) are ruled by a wide variety of authoritarian, autocratic, despotic, tyrannical, and totalitarian regimes. A rough classification would include five categories.

1) Traditional autocracies. These are the countries, like Saudi Arabia and the Gulf sheikhdoms, where established dynastic regimes rest on the traditional props of usage, custom, and history. These regimes are firmly authoritarian in character, but the same traditions that sustain them also bind them: their legitimacy relies heavily on acceptance, and too much open repression would shatter it. Their props are not quite what they used to be, however, having been partly undermined by new ideas and forces. The rulers use modern devices to help maintain themselves, but the same devices—especially electronic communications media—are now also available to those who would overthrow the existing order.

The Iranian Revolution, which overthrew the Shah in 1979, was the first electronic revolution in history. It will not be the last. Ayatollah Khomeini could do nothing while he was in Iran, and very little from nearby Iraq. But when he went to Paris and began recording cassette tapes and calling Iran via the direct-dial telephone system that the Shah had installed, he reached a vast audience, with results we know all too well. Satellite television, the fax machine, and electronic mail can all carry the message of subversion in ways difficult to prevent or control. The methods used by the Islamic revolutionaries against the Shah are now being used—in a more sophisticated form—by those who seek to overthrow the Islamic Republic. Other dissident groups—ethnic, religious, ideological—are using the same methods against the regimes that rule in their countries.

2) Modernizing autocracies. These are regimes—one thinks of Jordan, Egypt, and Morocco in particular—that have their roots in traditional autocracy but are taking significant steps toward modernization and democratization. None really fits the description of liberal democracy as given above, but none is anything like a total autocracy, either. All three are moving toward greater freedom. Difficulties, setbacks, and problems may abound, but the basic direction of change is clear.

3) Fascist-style dictatorships. These regimes, especially the one-party Ba'athist governments in Hafiz al-Assad's Syria and Saddam Hussein's Iraq, are modeled on European fascism. In matters of precept, practice, and style, they owe a great deal to the example of Benito Mussolini and, to a lesser extent, Adolf Hitler.

4) Radical Islamic regimes. There are two of these so far, Iran and Sudan. There may be others to follow, perhaps in Afghanistan or Algeria, though the latter possibility now seems to be dwindling rather than growing. Egypt has a potent radical Islamic movement, but the Egyptian political class also has a remarkable knack for maintaining itself in power. Moreover, the threat to the sovereign state posed by pan-Islamic radicalism has been greatly exaggerated. Khomeini used to say that there were no frontiers in Islam, but he also stipulated in the constitution that the president of the Islamic Republic of Iran must be of Iranian birth and origin. In Khomeini's own practice, let alone that of his successors, the Iranian element remained paramount. Elsewhere, there is a similar disinclination among even the most fanatical Islamic groups to sink their national or territorial integrity into some larger whole.

5) The Central Asian republics. A final group of countries, classifiable more by history and geography than by regime type, are the six former Soviet republics with mostly Muslim populations, sometimes known nowadays as "the five 'stans" plus Azerbaijan. I can venture no characterization of the regimes in these countries, but will only observe that they seem to be having the same problems disentangling themselves from their former imperial masters as the Egyptians, North Africans, Syrians, and Iraqis had with their respective former masters earlier in this century. After the formal recognition of independence comes the postimperial hangover, a period of interference, unequal treaties, privileges, basing agreements, and so on. The big difference this time, of course, is that the former colonial peoples are dealing not with London or Paris, but with Moscow. This may give rise to different results.

Muslims Outside the Middle East

There are also hundreds of millions of Muslims in South and Southeast Asia, but space limitations and my own relative ignorance of these lands lead me to offer only a brief and superficial impression of what is happening in them. Pakistan, Bangladesh, Malaysia, and Indonesia all appear to resemble Egypt or Morocco more than Syria or Iraq, which is encouraging. I say that the South Asian countries resemble the Middle Eastern or North African countries (and not vice versa) for a reason. There are almost as many Muslims in Indonesia, for example, as in the whole of the Arab world, but the lines of influence run from the latter to the former. The historical heartlands of Islam have hitherto enjoyed the kind of influence in the Islamic world that the outlying regions could rarely, if ever, achieve. With the overwhelming numerical preponderance of South and Southeast Asian Islam and the growing importance of the Islamic communities in the West, this may change.

Another relatively small group of Muslims who may matter a great deal are those adherents of Islam who have emigrated to non-Muslim countries in Western Europe and North America. These groups are extremely important, not so much because of what is happening in the countries of their present residence, as because of the impact that they have on their countries of origin. As Muslim minorities go, of course, they are a tiny handful. India's Muslim minority (equal to 11 percent of its total population) is by far the largest concentration of Muslims in a non-Muslim country. Indeed, only two other countries (Indonesia and Bangladesh) have more Muslims living within their borders. In the Middle East, there is a sizeable Muslim minority in Israel. Ethiopia, a Christian country whose church traces its origins to apostolic times, has a significant Muslim minority, and many other countries in sub-Saharan Africa have Muslim majorities or substantial minorities.

There are also old Muslim minorities in Europe, in the Balkan states, and above all in the Russian Federation itself, which may be as much as 15 percent Muslim.

Like Khomeini amid the Iranian-exile community in the 1970s, some of the political groups that move among the new Muslim communities in Europe and North America are seeking to recruit support for struggles against those in power at home. The separatist movement of Turkish Kurds, for instance, is highly active among the Kurdish population in Germany. The Islamic-fundamentalist movement in North Africa collects money, buys weapons, and organizes in France, and various movements are now using the United States in the same way.

The vast majority of Muslim immigrants in Western Europe and North America, it should be noted, has no interest in extremist or revolutionary movements. On the contrary, these immigrants are increasingly taking part (sometimes as citizens) in the democratic processes of their adopted societies while remaining in touch with their countries of origin. The views that they form as a result of their experience of democracy may well be among the most significant factors shaping the political future of the Islamic world.

Religion and the State

In Islam, as was mentioned above, there is from the beginning an interpenetration, almost an identification, of cult and power, or religion and the state: Mohammad was not only a prophet, but a ruler. In this respect, Islam resembles Old Testament Judaism and looks quite different from Christianity. Christianity, to repeat, began and endured for centuries under official persecution. Even after it became the state religion of Rome under the Emperor Constantine in the fourth century, a distinction was maintained between spiritual and temporal powers. Ever since then, all Christian states without exception have distinguished between throne and altar, church and state. The two powers might be closely associated, as under the caesaropapism of the Byzantine Empire, or they might be separated; they might work in harmony or they might come into conflict; one might dominate for a time and the other might displace it; but the duality remains, corresponding to the distinction in Christian Rome between *imperium* (imperial power) and *sacerdotium* (priestly power).

Islam in its classical form has no organizational equivalent. It has no clergy or clerical hierarchy in anything like the Christian sense of the word, and no ecclesiastical organization. The mosque is a building, not an institution in the sense that the church is. At least this was so until comparatively recently, for Khomeini during his rule seems to have effected a kind of "Christianization" of Iran's Islamic institutions, with himself as an infallible pope, and with the functional equivalent of a hierarchy of archbishops, bishops, and priests. All of this was totally alien to Islamic tradition, and thus constituted an "Islamic revolution" in a sense quite different from the one usually conveyed by references to Khomeini's legacy.

Islamic civilization has produced a wealth of theological, philosophical, and juridical literature on virtually every aspect of the state, its powers, and its functions. What is not discussed to any great extent is the difference between religious and temporal powers. The words for "secular" and "secularism" in modern Islamic languages are either loanwords or neologisms. There are still no equivalents for the words "layman" and "laity." Jurists and other Muslim writers on politics have long recognized a distinction between state and religion, between the affairs of this world and those of the next. But this in no way corresponds to the dichotomy expressed in such Western pairs of terms as "spiritual" and "temporal," or "lay" and "ecclesiastical." Conceptually, this dichotomy simply did not arise. It has arisen now, and it may be that Muslims, having contracted a Christian illness, will consider a Christian remedy, that is to say, the separation of religion and the state.

As a rule, gradual and unforced change is better than sudden and compulsory change. Democracy cannot be born like Aphrodite from the sea foam.

Of course, I am well aware that the Reformation was a stage in the evolution of Christendom and the Enlightenment a stage in the history of Europe, and I am not suggesting that the past of the West can somehow be grafted onto the future of Islam. There is no reason whatever why the Muslims can or should be expected to follow precisely the same pattern, by the same route. If they take up the challenge at all, they will have to tackle it in their own way. So far, alas, there is little sign that they are willing to take it up, but one may hope.

Turkey alone has formally enacted the separation of religion and the state. Its constitution and laws declare it a secular republic. In many practical respects, however, Islam remains an important and indeed a growing factor in the Turkish polity and in the Turks' sense of their own identity.

As a rule, gradual and unforced change is better than sudden and compulsory change. Democracy cannot be born like Aphrodite from the sea foam. It comes in slow stages; for that reason, places like Egypt and Jordan, where there is evolution in a broadly democratic direction, seem to offer the best prospects. In Iraq and Syria, an overthrow of the present dictators is unlikely to lead to the immediate establishment of a workable democracy. The next change of regime in those countries will probably just produce less-brutal dictatorships, which might then evolve into reforming autocracies in the Egyptian or Jordanian style.

That would not be democracy, but it would be a huge step forward nonetheless.

The places that offer the best prospects for democracy are those where there is a process of gradual change in the direction of freer institutions. Democracy usually evolves out of a movement toward freedom. The liberal democracies of the West certainly did not come about all at once. One need only think of the history of slavery in the United States or the disenfranchisement of women in most of the Western world to see that, even under favorable conditions, democratic progress takes time and effort and may be hard-won indeed.

Imperialist powers deprived most of the Islamic world of sovereignty; the prime demand, therefore, was for independence. Foreign rule was equated with tyranny, to be ended by whatever means possible. But tyranny means different things to different people. In the traditional Islamic system, the converse of tyranny is justice; in Western political thought, the converse of tyranny is freedom. At the present day, most Islamic countries are discovering that while they have gained independence, they enjoy neither justice nor freedom. There are some—and soon, perhaps, there will be many more—who see in democracy the surest way to attain both.

14

TWO VISIONS OF REFORMATION

Robin Wright

Robin Wright *is diplomatic correspondent for the* Washington Post *and former global-affairs correspondent for the* Los Angeles Times. *She is author of* The Last Great Revolution: Turmoil and Transformation in Iran *(2001),* In the Name of God: The Khomeini Decade *(1990), and* Sacred Rage: The Wrath of Militant Islam *(1985). This essay originally appeared in the April 1996 issue of the* Journal of Democracy.

Of all the challenges facing democracy in the 1990s, one of the greatest lies in the Islamic world. Only a handful of the more than four dozen predominantly Muslim countries have made significant strides toward establishing democratic systems. Among this handful—including Albania, Bangladesh, Jordan, Kyrgyzstan, Lebanon, Mali, Pakistan, and Turkey—not one has yet achieved full, stable, or secure democracy. And the largest single regional bloc holding out against the global trend toward political pluralism comprises the Muslim countries of the Middle East and North Africa.

Yet the resistance to political change associated with the Islamic bloc is not necessarily a function of the Muslim faith. Indeed, the evidence indicates quite the reverse. Rulers in some of the most antidemocratic regimes in the Islamic world—such as Brunei, Indonesia, Iraq, Oman, Qatar, Syria, and Turkmenistan—are secular autocrats who refuse to share power with their brethren.

Overall, the obstacles to political pluralism in Islamic countries are not unlike the problems earlier faced in other parts of the world: secular ideologies such as Ba'athism in Iraq and Syria, Pancasila in Indonesia, or lingering communism in some former Soviet Central Asian states brook no real opposition. Ironically, many of these ideologies were adapted from the West; Ba'athism, for instance, was inspired by the European socialism of the 1930s and 1940s. Rigid government controls over everything from communications in Saudi Arabia and Brunei to foreign visitors in Uzbekistan and Indonesia also isolate their people from democratic ideas and debate on popular empowerment. In the largest and poorest Muslim countries, moreover, problems common to developing states, from illiteracy and disease to poverty, make simple survival a priority and render democratic politics a seeming luxury. Finally, like their non-Muslim neighbors in Asia and Africa, most Muslim societies have no local history of democracy on which to draw. As democracy has blossomed in Western states over the past three centuries, Muslim societies have usually lived under colonial rulers, kings, or tribal and clan leaders.

In other words, neither Islam nor its culture is the major obstacle to political modernity, even if undemocratic rulers sometimes use Islam as their excuse.[1] In Saudi Arabia, for instance, the ruling House of Saud relied on Wahabism, a puritanical brand of Sunni Islam, first to unite the tribes of the Arabian Peninsula and then to justify dynastic rule. Like other monotheistic religions, Islam offers wide-ranging and sometimes contradictory instruction. In Saudi Arabia, Islam's tenets have been selectively shaped to sustain an authoritarian monarchy.

In Iran, the revolution that overthrew the Shah in 1979 put a new spin on Shi'ite traditions. The Iranian Shi'ite community had traditionally avoided direct participation by religious leaders in government as demeaning to spiritual authority. The upheaval led by Ayatollah Ruhollah Khomeini thus represented not only a revolution in Iran, but also a revolution within the Shi'ite branch of Islam. The constitution of the Islamic Republic, the first of its kind, created structures and positions unknown to Islam in the past.

Yet Islam, which acknowledges Judaism and Christianity as its forerunners in a single religious tradition of revelation-based monotheism, also preaches equality, justice, and human dignity—ideals that played a role in developments as diverse as the Christian Reformation of the sixteenth century, the American and French revolutions of the eighteenth century, and even the "liberation theology" of the twentieth century. Islam is not lacking in tenets and practices that are compatible with pluralism. Among these are the traditions of *ijtihad* (interpretation), *ijma* (consensus), and *shura* (consultation).

Diversity and Reform

Politicized Islam is not a monolith; its spectrum is broad. Only a few groups, such as the Wahabi in Saudi Arabia, are in fact fundamentalist. This term, coined in the early twentieth century to describe a movement among Protestant Christians in the United States, denotes passive adherence to a literal reading of sacred scripture. By contrast, many of today's Islamic movements are trying to adapt the tenets of the faith to changing times and circumstances. In their own way, some even resemble Catholic "liberation theology" movements in their attempts to use religious doctrines to transform temporal life in the modern world. The more accurate word for such Muslim groups is "Islamist." The term is growing in popularity in Western academic and policy-making circles, since it better allows for the forward-looking, interpretive, and often innovative stances that such groups assume as they seek to bring about a reconstruction of the social order.

The common denominator of most Islamist movements, then, is a desire for change. The quest for something different is manifested in a range of activities, from committing acts of violence to running for political office. Reactive groups—motivated by political or economic insecurity, questions of identity, or territorial disputes—are most visible because of their aggressiveness. Extremists have manipulated, misconstrued, and even hijacked Muslim tenets. Similar trends have emerged in religions other than Islam: the words "zealot" and "thug" were coined long ago to refer, respectively, to Jewish and Hindu extremists. Contemporary Islamic extremists have committed acts of terrorism as far afield as Buenos Aires, Paris, and New York, and they have threatened the lives of writers whom they regard as blasphemous from Britain to Bangladesh.

At the opposite end of the spectrum are proactive individuals and groups working for constructive change. In Egypt, Islamists have provided health-care and educational facilities as alternatives to expensive private outlets and inadequate government institutions. In Turkey, they have helped to build housing for the poor and have generally strengthened civil society. In Lebanon, they have established farm cooperatives and provided systematically for the welfare of children, widows, and the poor. In Jordan, Yemen, Kuwait, and elsewhere, they have run for parliament. The specific motives vary from religiously grounded altruism to creating political power bases by winning hearts and minds. But in diverse ways, they are trying to create alternatives to ideas and systems that they believe no longer work.

Less visible but arguably more important—to both Muslims and the world at large—is a growing group of Islamic reformers. While reactive and proactive groups address the immediate problems of Islam's diverse and disparate communities, the reformers are shaping thought about long-term issues. At the center of their reflections is the question of how to modernize and democratize political and economic systems in an Islamic context. The reformers' impact is not merely academic; by stimulating some of the most profound debate since Islam's emergence in the seventh century, they are laying the foundations for an Islamic Reformation.

The stirrings of reform within Islam today should not be compared too closely with the Christian Reformation of almost five hundred years ago. The historical and institutional differences between the two faiths are vast. Nonetheless, many of the issues ultimately addressed by the respective movements are similar, particularly the inherent rights of the individual and the relationship between religious and political authority.

The seeds of an Islamic Reformation were actually planted a century ago, but only among tiny circles of clerics and intellectuals whose ideas were never widely communicated to ordinary believers. At the end of the twentieth century, however, instant mass communications, improved education, and intercontinental movements of both people and ideas mean that tens of millions of Muslims are exposed to the debate. In the 1980s, interest in reform gained momentum as the secular ideologies that succeeded colonialism—mostly variants or hybrids of nationalism and socialism—failed to provide freedom and security to many people in the Muslim world. This sense of ferment has only grown more intense amid the global political upheaval of the post–Cold War world. Muslims now want political, economic, and social systems that better their lives, and in which they have some say.

The reformers contend that human understanding of Islam is flexible, and that Islam's tenets can be interpreted to accommodate and even encourage pluralism. They are actively challenging those who argue that Islam has a single, definitive essence that admits of no change in the face of time, space, or experience—and that democracy is therefore incompatible or alien. The central drama of reform is the attempt to reconcile Islam and modernity by creating a worldview that is compatible with both.[2]

Two Middle Eastern philosophers symbolize the diverse origins of Islamist reformers and the breadth of their thought. Abdul Karim Soroush is a Shi'ite Muslim and a Persian from Iran. He is a media-shy academic who has experienced almost a generation of life inside an Islamic republic. Sheikh Rachid al-Ghannouchi is a Sunni Muslim and a Tunisian Arab. He is the exiled leader of Hezb Al-Nahda (Party of the Renaissance), a movement intent on creating an Islamic republic in Tunisia. Over the past three years, Soroush and Ghannouchi have produced some of the most far-reaching work on the question of Islam and democracy.

Abdul Karim Soroush

Soroush supported Iran's 1979 revolution and took an active role in revising university curricula during its early years. Since then, however, he has articulated ideas that the regime considers highly controversial. Ranking officials such as Ayatollah Ali Khamenei, the successor to Ayatollah Khomeini, now Iran's Supreme Leader, have increasingly framed public remarks as implicit but unmistakeable responses to Soroush's articles and speeches. Some of Soroush's ideas amount to heresy in the regime's eyes, and the tenor of Khamenei's statements has become increasingly hostile. In a November 1995 address commemorating the 1979

U.S. Embassy takeover, Khamenei spent more time condemning Soroush's ideas than lambasting the United States or Israel.

The degree to which Soroush now frames the debate in Iran was revealed by two unusual events that took place in the autumn of 1995. At Tehran University, more than a hundred young members of Ansar (Helpers of the Party of God) physically attacked and injured Soroush as he attempted to give a special address that the Muslim Students' Association had invited him to deliver. Some among the two thousand students who had assembled to hear him were also injured. The attack then sparked a pro-Soroush demonstration on campus. A new law imposing severe penalties on anyone associating with critics and enemies of the Islamic Republic was widely thought to be aimed at undermining Soroush's growing support.

> *Soroush argues that there is no contradiction between Islam and the freedoms inherent in democracy.*

Educated in London and Tehran in both philosophy and the physical sciences, Soroush has recently taught at the Institute for Human Research and at Tehran University's School of Theology. His columns have been the centerpiece of *Kiyan* (a Farsi word that can mean "foundation" or "universe"), a bimonthly magazine founded in 1991 primarily to air his views and the debate that they have sparked. For years he also gave informal talks at Tehran mosques that were usually packed by followers ranging from young clerics to regime opponents, intellectuals, political independents, and government technocrats. But in the fall of 1995, the government banned him from giving public lectures or instruction and from publishing. He has been effectively forced from public view, and his academic career in Iran has been ended.

Soroush's writings on three subjects are particularly relevant. At the top of the list is democracy. Although Islam literally means "submission," Soroush argues that there is no contradiction between Islam and the freedoms inherent in democracy. "Islam and democracy are not only compatible, their association is inevitable. In a Muslim society, one without the other is not perfect," he said in one of several interviews in Tehran and Washington, D.C., in 1994 and 1995.

His advocacy of democracy for the Islamic world rests on two pillars. First, to be a true believer, one must be free. Belief attested under threat or coercion is not true belief. And if a believer freely submits, this does not mean that he has sacrificed freedom. He must also remain free to leave his faith. The only real contradiction is to be free in order to believe, and then afterward to abolish that freedom. This freedom is the basis of democracy. Soroush goes further: The beliefs and will of the majority must shape the ideal Islamic state. An Islamic democracy can-

Excerpts from Notes by Robin Wright on Lectures and Interviews Given by Abdul Karim Soroush, April–May 1995

Freedom of Faith: *In a democracy what you really want is freedom of faith. The other thing is this: justice is important. That is not the consequence of the rules of the shariʻa, but something that rules over the shariʻa. The third thing is this: There is no authority on matters religious. So you have to build a society in such a way as to accommodate these principles.*

Text and Context: *How do we reconcile the immutable principles of religion with the changing conditions of the world? The solution will be like this: We have to find something that is at the same time both changeable and immutable. And what is that?*

It is the revealed text itself. It is immutable and changeable at the same time. It has been revealed to the heart of the Prophet, and so it should be kept intact and nobody is permitted to tamper with it. At the same time, there is the interpretation of the text. That is changeable. No interpretation is without presuppositions. These presuppositions are changeable since the whole knowledge of mankind is in flux. It is age-bound, if you like.

Now, the knowledge of the age is always in flux. At the end of history—and I am not sure we are at the end of history, as some American philosophers suggest—we can know which knowledge is immutable and which not. But not now.

This is how I express the situation: The text is silent. We have to hear its voice. In order to hear, we need presuppositions. In order to have presuppositions, we need the knowledge of the age. In order to have the knowledge of the age, we have to surrender to change. So we have here the miraculous entity that is changing but at the same time is immutable.

Religion and Reason: *The ancient world was based on a single source of information: religion. The modern world has more than once source: reason, experience, science, logic. Modernism was a successful attempt to free mankind from the dictatorship of religion. Postmodernism is a revolt against modernism—and against the dictatorship of reason. In the age of postmodernism, reason is humbler and religion has become more acceptable. To me, the reconciliation between the two has become potentially more visible.*

not be imposed from the top; it is only legitimate if it has been chosen by the majority, including nonbelievers as well as believers.

Second, says Soroush, our understanding of religion is evolving. Sacred texts do not change, but interpretation of them is always in flux because understanding is influenced by the age and the changing conditions in which believers live. So no interpretation is absolute or fixed for all time and all places. Furthermore, everyone is entitled to his or her own understanding. No one group of people, including the clergy, has the exclusive right to interpret or reinterpret tenets of the faith. Some understandings may be more learned than others, but no version is automatically more authoritative than another.

Islam is also a religion that can still grow, Soroush argues. It should not be used as a modern ideology, for it is too likely to become totalitarian. Yet he believes in *shari'a,* or Islamic law, as a basis for modern legislation. And *shari'a,* too, can grow. "*Shari'a* is something expandable. You cannot imagine the extent of its flexibility," he has said, adding that "in an Islamic democracy, you can actualize all its potential flexibilities."

The next broad subject that Soroush addresses is the clergy. The rights of the clergy are no greater than the privileges of anyone else, he argues. Thus in the ideal Islamic democracy, the clergy also have no *a priori* right to rule. The state should be run by whoever is popularly elected on the basis of equal rights under law.

Soroush advocates an even more fundamental change in the relationship between religion and both the people and the state. Religious leaders have traditionally received financial support from either the state (in most Sunni countries) or the people (in Shi'ite communities). In both cases, Soroush argues, the clergy should be "freed" so that they are not "captives" forced to propagate official or popular views rather than the faith of the Koran.

A religious calling is only for authentic lovers of religion and those who will work for it, Soroush says. No one should be able to be guaranteed a living, gain social status, or claim political power on the basis of religion. Clerics should work like everyone else, he says, making independent incomes through scholarship, teaching, or other jobs. Only such independence can prevent them—and Islam—from becoming compromised.

Finally, Soroush deals with the subject of secularism. Arabic, the language of Islam, does not have a literal translation for this word. But the nineteenth-century Arabic word *elmaniyya*—meaning "that which is rational or scientific"—comes close. In this context, Soroush views secularism not as the enemy or rival of religion, but as its complement: "It means to look at things scientifically and behave scientifically—which has nothing to do with hostility to religion. Secularism is nothing more than that."

Modernism, according to Soroush, represented a successful attempt to challenge the "dictatorship of religion" by increasing the emphasis placed upon unaided reason in the conduct of human affairs. He maintains that the tension between reason and religion since the sixteenth century has been "welcome and beneficial for both" and has opened the way for an eventual *postmodern* reconciliation between the two.

Soroush's thought has wide-ranging implications. His work often echoes themes that lay behind the Christian Reformation. He shows how to empower Muslims by establishing a role for the individual—as a believer and as a citizen. Soroush refines, even downgrades, the role of the clergy—a particularly sensitive topic in Iran, for Shi'ite Islam stresses the doctrinal and interpretive authority of clerics far more than does Sunni Islam. Soroush also redefines, and to some degree separates, the relative roles and powers of the mosque—religious jurisprudence—and the state. The adoption of his ideas would signify a stunning shift for the only major monotheistic religion that provides a highly specific set of rules by which to govern society as well as a set of spiritual beliefs.

In a spirit similar to the one that characterized the Christian Reformation, he argues against rigid thinking and elitism. Soroush is a believing Muslim and has no wish to abandon the values of his faith; rather, he wants to convince his fellow Muslims of the need to face modernity with what he calls a spirit of "active accommodation . . . imbued or informed with criticism." By pointing the way to innovative interpretations of the Koran and the *shari'a,* he provides a foundation for a pluralist and tolerant society.

Rachid al-Ghannouchi

While Soroush prefers the cosmic overview, Rachid al-Ghannouchi's thinking is rooted in his experiences in Tunisia, and then applied to other Muslim societies. He has also been heavily influenced by Third World nationalism and the views of intellectuals from the global South who see their region as locked in a struggle against Northern "neocolonialism." A popular philosophy teacher and speaker educated in Damascus and Paris, Ghannouchi founded the Mouvement de la Tendance Islamique (MTI) in 1981 during a brief interlude of Tunisian political liberalization. Tunisia's government refused to legalize the MTI, however, citing laws that excluded religious parties from politics. Ghannouchi persisted in calls on the regime to share power by introducing political pluralism and economic justice. He was jailed from 1981 to 1984; after his release, the authorities forbade him to teach, speak in public, publish, or travel.

In 1987, Ghannouchi was again arrested and charged with plotting to overthrow the government. He was released after a bloodless coup in November 1987, which led to another brief political thaw. The MTI,

Excerpts from a Lecture by Sheikh Rachid al-Ghannouchi
Chatham House, London, 9 May 1995

The Koran acknowledges the fact that conflict and competition are natural features of development and of the balance of power within each individual, within each society, and at the global level. However, while the Koran calls for jihad *as well as the use of peaceful means to establish justice and equality, it condemns aggression and oppression and warns against falling captive to selfishness and lust. Furthermore, the Koran recognizes the legitimate right of an oppressed to resist and even fight in order to deter oppression, but it warns against the perpetration of injustice.*

Koranic teachings encourage humans to seek justice and to cooperate . . . in serving the interests of humanity, which is perceived as a single family that . . . is created by One Creator. . . . Thus Islam recognizes as a fact of life the diversity and pluralism of peoples and cultures, and calls for mutual recognition and co-existence. . . .

Contrary to the claims of Huntington and his colonial ancestors, such differences do not justify war but provide a good ground for richness, plurality, and cooperation through complementarity rather than incongruity. . . . [D]iversity is a challenge that provokes and awakens the powers of creation and innovation in nations, ridding them of laziness and flaccidity. . . .

While on the one hand Islam guarantees the right of its adherents to ijtihad *in interpreting the Koranic text, it does not recognize a church or an institution or a person as a sole authority speaking in its name or claiming to represent it. Decision making, through the process of* shura, *belongs to the community as a whole. Thus the democratic values of political pluralism and tolerance are perfectly compatible with Islam.*

Outside its own society, Islam recognizes civilizational and religious pluralism and opposes the use of force to transfer a civilization or impose a religion. It condemns the use of religion for material or hegemonic purposes. . . .

Once the Islamists are given a chance to comprehend the values of Western modernity, such as democracy and human rights, they will search within Islam for a place . . . [to] implant them, nurse them, and cherish them just as the Westerners did before, when they implanted such values in a much less fertile soil.

renamed Al-Nahda in early 1989 to remove religious overtones, was promised a place at the political table. But by the time of the April 1989 legislative elections, the thaw was over. Reforms were stalled and confrontations mounted. Ghannouchi went into voluntary exile. The government charged Al-Nahda with plotting a coup; the party was outlawed and Ghannouchi was sentenced *in absentia* to life imprisonment. Britain granted him political asylum in 1993, and he is now the most prominent Islamist leader living in the West.

Ghannouchi is controversial. In speeches and interviews, he often declares himself to be "against fundamentalism that believes it is the only truth and must be imposed on all others," yet he has visited Tehran, has traveled briefly on a Sudanese passport when he went into exile, and has condemned Zionism and Westernization. His 1993 book *Civil Liberties in the Islamic State* is dedicated to dozens of people, including "the forerunners of Islamic liberalism in the women's movement" and prisoners of conscience of every creed. But it is also dedicated to an imprisoned Hamas leader, to the late Ayatollah Khomeini, and to Malcolm X.

Of all the major Islamist leaders, however, Ghannouchi seems to have expanded his thinking the most in recent years. In Tunisia, his understanding of democracy was a matter of theory only. He used to say that, as an Islamist, he was not afraid of ideas and wanted a free dialogue with believers in different faiths and political systems. Since the beginning of his exile in 1989, he has traveled in Europe and the United States, come into contact with a wide range of policy makers and opinion leaders, and experienced the workings of different democratic systems firsthand. His years of exile have tempered some of the well-worn jingo common in Islamist parlance. Although the field of comparison is small, Ghannouchi now ranks among Islamism's most accessible and mature thinkers on the issue of democracy. Whatever happens in Tunisia or to Al-Nahda, his contributions will remain important to Islamic thought.

Ghannouchi advocates an Islamic system that features majority rule, free elections, a free press, protection of minorities, equality of all secular and religious parties, and full women's rights in everything from polling booths, dress codes, and divorce courts to the top job at the presidential palace. Islam's role is to provide the system with moral values.

Islamic democracy is first the product of scriptural interpretation. "Islam did not come with a specific program concerning our life," Ghannouchi said in one of several interviews between 1990 and 1995. "It brought general principles. It is our duty to formulate this program through interaction between Islamic principles and modernity." Believers are guaranteed the right of *ijtihad* in interpreting the Koranic text. Their empowerment is complete since Islam does not have an institution or person as a sole authority to represent the faith—or contradict their interpretations. The process of *shura,* moreover, means that decision making belongs to the community as a whole. "The democratic values of political pluralism and tolerance are perfectly compatible with Islam," he maintains.

Second, Islamic democracy is also a product of recent human experience. The legitimacy of contemporary Muslim states is based on liberation from modern European colonialism, a liberation in which religious and secular, Muslim and Christian, participated together. "There is no room to make distinctions between citizens, and complete equality is the base of any new Muslim society. The only legitimacy is the legitimacy of elections," he said. "Freedom comes before Islam and is the step leading to Islam."

Ghannouchi concedes that Islam's record in the areas of equality and participation has blemishes. Previous Muslim societies were built on conquest. But he contends that the faith has also traditionally recognized pluralism internally, noting the lack of religious wars among Muslims as proof of Islam's accommodation of the Muslim world's wide diversity. Citing the Koran, he explains that Islam condemns the use of religion for material or hegemonic purposes: "O mankind! We created you from a single [pair] of a male and a female, and made you into nations and tribes, that ye may know each other, not that ye may despise [each other]" (Sura 49:13).

Ghannouchi calls the act of striking a balance between holy texts and human reality *aqlanah,* which translates as "realism" or "logical reasoning." *Aqlanah* is dynamic and constantly evolving. As a result Ghannouchi, like Soroush, believes that Islam and democracy are an inevitable mix. In a wide-ranging address given in May 1995 at the Royal Institute of International Affairs in London, he said: "Once the Islamists are given a chance to comprehend the values of Western modernity, such as democracy and human rights, they will search within Islam for a place for these values where they will implant them, nurse them, and cherish them just as the Westerners did before, when they implanted such values in a much less fertile soil." He pledged Al-Nahda's adherence to democracy and the alternation of power through the ballot box, and called on all other Islamist movements to follow suit in unequivocal language and even in formal pacts signed with other parties.

Ghannouchi's acceptance of pluralism is not limited to the Islamic world. Responding to Samuel P. Huntington's widely discussed essay on the "clash of civilizations,"[3] Ghannouchi contends that cultural or religious differences do not justify conflict, but instead can provide ground for cooperation rooted in a mutual recognition of complementarity. "We appeal for and work to establish dialogue between Islam and the West, for the world now is but a small village and there is no reason to deny the other's existence. Otherwise we are all doomed to annihilation and the destruction of the world," he said in a 1994 interview.[4] In his 1995 London address, he added: "Islam recognizes as a fact of life the diversity and pluralism of peoples and cultures, and calls for mutual recognition and coexistence. . . . Outside its own society, Islam recognizes civilizational and religious pluralism and opposes the use of force to transfer a civilization or impose a religion."

A Long Way To Go

Christianity's Reformation took at least two centuries to work itself out. The Islamic Reformation is probably only somewhere in early midcourse. And the two movements offer only the roughest of parallels. The Christian Reformation, for example, was launched in reaction to the papacy and specific practices of the Catholic Church. In contrast, Islam has no central authority; even the chief ayatollah in the Islamic Republic of Iran is the supreme religious authority in one country only.

But the motives and goals of both reformations are similar. The Islamic reformers want to strip the faith of corrupt, irrelevant, or unjust practices that have been tacked on over the centuries. They are looking to make the faith relevant to changing times and conditions. They want to make the faith more accessible to the faithful, so that believers utilize the faith rather than have it used against them. And they want to draw on Islam as both a justification and a tool for political, social, and economic empowerment.

The Islamic reformist movement has a very long way to go. Although there are a handful of others besides Soroush and Ghannouchi making serious or original contributions to the debate, they still represent a distinct minority. The changes that they seek to promote will experience bumps, false starts, and failures, and may take a long time. Yet the Islamic Reformation represents the best hope for reconciliation both within Islam and between Islam and the outside world.

NOTES

1. Olivier Roy, *The Failure of Political Islam,* Carol Volk, trans. (Cambridge: Harvard University Press, 1994), esp. 1–27.

2. See John Voll, *Islam: Continuity and Change in the Modern World* (Syracuse: Syracuse University Press, 1995).

3. Samuel P. Huntington, "The Clash of Civilizations?" *Foreign Affairs* 72 (Summer 1993): 22–49.

4. "Dr. Rachid Gannouchi: Tunisia's Islamists Are Different from Those in Algeria," interview by Zainab Farran in *Ash-Shiraa* (Beirut), October 1994, 28–32.

15

THE CHALLENGE OF SECULARIZATION

Abdou Filali-Ansary

Abdou Filali-Ansary *is cofounder and former editor of the Moroccan quarterly* Prologues: revue maghrébine du livre, *a French-Arabic journal of philosophy, literature, and the social sciences based in Casablanca. He is author of* Réformer l'Islam? Une introduction aux débats contemporains *(2003). The present essay originally appeared in the April 1996 issue of the* Journal of Democracy.

Robin Wright and Bernard Lewis both seem to address the question of whether there is an "Islamic Reformation" going on now, and if there is, what content, direction, and influence it is likely to have. The raising of this question betokens an important shift in the way that Western observers view the Islamic world. Wright and Lewis implicitly acknowledge that behind the confrontations and violence that we witness today in many Muslim societies, there lies a situation marked by some kind of pluralism and opposition of ideas. In other words, there is not merely a fight, but a debate. To recognize this is already to take a giant step away from the familiar Western academic and journalistic stereotypes of Muslim societies as places overwhelmed by religious fanaticism, rejection of "the other," and crises of identity.

The dramatic importance of the question under discussion should need no emphasis: Islam, one of the major world religions, may be living through a turning point in its history, one that will bring it face-to-face with the challenges of the human condition at the beginning of the twenty-first century.

Bernard Lewis proceeds according to his well-known "macrohistorical" approach. He casts his gaze across large spans of history, constitutive elements of Islamic faith, and some features of Middle Eastern languages in order to construct a grand schema that explains what is happening now and illuminates its links with the mainstream of Islamic (and also Middle Eastern) history. He draws on a larger arsenal of disciplines (history, theology, linguistics) than does Wright, and discusses a greater variety of subjects (religious beliefs, historical facts, linguistic usages and concepts) in order to create a highly seductive synthesis of his own.

While Lewis acknowledges that the term "Islam" can be confusing, he himself is not always sufficiently careful in his use of it. He goes back and forth from Islam as a religion to Islam as a historical civilization, from detailed observations to general remarks. He seems to be guided by the "inner logics" that he sees lurking behind the observed data, molding attitudes, behaviors, and ways of understanding. His conclusions about the present situation point to a clash of such logics, one that pits Muslim communities against their Western counterparts. These inner logics are what he considers to be the true core of observed reality; facts, which appear on the surface, manifest the core imperfectly, much as the shadows that flicker on the wall of Plato's cave provide only a crude representation of the realities that give them shape.

Robin Wright, in contrast, adopts an approach at loggerheads with the one prevailing in specialized academic circles. She prefers to try to understand the debate by "listening" to two of its key participants: Iranian philosopher Abdul Karim Soroush and Tunisian political leader Sheikh Rachid al-Ghannouchi. Wright assumes that ideas, not conscious or unconscious determinisms, rule human societies, which simply cannot be understood through external observation or historical reconstruction alone. This, it would seem, is why she has chosen, among living Muslim thinkers, to discuss two prominent and highly controversial figures, each of whom is thought to exert a large (and in all likelihood growing) influence on thoughtful people in the Muslim world.

Strange Companions

This approach, much simpler than Lewis's and apparently without major risks, nonetheless raises a troubling question: How and why did Wright choose her two subjects? In posing this question I intend much more than the usual perfunctory observation, to be completed by remarks about the complexity of the situation, the availability of a large set of potential subjects, and the unavoidable arbitrariness of choice. In no way can one say that the two thinkers presented are minor, ordinary, or random specimens of contemporary Islamic thought. Indeed, they are generally considered to represent something close to opposite extremes on a spectrum: Ghannouchi is a main representative of Islamist attitudes and thought (and faces persecution from his government for that); Soroush is a formidable intellectual opponent of Islamism (for which he, too, faces persecution from his government). These considerations are by no means peripheral; they must be taken into account in any analysis that groups these two men together as workers in a single project. In fact, Wright's surprising decision to group them together is not devoid of logic, but it is a logic that she does not elaborate.

In what way can we consider *both* Ghannouchi and Soroush—the Islamist and the critic of Islamism—to be representatives of an ongoing "Islamic Reformation"? Is the opposition between the tendencies that they represent merely apparent, or do we face two opposite ways of reforming Islam?

Soroush wants to make the followers of Islam more inwardly Muslim by enabling them to adopt a piety based on free adherence and personal commitment rather than custom, habit, and conformism.

It should be observed beforehand that many controversies surrounding Islamic thought focus so heavily on semantics, on names for ideas and persons, that the real issues often disappear from sight. Many thinkers who are called or who call themselves "Islamists" make such large concessions to the power of unaided human reason that one may wonder what is left to render their thought Islamic. On the other hand, many secularists, especially nationalists, pay such reverence to Islamic dogmas that one may wonder if reason has any role left to play in their thought. The whole confrontation sometimes seems like so much posturing, where the real choices are never clarified or faced.

Does this apply to Soroush and Ghannouchi? Both, it is true, seem to accept Islam as a point of reference and to concentrate their efforts in an attempt, as Wright says, "to reconcile Islam and modernity by creating a worldview that is compatible with both." There is, however, an important difference masked by their apparent allegiance to the same flag. For Ghannouchi, the principal question is always how to free the community from backwardness and dependence on "the other." However significant his concessions in favor of democracy and freedom of thought, the community—not the individual—remains for him the ultimate reality and objective. Democracy and freedom of thought are instruments that Muslims should use to achieve their community's goals and defend its interests. They are tools for raising the community of Muslims to the level of power and efficiency that Western nations currently enjoy. Muslims can use these tools, argues Ghannouchi, because they work and because they are not opposed to Islamic principles, which remain the ultimate standard.

Soroush is not interested in showing Muslims how to achieve a more advantageous competitive position in the struggle with "the other." For him, the main adversary dwells within Muslims themselves, or rather within a complex of traditions that has long barred Muslims from the free implementation of reason and from direct contact with the sources of their faith. The urgent task is therefore to free Muslims from Islam understood as a social and historical heritage, as a set of overwhelming external conventions defining views and behavior, or, to use Henri

Bergson's expression, as a "closed religion."[1] Soroush wants to make followers of Islam more inwardly Muslim by enabling them to adopt a piety based on free adherence and personal commitment rather than custom, habit, and conformism. He argues further that this turn toward Islam understood as an "open religion" represents not a radical innovation, but rather a return to the original essence of the faith in its purity. For him, the basic reality and objective is the person, the individual believer. In this, Soroush is closer to modern humanism and is a true reformer. Ghannouchi, by contrast, is not.

Responses to Secularization

Taken together, Soroush and Ghannouchi illustrate the broad alternatives offered by the situation in which Muslim societies now find themselves as they face the inescapable challenges of secularization in the modern world. It should be stressed that secularization is a comparatively recent phenomenon. It began in Western Europe and has spread throughout the world. Its pace and exact form have varied a great deal from place to place, depending on a host of political, sociological, economic, and other variables. The world's religions have adopted varying responses to it, usually featuring some mixture of adaptation and self-defense designed to meet the new conditions. In short, societies have shown different ways of responding to the secularizing tendency.

Muslim societies have not experienced secularization as an internal or autonomous move. (Some scholars believe that such a move did begin within Islamic societies in the eighteenth century, but was never allowed to unfold autonomously.) External influences either started the secularization process or disrupted it (another point on which historians disagree). But secularization is already a reality in the Muslim world. No Muslim society today is governed solely with reference to religious law; religious traditions no longer possess absolute or near-absolute predominance (except perhaps in some remote rural areas); and newly emerging leadership classes are almost everywhere displacing or marginalizing the clerisy of theologico-legal experts who used to control meaning and organization in these societies. Yet even while all this has been happening, Islamic reformation has not yet been accomplished. In the Muslim world, secularization is preceding religious reformation— a reversal of the European experience in which secularization was more or less a consequence of such reformation.

Wright's examination of Soroush and Ghannouchi offers us excellent examples of the responses that this evolution has elicited. These responses point in two opposite directions. There are voices, like Ghannouchi's, calling for a return to the "implicit constitution"[2] that Islam is supposed to have provided (and which may not be opposed to democracy, or may even find in it a good expression of some of Islam's requirements). These are typically calls to resist "Westernization" and to return to the original (and never fully implemented) Islamic constitution via a course of general reform that usually involves the moralization of public affairs and of political and social relationships. Appeals like these are reminiscent of the "natural and cyclical reflex" to seek a purified and more forceful version of Islam that the fourteenth-century Arab historian Ibn Khaldun observed in Muslim societies whenever rulers exceeded the limits of the tolerable. For all their sincerity and effectiveness in terms of influence on the masses, such appeals grow out of attitudes that are trapped in the past. They can in no way lead to a real democratization of society.

By refusing to make religion the only means of reforming society, the other and opposed response tries to free Muslims from the "Khaldunian" cycle of rigorous reform enforced by an energetic outgroup, followed by the corruption and enervation of the reformers. This view recommends the reform of religious feeling and belief as the best means of making men free and responsible, and of placing them on the surest path to ordered and enduring liberty.

Soroush surely belongs to what Wright describes as "a growing group of Islamic reformers" who "are shaping thought about long-term issues," and whom she contrasts to "reactive and proactive groups [that] address the immediate problems of Islam's diverse and disparate communities." Ghannouchi, clearly, belongs with these latter groups. If we adopt the comparison with what happened in Christendom, the dividing line between Soroush and Ghannouchi is more or less equivalent to the one that separated the Reformation from the Counterreformation.

NOTES

1. Henri Bergson, *The Two Sources of Morality and Religion,* trans. R. Ashley Audra (Notre Dame: University of Notre Dame Press, 1977; orig. publ. 1932).

2. See Ernest Gellner's comments on Islam as an "entrenched constitution" in his *Postmodernism, Reason, and Religion* (London: Routledge, 1992), 12, 16.

16

THE SOURCES OF ENLIGHTENED MUSLIM THOUGHT

Abdou Filali-Ansary

Abdou Filali-Ansary *is cofounder and former editor of the Moroccan quarterly* Prologues: revue maghrébine du livre, *a French-Arabic journal of philosophy, literature, and the social sciences based in Casablanca. He is author of* Réformer l'Islam? Une introduction aux débats contemporains *(2003). The present essay originally appeared in the April 2003 issue of the* Journal of Democracy.

To begin, how appropriate is the term "liberal Islam" for the current of thought to which we are referring? There has in fact been a great deal of general hesitation on this question. To mention but a few of the alternatives proposed lately, there are: "reformed Islam," "modern Islam," "protestant Islam," "positive Islam," "the Islam of modernity," "enlightened Islam," and on they go. But "liberal Islam" is the one that seems to be the most widely accepted nowadays.

How adequate is it? "Liberal" in the strict political sense, is the opposite of "totalitarian" or "authoritarian" and, as an adjective, refers in principle to an ideology or set of overlapping ideologies. Applying it to a world religion presupposes the assimilation of that religion to a common framework with a secular ideology. Is this semantically adequate, intellectually accurate, or morally appropriate? There are grounds for skepticism on all three counts. Can we consider a world religion as being commensurable with an ideology? If so, are we aware of all the assumptions we make in doing so and the consequences that they entail? World religions have been with us for centuries, having shaped common understandings for many generations. Indeed, the ethical views that prevail in our societies are directly linked to the teachings of these religions, even if many around us no longer accept religious traditions as vessels of the truth. Modern ideologies, on the other hand, have tended to be either short-lived frameworks for political action or conceptual platforms that remain objects of debate and, so, subject to constant redefinition.

The second word in the expression "liberal Islam" raises another series of concerns. "Islam" has been in use, among Muslims and non-Muslims, to refer to many different conceptions and phenomena at once. It is used—and this is important to note—to designate both the equivalent of what Christians call "Christianity" *and* that of what they call "Christendom." On the one hand, there are the beliefs, rites, and narratives associated with religion; and, on the other, there are the events and facts—including the various "layers" of interpretation proposed down through the generations—associated with its history. The use of the same term for these two sets of "objects" has led to a habitual blurring of any categorical distinction between them (broadly put, the distinction between "religion" and "history"), often implicitly or at best half-consciously, leaving people little aware of the intellectual consequences involved. It thus creates misunderstandings between interlocutors and imprints a stamp of confusion on most debates. Marshall G.S. Hodgson, in his highly influential book *The Venture of Islam,*[1] coined the terms *Islamdom* and *Islamicate* in order duly to distinguish these objects from Islam itself.[2]

The problem is not, again, merely one of semantics or formal linguistic accuracy. It is a source of major confusions that, as we can see around us every day, lead many people to conflate norms and facts, and to combine beliefs and historical phenomena, in trite and damaging ways. Among those usually called "fundamentalists," it has become common to raise historical contingencies about Islam to the status of authoritatively normative models. Among social scientists, meanwhile, it has become almost as common to attempt to explain contemporary phenomena by recourse to religious precepts. An "ethos" specific to Muslims is often invoked as the "real" or "underlying" or "inside" explanation for this or that action or event, even where local and contingent causes (political, economic, or social) are clearly at work. There is today a widespread, almost Platonic, assumption of essentialism when it comes to Islam, which in turn reinforces the confusions created by its multiple and overlapping meanings.

The choice of terms here can have surprisingly far-reaching effects. For example, the very expression "liberal Islam" would, within Muslim societies, greatly handicap the acceptance of the very trends and approaches to which the phrase is meant to refer. "Liberal Islam" seems to set up a new strain of "Islam" alongside the existing ones—introducing new divisions or creating new partisan attitudes—and links it to what are perceived, accurately enough, as largely secular attitudes, Western in origin. The values associated with liberalism in Europe and North America are not expressed in the same terms as the religious and cultural values traditionally held by Muslims. Here, one thinks of the observation by Rifaa Tahtawi, a Muslim intellectual who traveled to Europe in the nineteenth century, that what Europeans called "liberty" referred to what Muslims called "justice." The use of the adjective "liberal" would not convey to Muslim publics the same positive connotation that it has in English and other European languages.

All right then, one might ask, what alternative do we have? Should we choose among the other proposed labels? Most of them, as mentioned earlier, use the name of Islam in a way that conflates religion and history, norm and fact. But there may be a salubrious alternative in the expression "enlightened Muslim thought." This phrase seems to convey an appropriate description of the turn that is now happening around us, since "enlightenment" points to the ideas of understanding and of openness to a tradition of critical thinking that is shared by European and Middle Eastern societies.

The Challenge of Modernity

The call for a "liberalization" or reformation of Islam has been heard regularly for more than a century. And among Muslims, the need for radical reform has been deeply felt since the eighteenth century. The term initially proposed by Muslim thinkers and political leaders was *Islah,* which means redress or reform.[3] Initially, and until the 1920s, it referred to the need for redressing the then-current state of affairs among Muslims, an idea that had more to do with curing social ills or reforming society than with reformulating religious dogmas. What it meant was reform of the popular *religiosity* and its related social behaviors, not the reexamination of orthodox *religious beliefs* by the protectors of orthodoxy. These protectors continued to hold their beliefs to be valid for all eternity and beyond the ambit of human criticism. In these views, a premodern idea of absolute truth prevailed, one taken to be fully transparent to the human mind. Any ills, dysfunctions, or negative tendencies in human life were considered matters of human frailty, ultimately traceable to ignorance, misunderstanding, or vice. Problems were never linked to the ways in which religious views were transmitted to and received in public consciousness. In other words, the reformist movement of the nineteenth and early-twentieth centuries never broached the question of the *historicity* of the established orthodoxy. This attitude still remains predominant among Muslims and within their societies, where the dominant conceptions of truth are linked to a premodern epistemology in which the external world is understood to be directly and passively accessible to the human mind.

Today, many Muslim scholars, who are in a way the heirs of the reformists, feel the need to fight this naïve and untenable attitude by stressing the inherent relativity of human interpretations. Thus is born the divide between fundamentalism or Islamism on the one hand (which is not so much literalist as it is simply premodern in an epistemological sense), and on the other hand those scholars (some of whom may be called modern and others of whom lean toward traditionalism) who agree on the intrinsic limitations of the human mind, the inaccessibility of absolute truth, and the need for more historically accurate readings of textual traditions. The reform or liberalization of Islam, even if called for from within different currents of thought, does not have the same meaning for these groups—traditionalists, fundamentalists, and modernists—since they are embedded in different epistemological views.

The call for reform and liberalization comes also, and insistently, from outside Muslim societies. It has seemingly taken the place of the assertions of Islamic backwardness that used to be widely heard in European intellectual and political circles in the nineteenth and early-twentieth centuries. Many non-Muslim scholars, journalists, and political leaders proclaim the need for the *aggiornamento* (updating), reform, or modernization (again, the exact terms vary) of Islam. The most striking thing about these calls is the dominant influence on them of a model drawn from Christian history, that of the Protestant Reformation. This model is taken to represent a turn in the history of Western religious communities during which views once held to be orthodox were thrown out and replaced by new ones more appropriate to the spirit of the time. Reformation necessarily meant revolution, with traditional religious doctrines being discarded and novel ones adopted. The model envisions a break or rupture that occurs at a particular moment and is propagated within the community at large. And this break is, in turn, a kind of "big bang" that leads to profound changes in prevailing attitudes. Such is clearly indicated by the numerous calls for the emergence (or appointment) of a "Muslim Luther" or the convening of a "Muslim Vatican II," to mention the religious event with which the term *aggiornamento* is most famously associated.

The truth of the matter is that there has been a great effervescence of thought among Muslim intellectuals since the late nineteenth century. One cannot help but be struck by the breadth, intensity, and sustained character of the debates that have been going on within the Muslim world for over a hundred years, a phenomenon for which there is no contemporary equivalent in any other religious or cultural community. One has to go back to sixteenth-century Western Europe—the age of the Reformation and its attendant wars of religion—in order to find a phenomenon of comparable nature and intensity. In the history of Muslims, one would have to go back to the Great Discord *(Fitna Kubra)* that followed the assassination in 656 C.E. of Uthman ibn Affan, the third caliph, in order to find such intense debates on basic issues.[4]

Since the nineteenth century, the main questions have been: How should Muslims face the challenges of modernity? What role should traditions play in the social and political order? And in what ways should ethical principles be conveyed and religious traditions implemented under contemporary conditions?

The quality and diversity of the answers that these questions have elicited vary so widely that it seems almost impossible to subject them to any kind of orderly or accurate classification. Some observers, such as Ernest Gellner, have gone back to Ibn Khaldun (1332–95) and tried to adapt his theory of historical cycles to contemporary phenomena.[5] Muslim societies, says Gellner, display a pattern in which moments of tension and the search for purification alternate with moments of relaxation and moral "realism." Contemporary calls for return to the pure forms of the faith and the strict implementation of all prescriptions show that we are now in a "tense" Gellnerian moment, while a "relaxed" moment tends to be characterized by fascination with Western, secular, modern forms of social and political life. The tokens of secularism and modernity have come to replace such traditional signs of "relaxation" as immorality or the lack of will—accounting for why the main opposition is now between fundamentalism and Western-inspired secularism. As Gellner correctly argues, what reshaped the cycle was modern mass education, which in widening access to the written cultural traditions, ended up strengthening the hand of fundamentalism. For the policies upon which this education was implemented were such that, instead of opening minds to critical inquiry and rational approaches, they favored a return to premodern views and attitudes. In this neo-Khaldunian view, the chances of a liberal, secularized Islam are, therefore, very limited. And, indeed, taking Ibn Khaldun's theory as a starting point is a path to reestablishing classical essentialism; it is another way of asserting that Islam always leads to similar patterns of behavior, as it did in the past, and as it must do in the present.

Similar classifications are normal in contemporary literature. Their common feature is to view contemporary debates among Muslims as a continuation of old confrontations, and to consider present-day realities as being determined by a remote history, on the assumption that earlier moments have imprinted rigid, stagnant, repetitive patterns.

One fairly refined variant of such classifications, however, is offered by Charles Kurzman. In the introduction to his widely read anthology *Liberal Islam,* he contrasts "liberal" Islam with "customary" and "revivalist" Islam, respectively. Customary Islam, "which represents the great majority of Muslims in most places and times," includes the diverse expressions of popular religiosity that prevail in premodern contexts: "The customary tradition is not a unitary phenomenon, since each region of the Islamic world has forged its own version of customary practice."[6] This seems to refer to what anthropologists describe as "popular" religiosity or "low Islam," in contrast to "high Islam," which is defined by the *ulama*—that is, by learned elites with access to written sources. The main opponent of this customary tradition is the "revivalist" tradition, "known variously as Islamism, fundamentalism, or Wahabism," which also seems to be modern expressions of what anthropologists called "high Islam."[7] Here, Kurzman is in line with anthropologists such Gellner: While Kurzman avoids using their terminology, he does, as they do, implicitly assume a direct continuity between premodern and modern Muslim societies. The customary and revivalist traditions are considered to be two rival forms engaged in constant competition, alternating between open hostility and mutual acceptance. But are the contemporary versions of these two traditions really reproductions of the high and popular Islam of old times? Or are they rather modern, "ideologized" forms of religious discourse? Experts have debated this question intensely for decades. The stakes are more than academic, too, for the debate's outcome has the potential decisively to shape how decision makers understand the basic issues and trends within contemporary Muslim societies.

The third, or "liberal," strain can be understood as the only one that genuinely accommodates the "fruits of modernity." In this sense, the liberal strain is something like a "branch" of traditionalism that is ready to make partial, and more or less consistent, concessions to modern ideas and ways of doing things. Liberal Islam is similar to revivalist Islam in its opposition to the notion that the merely customary has great authority. Yet liberalism distinguishes itself from revivalism by taking a far more positive attitude toward modernity. Or as Kurzman puts it, the liberal tradition's main feature is its

> critique of both the customary and revivalist traditions for what liberals sometimes term "backwardness," which in their view has prevented the Islamic world from enjoying the fruits of modernity: economic progress, democracy, legal rights, and so on. Instead, the liberal tradition argues that Islam, properly understood, is compatible with—or even a precursor to—Western liberalism.[8]

After expressing some perfunctory caveats—by observing, for example, that the three traditions "overlap and intervene and should not be considered mutually exclusive or internally homogeneous"—Kurzman claims that "as heuristic devices, the three labels provide significant insight into the recent history of Islamic discourses."

This is where Kurzman overlooks the essential point. On the one hand, the two first traditions (customary and revivalist) are *not* adequate as "heuristic devices" for understanding the present situation, since they imply a continuation of premodern attitudes and ignore or minimize the processes at work in modern contexts. The third category, the "liberal" one—to which his work wants to direct attention—becomes, by the same token, a mixture of extremely contrasting attitudes, assembled in one category based on the sole reason that they show some readiness to accommodate the "fruits of modernity."

This is clearly shown first by the history of the liberal trend that Kurzman outlines. He goes back to the eighteenth century to identify the birth of liberal Islam, naming Shah Wali-Allah (1703–62) as the initiator of the liberal tradition—yet acknowledges a little later that Wali-Allah "did not place any great stock in 'modern' forms of knowledge and deemed traditional Islamic scholarship to be sufficient to meet the demands of the contemporary world."

Kurzman then carries on with this "genealogy" by turning to the most renowned reformists of the nineteenth century: Jamal al-Din al-Afghani (1838–97), Sayyid Ahmed Khan (1817–98), and Muhammed Abduh (1849–1905). These "liberals," Kurzman ultimately concedes, "sought to impose themselves as tutelary authorities." They show "respect for modernity" by their willingness to introduce "Western subjects" into the traditional curriculum, but they still consider that the practice of *ijtihad* (or "rational inquiry")—which is supposed to open the way to modernization—is not open to anyone but should be restricted to competent religious scholars. One can only express skepticism at the idea of calling thought like this "liberal."

Kurzman's discussion of the "modes of liberal Islam" clearly implies the adoption of a category encompassing virtually anyone who shows any readiness to accommodate the fruits of modernity, including those who do no more than pay lip service to modern attitudes and practices. Here he proposes another triad, based on differing relationships to the primary sources of Islam: "the divinely revealed book (Qur'an) and the divinely inspired practice of the Prophet Mohammad (Sunna), which together constitute the basis for Islamic law *(shari'a)*." Not only does Kurzman reduce all debate over the category of liberal Islam to the issue of religious law and its relevance to contemporary conditions; he also arbitrarily defines the "modes" that he posits:

> The first mode takes liberal positions as being explicitly sanctioned by the *shari'a*; the second argues that Muslims are free to adopt liberal positions on subjects that the *shari'a* leaves open to human ingenuity; the third mode suggests that the *shari'a*, while divinely inspired, is subject to multiple human interpretations. I call these modes *liberal, silent* and *interpreted.*

In fact, the first of these "modes," the one which alleges that orthodox traditions contain all of the positive "fruits of modernity," is clearly the apologetic mode. This can be described more adequately as advocating what Said Amin Arjomand describes as a form of *Islamic modernism:*

> It can be said generally that the advocates of Islamic modernism throughout the twentieth century and the Muslim world maintained that Islam was the most perfect religion and therefore had the best answers to all problems of modern social and political organisation, purporting apologetically to deduce democracy, equality of women, and principles of social justice and human rights from its sources. To them Islam was the Straight Path and could generate the perfect modern social and political system by re-examining its fundamentals.[9]

Defined in such terms, this mode is anything but liberal. It is simply a set of formal (mostly verbal) concessions, the main idea being, as

Kurzman puts it, that "Islam is timeless and unchanging, and that Muslims must interpret the world of God as literally as possible." It is, in other words, a modernized formulation of the idea that Islam is the archetype of the world, or that it provides a "blueprint" for the social order—a notion that is clearly dear to "fundamentalists" and other radical opponents of liberalism. To insist on calling this a "mode" of liberal Islam only clouds the picture. It leads us to miss one of the basic dividing lines in the ongoing debates between Muslims, and it leads Kurzman to make mistakes such as calling the clear-cut conservative A. Alaoui M'daghri—a former Moroccan minister of Islamic affairs and prominent apologist for traditional Islam—part of the liberal trend.

This same problem is further confirmed by the two other modes that Kurzman discusses. *Silent* and *interpretive* are in fact two complementary and indivisible formulations of one and the same attitude, as better contemporary research reveals: The sacred texts do not provide a comprehensive and systematic body of laws. The rules they propose are a collection of moral injunctions, including some prescriptions, and convey an ethical outlook that defines the Islamic approach to life and its meaning. It befell later generations of Muslims to build legal systems, or rather methodologies, that enabled them to extract or develop new rulings from the original "scriptural" prescriptions. As they are based on empirical observations, both the silent and the interpretive "modes" in fact express a historicist approach to Muslim traditions. By calling these modes "historicist," I mean that they recognize basic historical facts and keep their distance from any ideological attitude in which the development of systematic Muslim legal thought is understood as a simple explication of an "archetype" or "blueprint" itself deemed to be coeternal with the last message from God.

I would propose, then, to redraw Kurzman's categories: The first group, on my view, consists of traditional religious scholars, whose expertise covers mainly the late written works of Islamic law, and who remain faithful to the traditional worldview (combining premodern epistemological outlooks with traditional contents); the second group, radical Islamists, who combine traditional contents and premodern epistemological views with modern ideological attitudes; and the third, which I consider the most enlightened, those scholars who seek ways of reconciling modern epistemological views with a classical cultural and religious heritage.

Faith and Scholarship

In the 1920s—in 1924–25, to be precise—a very important divide opened up within the reformist movements that had been sweeping Muslim societies since the middle of the nineteenth century. The precipitating event was Kemal Atatürk's abrogation of the Islamic caliphate in Turkey; and the divide was in itself a major turn in the history of most Muslim societies, setting off developments that went in two different directions. One of these led to what we now call revivalism, fundamentalism, or Islamism, while the other gave birth to an enlightened approach to religious traditions. Traditional scholars "survived" in this context, and were attracted by one or the other of the two trends. After the abrogation of the caliphate—when the institution which symbolized the continuity and permanence of historical Islam was eliminated—a number of scholars turned away from those who called for its restoration, rejecting apologetic attitudes while remaining faithful to the fundamental ethical teachings that they drew from Muslim traditions. This was the beginning of a crucial evolution within Muslim intellectual life.

Thus while revivalism (or fundamentalism) was hardening and systematizing its ideology, some thinkers moved in the opposite direction and began—for the first time in a dozen centuries—to raise the basic, essential questions that had divided early Muslim communities, hoping to tackle these issues from fresh angles, or to propose new views based on a critical rethinking of the prevailing conceptions. Ali Abderraziq's 1925 essay asking "Was the Prophet a King?"[10] was path-breaking in more than one respect. It raised the issue of the relationship between religious and political authority and challenged Muslims to come up with new answers. The return of such a question, posed as it was in such a direct way, profoundly shook traditional learned elites throughout Muslim societies. Ali Abderraziq's question is still with us; indeed it is *the* question that most Muslim intellectuals take it upon themselves to attempt to answer.

So what has happened since the divide of the 1920s? The two tendencies coming out of it have crystallized even further: One claims that there is an essence of Islam, a single Islamic pattern that we can contemplate and study, and from which we can deduce the answer to any question that we may meet in the course of our lives. This is the prevailing idea of Islam among revivalists, fundamentalists, and Islamists, and also, in slightly different forms, within some scholarly circles in North American and European universities.[11] One can find many publications in which the claim is put forward that Islam is this or that discrete and homogenous thing, ignoring the diversity and the richness that have characterized the history of Muslims. The idea of *shari‘a* as a system of eternal prescriptions, drawn directly from sacred texts, is an illustration of this attitude. According to the rival point of view, which has been well documented by historical research, Islamic law is instead the outcome of processes that have unfolded over the course of Muslim history, and indeed often relatively late in that history. It belongs therefore to the realm of facts that can be "situated," *not* to the realm of principles and norms as such. It is the recognition of this distinction that defines the other great post-1925 tendency, the new attitude and approach that I refer to as "enlightened" Muslim thought.

This second tendency, which is enlightened and liberal in the sense given to these words in the West, is thus founded on modern epistemological premises that abandon ahistorical essentialism. It accepts the methods and suppositions of modern scholarship, and rejects the idea of Islam as an archetype of truth that can serve as a blueprint for social and political order. Enlightened Islamic thought accepts the legitimacy of attempting to link expressions of the sacred to the historical settings in which these expressions were formulated, and thus recognizes the historicity of these expressions. Yet it remains faithful to the idea of an "external" origin of the norms and views expressed by the Prophet, and it affirms their sacred character and universal validity. In other words, it accepts a principle of heterogeneity that makes room for both the universal and the particular; it sees prophetic prescriptions as being *universal* in that they are sacred in origin, conveying ethical principles which are intended for all humans and which converge with principles taught by other religious and philosophical traditions, and *particular* in that they express one historically bounded vision of such principles.

Since the 1920s, thinkers who work along these lines have emerged in many contexts. The most renowned are those whose writings have been composed in or translated into European languages, such as Ali Abderraziq, Fazlur Rahman, Mohamed Mahmoud Taha, Abdullahi An-Na'im, Mohamed Talbi, Mojtahed Shabestari, Abdelmajid Charfi, and Abdul Karim Soroush. It is striking how many corners of the Muslim world these thinkers hail from, including communities of new emigrants in Europe and North America. They do not form a "school" in any sense, for there is no direct or indirect affiliation among them. They speak different languages, pursue different disciplines, and reside in different countries. But they do share a strong "family resemblance." The avenue opened by this trend is commending itself to many, across cultures and disciplines, not as an eternal idea uncovered, or a potentiality unfolded at a moment in history, but as a "reading" that emerges out of the application of rigorous scholarship and hermeneutic insight to Muslim traditions. Enlightened Muslim thought is represented by a great diversity of thinkers and has emerged out of varying contexts, but it shares in common a tendency toward subtler views about truth and its relationship to reality than those dominant in antiquity.

Certain Muslim thinkers exemplify key aspects of this enlightened turn of mind (though this does not necessarily mean that they should be considered the leading lights in this relatively large intellectual family). Ali Abderraziq opened the way to the new approaches; Fazlur Rahman offered an in-depth theoretical articulation of them; and Abdelmajid Charfi and Abdul Karim Soroush initiated the process of building around them an institutionalized school of thought.

Ali Abderraziq (1888–1966) was the first who broke with the "reform-ist" trend and its mixture of premodern epistemological views of religious traditions and apologetic leanings. His famous question "Was the prophet a king?" signaled a fundamental break with classical or essentialist ideas and a turn toward critical reasoning. He challenged established views and submitted them to rational inquiry, raising the issues of their coher-ence and adequacy in light of the available textual and historical sources. His departure from the search for the eternal Islam was a reaction against traditionalist intellectual efforts to demonstrate the *precedence* of Islam over such modern values such as rationality, democracy, and human rights.

He also attempted to test the validity of orthodox views by examin-ing their internal logic. Traditional Muslims think that Mohammad founded a state by leading the first community of believers in Medina, even though the Koran famously denies that he could be a king or tem-poral ruler of any kind. Abderraziq examined the Koranic verses most often used to back up the claim that a particular form of state is pre-scribed by Islam and found that what these verses expressed were basic principles of consultation and obedience to "those in charge" (not nec-essarily to be understood as kings or political rulers of any kind). To corroborate his claims, he adduced extra-Koranic historical evidence showing that the first *ummah* (community) of believers whom Mohammad led from Mecca to Medina in 622 C.E. had none of the features of a polity.

Abderraziq's break with traditional notions stirred huge waves of protest, accusation, and attempted refutation. It is noteworthy that most of these hostile reactions came both from traditional clerics and from reformists (such as Rachid Rida) associated with what would later be-come known as Islamism. General readers, who for the first time in Muslim history could follow such a controversy through the press, showed not the slightest sign of hostility to Abderraziq's ideas. Their "silence" could not be understood as anything other than approval for what amounted to a systematic critique, by a Muslim intellectual writ-ing for fellow Muslims, of longstanding attempts to rationalize tyranny and theocracy with the stolen mantle of sacred tradition.

The second figure who illustrates the enlightened turn is Fazlur Rahman (1919–86). Like Abderraziq, he had a solid training in tradi-tional Muslim disciplines, but he also had a modern university education. As a scholar who possessed both traditional religious learn-ing and a knowledge of modern textual analysis, he was superbly equipped to widen the scope of rational inquiry into the elaborations and systems that Muslim scholars had built upon the basis of the early Islamic texts. His specialty was a systematic scrutiny of the historical processes that produced some of the basic conceptions prevailing among Muslims. And his appraisal of the ways in which orthodoxy was con-

structed was severely critical, and left no room for the assertion that
there is a venerable "Islamic system" that somehow "pre-includes"
modern norms.

Instead, Rahman perceived a specific moral "ethos" that emanated
from Islamic scriptures and the Prophet's example. He questioned traditional explanations of revelation that minimized Mohammad's role and
set the stage for the emergence of the doctrine that the Koran is eternal.
These ideas about the role of the Prophet in the transmission of revelation[12] stirred protests comparable to the ones that greeted Abderraziq in
1925. In an essay entitled *Islam and Modernity,* Rahman offered one of
the most radical reexaminations of the learned Muslim traditions and
their reproduction, showing how they were shaped by a mindset sharply
opposed to the ethos of the initial *ummah.*[13] And he pointed to the negative consequences of sacralizing such traditions and allowing them to
appear as the sole valid expressions of Islamic religious tenets.

Supporting the movement of enlightened thought is a trend that looks
at Muslim traditions as "layers" of narratives or forms of social organization, each referring to a common source, which can be studied as
objects of knowledge without necessarily assuming the validity of religious claims. Here, religious traditions are considered to be
accumulations of social institutions, written traditions, different myths,
and different forms of expression, which claim to refer to a common
core, and present themselves as expressions of something far beyond
ordinary human experience. Spokespersons for this trend include such
renowned scholars as Mohammed Arkoun or Ridwan Assayyid. One can
say that hundreds of scholars—Muslim and non-Muslim alike, and belonging to different disciplines and schools—are engaged in this
endeavor in universities and research institutions around the world. In
fact, we are now living through a period in which the history of Muslims
is being rewritten on a vast scale. New knowledge and new understandings are offering support to enlightened Muslims and giving radicals
more reasons for fear. The new learning does tend to favor the emergence of religious, moral, and sometimes intellectual relativism within
the circles of its adepts and those influenced by them. However, its
greatest impact has been its support for enlightened thinkers interested
in exploring implications for religious consciousness. In a way, one can
describe this tendency as one in which scholarship is being put in the
service of religious enlightenment.

At the edge of this current, Abdelmajid Charfi (b. 1944) is an example
of the enlightened Muslim intellectual as scholarly institution-builder.
Through his writing, his instruction of important young scholars, and
his work in organizing a department of religious studies within the University of Tunis, he has inaugurated one of the first new systematic
analyses of traditional Islamic dogmas, taking into account the views
and methods of contemporary social science, comparative religion, and

ethical reasoning. His *Islam Between Message and History* proposes a comprehensive alternative to the views held by Islamists and ultraconservatives. He draws a sharp distinction between the religious and ethical message of Islam and its reception within Muslim communities separated by time, space, and culture. He offers a new reading of one of the basic dogmas held by Muslims—namely, that of the end (or "sealing") of revelation. The traditional interpretation strengthens the finality of the scriptural prescriptions as the last and most accomplished expression of divine will. Charfi, building on both early traditional sources and modern scholarship, stresses that this new reading marks not merely the close of one period but also the opening of new horizons for the human venture, built on new knowledge, ethical experimentation, and the liberation of mind and will.

Finally, Abdul Karim Soroush emerges as a representative of a rich and powerful Iranian movement, which has attracted active thinkers from within both religious institutions and secular circles, and which benefits from a large following within Iranian society as a whole. This movement displays the clear influence of the Shi'ite learned traditions, where philosophy and rational theology have been cultivated without disruption for centuries. It firmly upholds the distinction between religious truths (absolute but inaccessible by themselves) from human knowledge (necessarily situated and thus relative). At the same time, it resists the reduction of religious principles to legalistic, external prescriptions by in-depth explorations of the ontological, eschatological, and ethical dimensions of religious experience, drawing clearly from the mystical heritage of Persia and the Middle East.

Belief and Identity

One of the most important consequences of the enlightened tendency—and one that further distinguishes it from the radical and traditionalist alternatives—is its capacity to distinguish between religious faith and assertions of collective identity. In the enlightened view, religion is a historically situated expression of spiritual visions and ethical ideals. Historical-critical analyses and other forms of scientific inquiry need not provoke fears of loss, whether of belief, social cohesion, or identity. These fears, which seem to have played an important role in the radicalization of Islamism, are defused within enlightened thought. Expressions of identity should be local, geographical, and cultural. The realization that Islam, properly understood, is *not* a system of social and political regulation frees up space for cultures and nations—in the modern sense of those words—to lay the foundations of collective identity. This opens the way, in turn, to the acceptance of a convergence with other religious traditions and universalistic moralities, beyond political and cultural boundaries and in more than formal terms.

It also opens the way to a full respect for civic spheres in which Muslims can coexist as equal citizens with non-Muslims. Moreover, both this acceptance and this respect are to enlightened Muslim minds matters of principle and not merely grudging tactical concessions (of the sort some Islamists make) to a prevailing but illegitimate balance of forces or a fashion of the day.

What is more, the enlightened turn recognizes that Islam's axial texts breathe a spirit of social justice, equality, and solidarity with the poor. Islam gave birth to a community based on the ideal of adherence to a common creed, and not to some tribal or ethnic sense of belonging. It remained throughout history a framework vindicating equality and generated repeated attempts to enact those principles in the sociopolitical order. Today, however, most of these aspirations can be channeled through established political institutions and forms of expression. Muslims are no longer obliged to "practice politics within religion"—that is, to adopt religious formulations in order to express political agendas, as was the case in premodern times.[14] The creation of political arenas where citizens have the benefit of freedom of expression and political action opens the way to modern types of collective behavior.

We may ask whether progress in modern scholarship, and the reduction of some conceptions held to be sacred to the status of historical expressions, would lead to relativism or "disenchantment"—a dissociation from faith in the spiritual and from those moral attitudes associated with it. The answer is "not necessarily." The idea behind enlightened Muslim thought is that even if we accept the historicity of traditions, even if we accept the point of view of modern scholarship, there is behind these traditions an "Otherness" that provides an insight into the meaning of existence and the basis of ethical principles. We have to accept what modern scholarship has brought to us, in particular the critical attitude to all religious traditions, ours as well as others'. But we have to assume that these traditions, despite their historicity, point to the divine and capture its inspiration and ethical guidance. This is, in a way, a reassertion of the "Rushdian" creed, the conception that Ibn Rushd (or Averroës, 1126–98) originally proposed, which was later misrepresented and rejected in Muslim societies as the theory of the "double truth." The Rushdian creed asserts the idea that reason understands its own incapacity to provide ethical guidance, and thus refers us to religion, but that religion itself points back to reason as the way to develop adequate ways and means of enacting ethical principles in historical settings. The truth is one, but it is apprehended at different levels and in different modes. Mohamed Abed Jabri identifies this aspect of the nature of truth as the postulate that lies at the foundation of modernity.[15] Ibn Rushd came from Spain, and his ideas were well known among the learned of Western Europe during the High and Late Middle Ages. It was indeed an acceptance of his insight among European Christians that helped to open the way to new understandings of the possible relationships between religion and sociopolitical order in Europe. There is no inherent reason why it cannot provide a foundation for such new understandings among Muslims as well.

NOTES

1. Marshall G.S. Hodgson, *The Venture of Islam: Conscience and History in a World Civilization,* 3 vols. (Chicago: University of Chicago Press), 1961–74.

2. Marshall G.S. Hodgson, *Rethinking World History: Essays on Europe, Islam and World History* (Cambridge: Cambridge University Press, 1993).

3. "Islah," in *Encyclopedia of Islam* (Leiden: Brill, 2001).

4. Hichem Djaït, *La grande discorde: Religion et politique dans l'Islam des origines* (Paris: Gallimard, 1989).

5. Ernest Gellner, "Flux and Reflux in the Faith of Men," *Muslim Society* (Cambridge: Cambridge University Press, 1981).

6. Charles Kurzman, *Liberal Islam: A Sourcebook* (New York: Oxford University Press, 1998), 3–14. The discussion of and quotes from Kurzman in the present essay all refer to these pages, which form his introduction to this volume.

7. Ernest Gellner, *Postmodernism, Reason and Religion* (London: Routledge, 1992).

8. Charles Kurzman, *Liberal Islam,* 6.

9. Said Amir Arjomand, "The Reform Movement and the Debate on Modernity and Tradition in Contemporary Iran," *International Journal of Middle Eastern Studies* (November 2002): 723.

10. See Ali Abderraziq, *L'Islam et les fondements du pouvoir,* trans. Abdou Filali-Ansary (Paris: La Découverte, 1994).

11. Again, Gellner gives one of its best formulations at the opening of one of his most important works, *Muslim Society* (Cambridge: Cambridge University Press, 1981), 1: "Islam is the blueprint of a social order. It holds that a set of rules exists, eternal, divinely ordained, and independent of the will of men, which defines the proper ordering of society. . . . In traditional Islam, no distinction is made between lawyer and common lawyer, and the roles of theologian and lawyer are conflated. Expertise on proper social arrangements, and on matters pertaining to God, are one and the same thing."

12. See Fazlur Rahman, *Islam,* 2nd ed. (Chicago: University of Chicago Press, 1979).

13. Fazlur Rahman, *Islam and Modernity* (Chicago: University of Chicago Press, 1984).

14. Mohamed Abed Jabri, *Al-'aql al-siyâsi al arabi: muhaddidâtuh wa tajalliyâtuh* (Arab political reason: Determinants and manifestations) (Casablanca: Al-Markaz Ath-Thaqafi al-Arabi, 1990).

15. Mohamed Abed Jabri, *Naqd al-'Aql al-'Arabi: Takwin al-'Aql al-'Arabi* (Critique of Arab reason, vol. I: The formation of Arab reason) (Casablanca: Al-Markaz Ath-Thaqafi al-Arabi, 1991).

17

THE ELUSIVE REFORMATION

Abdelwahab El-Affendi

Abdelwahab El-Affendi *is a senior research fellow at the Centre for the Study of Democracy, University of Westminster, and coordinator of the Centre's Project on Democracy in the Muslim World. His books include* Who Needs an Islamic State? *(1991) and* Rethinking Islam and Modernity *(2001). This essay originally appeared in the April 2003 issue of the* Journal of Democracy.

The overriding political problem with modern Islam is not just the embarrassing absence of democracy in most Muslim countries, but the more basic failure to provide any form of stable, and even minimally consensual governance at all. This problem is so glaring and of such long standing that it is difficult to dismiss out of hand the role of such "prepolitical" factors as culture and, in particular, religion in explaining it.

The more weight we ascribe to these "prepolitical" factors, the greater the need appears to be for a radical intellectual and ethical reorientation of Islam. But the argument that such a reorientation should take the form of an "Islamic Reformation" is nevertheless a precarious one. Despite the achievements of scholars who have followed the *sunna* (tradition) of Max Weber in using religion to explain social phenomena, it remains risky for social scientists to double as amateur theologians, especially when they want to speak in a prescriptive mode. This need not discourage us from dabbling in theology, as long as we remember that theology and political sociology are profoundly different enterprises. The greater risk is not that theology will corrupt social science, but the reverse. Social scientists have a dangerous tendency to take such theological concepts as "the rule of God" at face value and then run away with them—projecting, for example, simplistic contrasts with the political concept of "the rule of man."

The question of whether liberal democracy can be given a "truly" Islamic basis is unanswerable, since there cannot conceivably be any Islamic democratic movement which is untouched by the influences and challenges of Western liberal-democratic thought and practice. Meanwhile, any modern Islamic reform movement trumpeting its liberal-democratic potential begs the question of whether religious-cum-cultural reform is a precondition for democratization, since to cite favorably the presumed liberal-democratic potential of a particular interpretation of Islam is to assume that there is already a broad Muslim constituency for liberalism and democracy as things desirable in and of themselves.

Not all those classified as "Muslim liberals" base their liberalism on theological assumptions; in fact the majority do not. But the conceptual amalgam that travels under the "Muslim liberal" label is more problematic than the easy combination of adjectives suggests—and not only because the term "liberal" is as hotly contested as it is. Islamic liberalism is often defined as a tendency that "share[s] common concerns with Western liberalism,"[1] in particular the privileging of "rational discourse" that aims primarily at "agreement based on goodwill" among participants in public life.[2] This appears to be a circular definition, tautologically generating the conclusion that "liberal Islam" is more congenial to democracy than other modes of Islam. If Muslim liberals are by definition those who share Western liberal democratic ideals, and if non-liberals are those who do not, then it goes without saying that "Muslim liberalism" is the intra-Islamic tendency that would promote liberal democracy within Islam.

It is significant, though, that reality does not accord with this "tautology." Those groups and thinkers who have gone the furthest in promoting "liberal" theologies within Islam (like the Ahmadis in Pakistan, the Bahais in Iran, or the Republican Brothers in Sudan) have been less inclined toward modern liberal democracy than toward positions of the sort taken by such early-modern Western liberals as John Locke, Jeremy Bentham, or James Madison, all of whom were at best "reluctant democrats."[3] Nor is it difficult to see why, since most of these reformist schools of Islam were often marginalized and even persecuted.

Liberalism—understood broadly as support for individual autonomy and the political and civil liberties that underpin it—has not always been democracy-friendly.[4] Liberals have often worried that empowered but misguided masses can threaten fundamental rights and liberties, especially property rights. In spite of the intimate relationship that is now thought to hold between liberalism and democracy, significant tensions persist between them—with certain tenets of classical liberalism even being arguably "profoundly hostile to democracy."[5]

Governance and Belief

It goes without saying that Islamic teachings, traditionally understood, certainly conflict with aspects of Western liberalism, but that does not in itself mean that they are an obstacle to democracy. Any set of religious beliefs, even beliefs based on caste stratification, could be compatible with democracy (understood as consensual popular rule) if they are shared by all members of the community. On the other hand, differing and incompatible versions of beliefs would make democratic consensus difficult, regardless of their content.

One could, at this point, venture the counterintuitive thesis that not only Islam, but all religion is essentially "democratic," in the sense that religion as a matter of individual conscience can only be espoused freely. Religious communities—from the early Hebrews to early Christians, and down to the Pilgrims, Mormons, and Nation of Islam—depended for their existence on the continuous promotion of consensus. Otherwise they tended to fragment very quickly. Like any source of moral or spiritual values, religion can be deployed as an element of intimidation and coercion against dissidents (actual and potential), but that can only happen once the values in question have been widely accepted and have become constitutive of the community itself. The central problem that religion poses for democracy (or any form of government) is that strongly held beliefs or loyalties can also make consensus hard to secure.

Muslim communities have responded positively both to democracy and to most aspects of liberalism. Limits on state authority, the separation of powers, and constitutionalism in general, have traditionally found strong support in Muslim circles. For evidence one could point to the constitutionalist movements that emerged in Iran, Egypt, and the Ottoman Empire during the nineteenth century. And upon gaining independence from colonial rule, almost all Muslim countries adopted some form of protodemocratic rule. Many leading reformers put forth theological-political arguments for the compatibility of democracy and Islam. For the most part, however, these countries were run by instinctive liberals who did not bother to offer religious arguments for their political beliefs. The "founding fathers" in countries like Pakistan and Malaysia fit this mould, as did the monarchies of postindependence Iraq, Morocco, Egypt, Jordan, and Libya. The subsequent collapse of protodemocracy from one Muslim country to the next coincided with general trends in the wider Third World, and had more to do with secular ideologies such as socialism and nationalism rather than shifts in religious thought.

All dictatorships in the Muslim world in fact remain secular—as they must, since dictatorships are by definition political systems that subordinate all values and considerations, including religious ones, to regime survival. Even where dictatorships venture a theological justification, they do not lose this secular character. Ayatollah Khomeini's doctrine of the "absolute jurisdiction of the jurist" *(Mutlaq Velayat-e-Faqih),* enunciated in 1988, demonstrates as much, based as it is on the argu-

ment that the survival of the Islamic state is the supreme value to which
all other religious obligations must be subordinated. But unless the
theological principle in question has real majority support, the regime's
continuing survival cannot be ascribed to its theological credentials,
but more to its secret police or petrodollars.

The Islamist Challenge

In the twentieth century, a rising number of Muslim thinkers *did* attempt to produce religious arguments against democracy and in favor
of more "authentic" Islamic models, such as that of *shura* (consultative
system) or various kinds of guardianship by religious scholars. Sayyid
Abu'l-A'la Mawdudi (1903–79) from the Indian subcontinent, Sayyid
Qutb (1906–66) from Egypt, and Ayatollah Ruhollah Khomeini (1900–
89) from Iran argued that the democratic idea of popular sovereignty
directly contradicted the sovereignty of God.[6] Yet all these authors advocated some form of modern constitutional practice—albeit always with
the proviso that some (variously defined) religious authority should have
a final veto on the decisions of elected bodies. But these thinkers, like
those theologians who serve as apologists for existing autocracies today, have enjoyed little popular support.

The rising popularity of Islamist trends has posed a dual challenge
for democratization. On one hand, it has created a fear among liberals
that democratic forms may hand power to illiberal Islamists. On the
other, despots have used the Islamist threat to resist pressures to democratize—often with support from some local liberals and major
foreign powers. Moreover, disillusionment among many Muslims with
contemporary experiments in Islamization (in Iran, Pakistan, Afghanistan, Sudan, and Saudi Arabia) has given rise to new liberal tendencies
that claim the Islamic mantle and marshal religious arguments. Some
commentators see these new tendencies as sure signs of a shift toward liberalism in the Muslim world, especially in Iran, where
disillusionment with the Islamic "republic of virtue" is at its most
acute:

> If, as the Christian West has shown, widespread disenchantment with
> attempts to create a "City of God" on Earth ultimately fuels the rise of a
> democratic "City of Man," then Islamic civilization is on the verge of a
> decisive, and familiar, breakthrough.[7]

Charles Kurzman distinguishes three strands of Islamic liberalism.
One argues that Islamic teachings are essentially liberal; another argues
that Islamic teachings are neutral toward liberalism; a third accepts that
there is a conflict between liberalism and traditional Islam but argues
that they can be reconciled through a process of mutual reinterpreta-
tion.[8] The new trends belong to this third or "revisionist" strand—a

category represented by important movements such as Nahdatul Ulama in Indonesia and the reformism behind President Mohammad Khatami in Iran, as well as by individuals such as Iran's Abdul Karim Soroush. For our purposes, the first two categories can be referred to as modes of "traditional" Islamic liberalism and the third, as "critical" Islamic liberalism.

Yet one can point beyond these to a fourth category, one exemplified by emerging parties such as Justice and Development in Turkey and Morocco or Ennahada in Tunisia, movements such as the Muslim Youth Movement of Malaysia or certain splinters from the Muslim Brotherhood in Egypt and Syria, and personalities such as Tarek al-Bichri in Egypt. These groups combine traditional with critical liberalism in that they show a full awareness of, and sympathy with, the revisionist trends, but they do not themselves explicitly make revisionist arguments. Instead, they self-consciously (if often tacitly) prefer to postpone or bypass the thorny issues implied by a commitment to both liberalism and Islam.

The positive aspect of these new trends is that they have helped to create prodemocracy coalitions by deliberately removing some of Islam's most contentious theological-political issues from the table, at least for the short to medium term. But unlike most traditional Islamic liberals, who were often unaware of or unconcerned with divisive issues, the new Islamic liberals are acutely aware of them and know that at some point they will need to defend their own stance on these hard questions, even if it is wise to get them off the front burner of politics for now. In places like Iran, the new liberalism has managed to generate broad coalitions that encompass critical Islamic liberalism, traditional liberalism, and even plain secular liberalism. As a result, it has managed to secure wide popular support for its programs of reform, as indicated by the landslide victory Khatami secured in the last presidential and parliamentary elections in Iran.

The rise of such a coalition does not, of course, prevent rivals from raising the issues that the new movements have wanted to keep off the agenda, and thus from reopening the battles anew. But these critics are less likely to mobilize significant popular support, and so less likely to destabilize the system. Recent elections in Turkey, Egypt, Indonesia, Morocco, Pakistan, and Malaysia have shown that radical parties, such as the Islamic Party of Malaysia or Fazilet in Turkey, do not enjoy significant popular support. Violent Islamist organizations, such as Egypt's Islamic Group, are even more isolated. The resulting stability may make it possible to debate these issues in a calmer atmosphere and maybe even to resolve them.

It can, in conclusion, be said that an "Islamic Reformation" is neither necessary nor sufficient for enabling Muslims to build stable and consensual political institutions. A reformation may be a desirable thing; that is a matter for Muslim believers to decide. But its prospect is unlikely to improve the outlook for political stability in the short term. Like the Christian Reformation before it, it would more likely be a dauntingly divisive and bloody affair.

NOTES

1. Charles Kurzman, "Liberal Islam: Prospects and Challenges," *MERIA Journal* 3, No. 3 (September 1999), available online at *http://meria.idc.ac.il/journal/1999/issue3/jv3n3a2.html*.

2. Leonard Binder, *Islamic Liberalism: A Critique of Development Ideologies* (Chicago: University of Chicago Press, 1998), 1–5, 358–59.

3. David Held, *Models of Democracy,* 2nd ed. (Stanford: Stanford University Press, 1996), 100.

4. Marc F. Plattner, "From Liberalism to Liberal Democracy," *Journal of Democracy* 10 (July 1999); David Beetham, "Liberal Democracy and the Limits of Democratization," in David Held, ed., *Prospects for Democracy: North, South, East, West* (Cambridge: Polity Press, 1993).

5. David Beetham, "Liberal Democracy and the Limits of Democratization," 58.

6. Abdelwahab El-Affendi, *Who Needs an Islamic State?* (London: Grey Seal Books, 1991), 49–56.

7. See the editors' introduction in Mahmoud Sadri and Ahmed Sadri, eds., *Reason, Freedom and Democracy in Islam: Essential Writings of Abdolkarim Soroush* (Oxford: Oxford University Press, 2000).

8. Charles Kurzman, "Liberal Islam."

18

THE SILENCED MAJORITY

Radwan A. Masmoudi

Radwan A. Masmoudi *is the founder and president of the Washington, D.C.–based Center for the Study of Islam and Democracy* (www.islam-democracy.org). *He is also editor-in-chief of the Center's quarterly publication,* Muslim Democrat, *and the author of numerous articles on democracy, diversity, and human rights in Islam. This essay originally appeared in the April 2003 issue of the* Journal of Democracy.

Liberal Islam is a branch, or school, of Islam that emphasizes human liberty and freedom within Islam. Liberal Muslims believe that human beings are created free—a concept that is so important to highlight in the Muslim world today—and that if you take away or diminish freedom, you are in fact contradicting human nature as well as divine will. While some people want to impose their views on others, liberal Muslims insist that people—both men and women—must be free to choose how to practice their faith. This is in accordance with the basic teaching of the Koran that "there can be no compulsion in religion." Forcing religion on people contradicts a basic requirement of religion: that human beings are supposed to come to God of their own free will.

Unlike the rather starkly opposed "liberalisms" of the United States and Europe, respectively, Islamic liberalism emphasizes *both* the liberty of the community *(ummah)* from occupation and oppression, and at the same time the liberty of the individual within the community. Nor does it conflate the latter with the former: Like classical libertarians such as Frédéric Bastiat, Ludwig von Mises, or Friedrich von Hayek, Islamic liberalism places explicit emphasis on limited government, individual liberty, human dignity, and human rights. "Moderate Islam" is another description often used for the ideas and representative figures that I have in mind. But "moderate" does not precisely capture the pervasive ideological orientation suggested here. The main pillars of Islamic liberalism are:

Liberty *(hurriya)*—Human beings are created free and must remain free; freedom of thought, freedom of religion, and freedom of movement are essential to life as envisaged by our creator. Without freedom, life and religion have no meaning and no flavor. God, in his unlimited wisdom, intended human beings to be free; free to believe or disbelieve and free to practice or not practice. It is wrong and counterproductive to impose religion on people, and it is also against the will of God.

Justice *(adl)*—Equality before God must translate into equality on earth. Only God can be the judge of who is best among us. Justice must be upheld for everyone—man or woman, Muslim or non-Muslim, friend or foe, Arab or non-Arab. Justice means that every human being is treated fairly and equally by society and by the government. Injustice toward a single human being is an injustice toward all and an affront to the Almighty God.

Consultation *(shura)*—God is against oppression and dislikes oppressors. The affairs of the community and the society must be decided through mutual consultation and consent. Consultation must include all members of the community and must be binding on the rulers or officeholders. Prophet Mohammad, who died without designating a ruler, indicated to his companions that they must elect the ruler themselves and that the ruler must be held accountable to them.

Rational interpretation *(ijtihad)*—God has prescribed important goals for believers to achieve on earth (such as *shura,* justice, freedom, dignity, and peace). However, the way to achieve these objectives is mostly left up to Muslims themselves, who must decide using reason, knowledge, and faith what is best for them and for their community. Islam has no clergy and no hierarchy, and therefore all Muslims must voice their opinion, in light of the teachings of Islam and the changing needs and priorities of society. It is vital for the Muslim *ummah* today that the doors of *ijtihad*—closed for some 500 years—be reopened.

There are *many* scholars and leaders for this growing movement in the Muslim world, although they are not well known in the West. They include Tarek al-Bichri and Saleem al-Awwa (Egypt), Mohamed Talbi (Tunisia), Anwar Ibrahim (Malaysia), Fathi Osman, Aziza al-Hibri, and Abdulaziz Sachedina (United States), Shafeeq Ghabra (Kuwait), Abdelwahab El-Affendi (Sudan), Nurcholish Madjid (Indonesia), Ibrahim al-Wazir (Yemen), and Abdul Karim Soroush (Iran).

Why Is It Silent?

The good news is that liberal Islam represents the overwhelming majority within the Muslim world today. The bad news is that it is a silent majority—or perhaps more accurately, a *silenced* one. There are two minority groups in the Muslim world that are fighting, literally, over political control: secular extremists and religious extremists. For the most part, secular extremists are in power, as they have been for the last 50 years, but they have lost legitimacy largely because of their unabashed and relentless efforts to impose their views on society. The religious extremists also want to impose their views, but many of them are in jail, or in hiding. They are not in power, except in two or three countries. They have also lost legitimacy because they advocate violence. Between these two extremes, we find the majority of the people, who want to practice their religion faithfully, but who also want to live in the modern age; that is, they want a modern, moderate, and appropriate interpretation of Islam.

Is Liberal Islam Likely to Grow?

In the long run, yes, because it is the only alternative that combines faith and reason. In the short run, it depends: Liberal Muslims are caught between a rock and a hard place. The rock is the state (and its internal police forces, or *mukhabarat*) in the oppressive form it predominantly takes in the Muslim world, which is constantly pounding society in general. These states do not like liberal Islam because it threatens the corrupt status quo that they sustain. Because these states often do not distinguish between liberal and fundamentalist Islam, they tend to perceive religion itself as a threat. In the Muslim world, the state has often taken the stand that you are "with us or against us," and if you try to criticize it in any way, you are automatically seen as a threat and silenced. The hard place is the aggregation of fundamentalist groups who want to monopolize Islam. These groups accuse anyone talking of moderation, patience, legitimacy, reason, and pragmatic thinking of being un-Islamic or anti-Islam. The religious authorities in most Muslim countries have little credibility because they so often accede to the enormous pressure they are under either to side with the state or to side with the fundamentalists.

The key to the success of liberal Islam is more freedom. Lack of freedom in Muslim countries is stifling society, preventing any debate on what is wrong with the Muslim world today. You add to the lack of freedom a loss of dignity, a sense of hopelessness and despair, and you have a fertile ground for all kinds of extremism and violence. Hence, the solution is to allow liberal Islam to grow, which means radically expanding freedom of the press, freedom of religion, freedom of thought, and freedom to form independent organizations. This is, of course, the essence of democracy.

Some claim that the Muslim world needs the rule of law, but not necessarily democracy. It is impossible to separate the two; ultimately, you cannot have rule of law without democracy. When the law comes from an illegitimate government, it is illegitimate, and its enforcement—in the absence of independent branches of government—leads to dictatorship.

The transition to democracy may take a few years. But it must be real, it must be sustained, and it must be irreversible. Governments in the Muslim world have become adept at promising democratic reforms while delivering more oppression. And this has created an environment of great disappointment and frustration.

The international community needs to exert sustained pressure on the existing governments to allow more freedom, because it is in their own interest and in that of their societies, as well as in the interest of peace and stability in the world. Of course, they will scream and complain of interference and demand that their "sovereignty" be respected. But we must insist, because this is the only way out of the terrible situation that we all find ourselves in.

Moderate and liberal Muslims should be allowed to have a voice. Repressive regimes must not be allowed to use the war on terrorism to silence all opposition or to lump all Islamists together. Those who advocate extremism and violence are the enemies of mankind and of Islam and must be stopped before they bring havoc and mayhem to their own countries and to the world. Real and genuine reforms are needed, and liberal and moderate voices cannot be heard in an environment of fear and repression.

The international community should make democratic reforms in the Muslim world a priority. As a start, the United States and European countries must stop supporting dictators in the name of stability. We all know that the stability provided by dictators is an illusion that only breeds violence and extremism. To promote peace and strengthen the voices of liberal Islam, Muslim countries must gain experience with democratic institutions and practices. Experience with democracy will allow Islamic movements to become more moderate and adapt their visions, thoughts, and strategies to the needs of their societies and the requirements of the twenty-first century. The contrasting examples of Turkey and Algeria are very telling in this regard. Staunchly secular Turkey allowed Islamists to participate in the political process and thus is on the road to becoming a model democratic state in the Muslim world. Algeria, however, chose to crack down harshly on its Islamist party in 1992 and is still recovering from a ten-year-old civil war, which has resulted in the deaths of more than 150,000 people and the radicalization of Islamist groups around the world.

A Glimmer of Hope

Liberal Islam is thriving and well in the United States and in Europe. Many free-thinking Muslims who could not tolerate the repressive environments of their own countries have escaped to the West, where they now live in freedom. They represent significant groups that can, and I believe will, play a major role in modernizing Islam and in promoting liberal and moderate views of Islam in the Muslim world. The reformation of Islam will require freedom and democracy, and right now, the only place where we have them is in the West. It is for this reason that I believe reformation will begin in the West. Muslims who live in the West are an important asset for liberal Islam, for all those who share its goals of peace, freedom, and democracy, and ultimately for the Muslim world itself.

It is imperative that U.S. Muslims play a leading role in reforming the Islamic world, principally by spreading understanding among Muslims generally, and their leaders in particular, of the values and merits of democracy. Friends of Islam and, indeed, everyone who hopes for peace and interfaith harmony should do all they can to support liberal Islam, the nascent voice of the Muslim world's silenced majority.

19

FAITH AND MODERNITY

Laith Kubba

Laith Kubba *is senior program officer for the Middle East at the National Endowment for Democracy. He was director of the international program of the Al-Khoei Foundation in London and founder of the Islam 21 project. He has been an active participant in a number of Iraqi democratic organizations and has served on the boards of such regional institutions as the Arab Organization for Human Rights and the International Forum for Islamic Dialogue. This essay originally appeared in the April 2003 issue of the* Journal of Democracy.

In assessing the nature of "liberal Islam" and its political prospects, we must of course devote careful scrutiny to the adjective that we are attaching to "Islam," for the term "liberal" has many meanings. Moreover, as Abdou Filali-Ansary reminds us, there is an even more fundamental question that must be defined when we examine the idea of "liberal Islam"—namely, what is "Islam"? The importance of this question can scarcely be understated. All too often, it is answered on the basis of seriously misleading assumptions about what is "naturally" the case that liberal Muslims must challenge or, as it were, "denaturalize" if they are to win the hearts and minds of their coreligionists around the world.

There is an unfortunate tendency among certain critics as well as certain supporters of the Muslim religion to conflate Islam as such with all sorts of attributes, practices, and institutions that are in fact quite exogenous to it. It is common, for example, to hear Islam equated with *shari'a* law, or *shari'a* with Islam. In this way, "Islam" has become a code word for such a wide range of ideas and things that its true meaning—within the Muslim world no less than outside it—has become almost completely obscured, suppressed, or lost. Among the sad results of this loss is the ease with which those who would naysay any new turn within the religion can do so simply by calling such a path "inauthentic." This is so whether the naysayers see themselves as critics or as supporters of Islam. In the face of this situation, we must clarify what authenticity truly means. A good way to start is to distinguish between the *core message* of Islam on the one hand, and on the other the often-problematic *baggage* that has come, over the course of centuries, to cluster around that message.

In trying to identify liberal, modernist, or—to use Filali-Ansary's term—enlightened Muslims, it is essential to ask: How should one define Islam? Does one look to the whole of the historical heritage and body of traditions that Muslims have inherited, or does one look to the revelation upon which all Muslims agree? To speak of Muslims is to speak of a vast number of people—almost a billion or more these days, and growing—from many countries, often with distinct heritages and traditions. To speak of the Koran is to speak of the one single book upon which the unity of the Muslim faith depends. The relationship between these diverse heritages and traditions, on one hand, and the revelation that unites all Muslims, on the other, is far from straightforward. To sort it out, one must know: What are the defining sources of Islam? This is a highly controversial issue among Muslims, and yet it is also a question that any serious defender (or any serious student, for that matter) of the liberal or modernist Muslim position cannot avoid asking.

A second and no less essential question is how Muslims deal with the sources that they take to be definitive of Islam. When we Muslims look to the revelation of the Koran and seek, as it were, to "translate" or "mediate" its message for the modern world—not just as it touches on our personal lives but as it relates to our social and political arrangements as well—how do we think about this translation or mediation? Do we accept all the historical baggage, all the interpretations that have been built up over the centuries in reference to the revelation of the Koran, as somehow authoritative over it? Given that at least some of these interpretations conflict with each other, do we have a way of fully and nonarbitrarily identifying any *one* of them with the authority of the Koran itself? Or do we, alternatively, understand these interpretations and narratives of Muslim history in a genuinely *historical* way—that is, relative to the circumstances in which they are written? This is a second key question, the answer to which profoundly determines our understanding of what it means to implement Islam in the modern world, and which is essential in defining who is a liberal or modernist Muslim and who is not.

My own view—and that of many others, including those involved in a very laudable project called Islam 21 *(www.islam21.net)*—is that the defining source of Islam is revelation itself. While there are profound sources of Islamic *inspiration* beyond the Koran and down through history—and while these sources must be taken seriously by anyone interested in the *meaning* of Islam—Islamic *authority* is the Koran's alone. The world's Muslim traditions have been formed under the deep influence of scripture; and it is certainly important to come to terms with the different messages and claims that have been variously derived from that influence. Scripture has *influenced* these traditions, even *formed* them, if you like. But it has not *sanctified* them, and it is a mistake to think that it has done so. Unless we diverge from what has for too long been taught among the *ulama*—unless we get beyond the outdated epistemology that underlies this teaching and the rationalizations for theological authority that derive from it—we risk not only retarding the political momentum of liberal Islam, but also impeding access to the true meaning of Islam itself.

The Clash of Attitudes

Given these points of divergence, how do they relate to the sort of nascent liberal evolution that is now taking place in the understanding and practice of Islam in public life in some quarters of the Muslim world? This question may turn partly on the prospects for liberal interpretations of scripture, but I think that it is more accurate to say that it turns on the prospects for *modern* interpretation of scripture; indeed, I think it turns on Muslim attitudes about modernity as such.

In this respect, we can identify two contemporary tendencies among Muslims: First, there is a *secularist* persuasion. Advocates of this view see the modern world in a positive light but also see modernity and Islam as inimical, and typically promote the former over the latter. This school of thought is famously prominent in Turkey, of course, but it also influences many other Muslim countries, and it has shown its advantages and limitations. But it is not the modernist tendency with the greater momentum. That momentum belongs to a second tendency: Muslims who insist that if we are to come to terms with the modern world, we must not abandon ourselves to a point of view that is wholly external to Islam in doing so.

If we look more closely at this second tendency, we can see within it a further division between two approaches. The first—which now predominates on the ground but is in fact the more intellectually and politically problematic—sees the modern world and what it offers negatively. It claims to embrace modernity but on distinctly "Islamic" terms. This is an implicit contradiction that cannot be resolved without addressing it at the core: In order to modernize our institutions, we Muslims must do more than grudgingly resign ourselves to modernity. Rather, we must embrace modernity's contributions to the common heritage of humanity and try to make the best of what modernity has to offer. As it happens, the trail that leads to the modern world has been blazed by Western countries. Yet modernity's benefits ought to be accepted not because they are Western, but because they are good and relevant.

A great many Muslims have a problem with this because 1)

modernity's terms of reference have not evolved from within our own heritage, and 2) because there is a perception of political conflict with the West, a perception that has grown largely out of a recent history of colonization. There is an ongoing bundle of issues associated with that history which exacerbates this anti-Western attitude and generates the well-known incoherence of wanting modernity's benefits (regardless of their original historical provenance) while at the same time condemning modernity itself as a "Western import" or a "foreign imposition."

The second approach—still nascent, but full of possibility—tries to address these issues more subtly and from a standpoint that rises above the grievances issuing from colonialism. In this view, tracing exactly where and how modern modes and orders evolved is less important than weighing their intrinsic merits. Aware of Islamic civilization's great and many contributions to the world, this approach seeks to take advantage of the best that humanity has to offer, precisely for the sake of pursuing such high Islamic ideals and virtues as truth, justice, charity, brotherhood, and peace.

A final point of divergence in trying to define who is a liberal or a modernist among Muslims lies in their attitudes regarding relations between tradition on the one hand, and politics or public life on the other. Here as elsewhere, we Muslims have too often conflated regional or local custom with Islam itself. A fundamental distinction needs to be made between the message of Islam and all the historical traditions that have accumulated around it over the years, not only in Arabia but throughout the world. All of these traditions have been conditioned by their times, by their human limitations, and they should not be confused with Islam itself.

As it is with respect to specific manifestations of religion, so it is with respect to the relationship between religion and public life. Here too, the traditions of interpretation that have grown up around Islam are not themselves sanctified by Islam. Muslims accordingly can and should approach these traditions in a spirit of liberty, modernizing them, adapting them, stretching them. And they can do so from within an authentically Muslim framework, while at the same time taking their lead from the West in some respects, because there is nothing in the origins and nature of Islam itself that precludes doing so.

Take, for example, the role of women—or to be more precise the segregation of men and women that has been practiced so ubiquitously throughout Muslim history. There is no justification at all for this in our religion's original message. It has come from extra-Islamic cultural sources, been transposed into an Islamic idiom, and labeled with the name of Islam. Again, if we refer to the Koran, I can have one copy and nobody worldwide will disagree with what that copy says. But if we refer to *shari'a* law there is no holy book called *Shari'a*. And if we refer to Muslim traditions, there is no specific collection of Muslim traditions. There are only collections. They have a flavor of Islam, and they have certainly come to relate themselves to, and often define themselves in terms of, Islam; but they need not be dealt with by faithful Muslims as coextensive with Islam or as sharing in its sanctity.

This is no less true when it comes to questions of government and politics. For many Muslims, the model of the first Islamic community that came into being after the *hajj* to Medina in 622 C.E. provides the conceptual framework for any Islamic political order. Indeed, the very name Medina is symbolic of an ideal: The town's pre-Islamic name was Yathrib, and it became known by its current name of al-Medina (which means "the city" in Arabic) as a token of its importance in Islamic history. For this reason, it is quite poignant, I think, to consider what *modern* Medina is, how this city has evolved over time, what it has become. Thus considered, Medina makes an excellent reference point for thinking about liberal Islam. It has been 28 years since I first visited Medina in 1975, but when I think of what I saw there even then, I wonder about what civic life must have been like during the early Muslim centuries, and what it is like now in that complex, cosmopolitan metropolis that remains one of the holiest places in the Islamic world.

Thinking about the Medina of old helps us to grasp the political concepts and principles that were at work during the seedtime of Islam, but in no way can that bygone city provide—nor was it ever meant to—a method of running the complex cities, states, and societies in which we live today. There is nothing in specifically Muslim history—not even the Ottoman Empire, which was multinational, religiously very tolerant by the standards of its time, and also the most recent Muslim society to rank as what we today would call a superpower—that can fully prepare us for the political and social challenges and opportunities that we Muslims face in the contemporary world.

Yet there is much in our faith and its legacy of ethical reflection and action that can guide us, even if our history hands us no ready-made recipes. Liberal, modernist Muslims look at modernity and see an opportunity as well as a challenge. To take advantage of the former, they know that they must confront the latter. Buoyed by their faith and ready to give their best in thought, word, and deed, they accept these twin historic tasks, the challenge no less than the opportunity, with confidence born out of a desire to secure for the nearly one-fifth of the world's population that is Muslim full access to all that is worthy in the common heritage of humankind.

20

TERROR, ISLAM,
AND DEMOCRACY

Ladan Boroumand and Roya Boroumand

Ladan Boroumand, a former visiting fellow at the International Forum for Democratic Studies, is a historian from Iran with a doctorate from the Ecole des Hautes Etudes en Sciences Sociales in Paris. Her sister Roya Boroumand holds a history doctorate from the Sorbonne, and specializes in contemporary Iran. She has served as a consultant on women's rights for Human Rights Watch in Morocco and Algeria. They are currently collaborating on a study of the Iranian Revolution and an Internet-based project to promote human rights education in Iran.

"Why?" That is the question that people in the West have been asking ever since the terrible events of September 11. What are the attitudes, beliefs, and motives of the terrorists and the movement from which they sprang? What makes young men from Muslim countries willing, even eager, to turn themselves into suicide bombers? How did these men come to harbor such violent hatred of the West, and especially of the United States? What are the roots—moral, intellectual, political, and spiritual—of the murderous fanaticism we witnessed that day?

As Western experts and commentators have wrestled with these questions, their intellectual disarray and bafflement in the face of radical Islamist (notice we do not say "Islamic") terrorism have become painfully clear. This is worrisome, for however necessary an armed response might seem in the near term, it is undeniable that a successful long-term strategy for battling Islamism and its terrorists will require a clearer understanding of who these foes are, what they think, and how they understand their own motives. For terrorism is first and foremost an ideological and moral challenge to liberal democracy. The sooner the defenders of democracy realize this and grasp its implications, the sooner democracy can prepare itself to win the long-simmering war of ideas and values that exploded into full fury on September 11.

The puzzlement of liberal democracies in the face of Islamist terrorism seems odd. After all, since 1793, when the word "terror" first came into use in its modern political sense with the so-called Terror of the French Revolution, nearly every country in the West has had some experience with a terrorist movement or regime. Why then does such a phenomenon, which no less than liberal democracy itself is a product of the modern age, appear in this instance so opaque to Western analysts?

Islamist terror first burst onto the world scene with the 1979 Iranian Revolution and the seizure of the U.S. embassy in Tehran in November of that year. Since then, Islamism has spread, and the ideological and political tools that have helped to curb terrorism throughout much of the West have proven mostly ineffective at stopping it. Its presence is global, and its influence is felt not only in the lands of the vast Islamic crescent that extends from Morocco and Nigeria in the west to Malaysia and Mindanao in the east but also in many corners of Europe, India, the former Soviet world, the Americas, and even parts of western China.

Before the Iranian Revolution, terrorism was typically seen as a straightforward outgrowth of modern ideologies. Islamist terrorists, however, claim to fight on theological grounds: A few verses from the Koran and a few references to the *sunna* ("deeds of the Prophet") put an Islamic seal on each operation. The whole ideological fabric appears to be woven from appeals to tradition, ethnicity, and historical grievances both old and new, along with a powerful set of religious-sounding references to "infidels," "idolaters," "crusaders," "martyrs," "holy wars," "sacred soil," "enemies of Islam," "the party of God," and "the great Satan."

But this religious vocabulary hides violent Islamism's true nature as a modern totalitarian challenge to both traditional Islam and modern democracy. If terrorism is truly as close to the core of Islamic belief as both the Islamists and many of their enemies claim, why does international Islamist terrorism date only to 1979? This question finds a powerful echo in the statements of the many eminent Islamic scholars and theologians who have consistently condemned the actions of the Islamist networks.

This is not to say that Islamic jurisprudence and philosophy propound a democratic vision of society or easily accommodate the principles of democracy and human rights. But it does expose the fraudulence of the terrorists' references to Islamic precepts. There is in the history of Islam no precedent for the utterly unrestrained violence of al-Qaeda or the Hezbollah. Even the Shi'ite Ismaili sect known as the Assassins, though it used men who were ready to die to murder its enemies, never descended to anything like the random mass slaughter in which the Hezbollah, Osama bin Laden, and his minions glory.[1] To kill oneself while wantonly murdering women, children, and people of all religions and descriptions—let us not forget that Muslims too worked at the World Trade Center—has nothing to do with Islam, and one does not have to be a learned theologian to see this. The truth is that contemporary Islamist terror is an eminently modern practice thoroughly at odds with Islamic traditions and ethics.[2]

A striking illustration of the tension between Islam and terrorism was offered by an exchange that took place between two Muslims in the French courtroom where Fouad Ali Saleh was being tried for his role in a wave of bombings that shook Paris in 1985–86. One of his victims, a man badly burned in one of these attacks, said to Saleh: "I am a practicing Muslim. . . . Did God tell you to bomb babies and pregnant women?" Saleh responded, "You are an Algerian. Remember what [the French] did to your fathers."[3] Challenged regarding the religious grounds of his actions, the terrorist replied not with Koranic verses but with secular nationalist grievances.

The record of Saleh's trial makes fascinating reading. He was a Sunni Muslim, originally from Tunisia, who spent the early 1980s "studying" at Qom, the Shi'ite theological center in Iran. He received weapons training in Libya and Algeria, and got his explosives from the pro-Iranian militants of Hezbollah. In his defense, he invoked not only the Koran and the Ayatollah Khomeini but also Joan of Arc—who is, among other things, a heroine of the French far right—as an example of someone who "defended her country against the aggressor." After this he read out long passages from *Revolt Against the Modern World* by Julius Evola (1898–1974), an Italian author often cited by European extreme rightists. This strange ideological brew suggests the importance of exploring the intellectual roots of Islamist terrorism.[4]

The Genealogy of Islamism

The idea of a "pan-Islamic"[5] movement appeared in the late nineteenth and early twentieth centuries concomitantly with the rapid transformation of traditional Muslim polities into nation-states. The man who did more than any other to lend an Islamic cast to totalitarian ideology was an Egyptian schoolteacher named Hassan al-Banna (1906–49). Banna was not a theologian by training. Deeply influenced by Egyptian nationalism, he founded the Muslim Brotherhood in 1928 with the express goal of counteracting Western influences.[6]

By the late 1930s, Nazi Germany had established contacts with revolutionary junior officers in the Egyptian army, including many who were close to the Muslim Brothers. Before long the Brothers, who had begun by pursuing charitable, associational, and cultural activities, also had a youth wing, a creed of unconditional loyalty to the leader, and a paramilitary organization whose slogan "action, obedience, silence" echoed the "believe, obey, fight" motto of the Italian Fascists. Banna's ideas were at odds with those of the traditional *ulema* (theologians), and he warned his followers as early as 1943 to expect "the severest opposition" from the traditional religious establishment.[7]

From the Fascists—and behind them, from the European tradition of putatively "transformative" or "purifying" revolutionary violence that began with the Jacobins—Banna also borrowed the idea of heroic death as a political art form. Although few in the West may remember it today, it is difficult to overstate the degree to which the aestheticization of death, the glorification of armed force, the worship of martyrdom, and faith in "the propaganda of the deed" shaped the antiliberal ethos of both the far right and elements of the far left earlier in the twentieth century. Following Banna, today's Islamist militants embrace a terrorist cult of martyrdom that has more to do with Georges Sorel's *Réflexions sur la violence* than with anything in either Sunni or Shi'ite Islam.[8]

After the Allied victory in World War II, Banna's assassination in early 1949, and the Egyptian Revolution of 1952–54, the Muslim Brothers found themselves facing the hostility of a secularizing military government and sharp ideological competition from Egyptian communists. Sayyid Qutb (1906–66), the Brothers' chief spokesman and also their liaison with the communists, framed an ideological response that would lay the groundwork for the Islamism of today.

Qutb was a follower not only of Banna but of the Pakistani writer and activist Sayyid Abu'l-A'la Mawdudi (1903–79), who in 1941 founded the Jamaat-e-Islami-e-Pakistan (Pakistan Islamic Assembly), which remains an important political force in Pakistan, though it cannot claim notable electoral support.[9] Mawdudi's rejection of nationalism, which he had earlier embraced, led to his interest in the political role of Islam. He denounced all nationalism, labeling it as *kufr* (unbelief). Using Marxist terminology, he advocated a struggle by an Islamic "revolutionary vanguard" against both the West and traditional Islam, attaching the adjectives "Islamic" to such distinctively Western terms as "revolution," "state," and "ideology." Though strongly opposed by the Muslim religious authorities, his ideas influenced a whole generation of "modern" Islamists.

Like both of his preceptors, Qutb lacked traditional theological training. A graduate of the state teacher's college, in 1948 he went to study education in the United States. Once an Egyptian nationalist, he joined the Muslim Brothers soon after returning home in 1950. Qutb's brand of Islamism was informed by his knowledge of both the Marxist and fascist critiques of modern capitalism and representative democracy.[10] He called for a monolithic state ruled by a single party of Islamic rebirth. Like Mawdudi and various Western totalitarians, he identified his own society (in his case, contemporary Muslim polities) as among the enemies that a virtuous, ideologically self-conscious, vanguard minority would have to fight by any means necessary, including violent revolution, so that a new and perfectly just society might arise. His ideal society was a classless one where the "selfish individual" of liberal democracies would be banished and the "exploitation of man by man" would be abolished. God alone would govern it through the implementation of Islamic law *(shari'a)*. This was Leninism in Islamist dress.

When the authoritarian regime of President Gamal Abdel Nasser suppressed the Muslim Brothers in 1954 (it would eventually get around to hanging Qutb in 1966), many went into exile in Algeria, Saudi Arabia,[11] Iraq, Syria, and Morocco. From there, they spread their revolutionary Islamist ideas—including the organizational and ideological tools borrowed from European totalitarianism—by means of a network that reached into numerous religious schools and universities. Most young Islamist cadres today are the direct intellectual and spiritual heirs of the Qutbist wing of the Muslim Brotherhood.

The Iranian Connection

Banna and the Brotherhood advocated the creation of a solidarity network that would reach across the various schools of Islam.[12] Perhaps in part because of this ecumenism, we can detect the Brothers' influence as early as 1945 in Iran, the homeland of most of the world's Shi'ites.

Returning home from Iraq that year, a young Iranian cleric named Navab Safavi started a terrorist group that assassinated a number of secular Iranian intellectuals and politicians. In 1953, Safavi visited Egypt at the Brothers' invitation and presumably met with Qutb. Although Safavi's group was crushed and he was executed after a failed attempt on the life of the prime minister in 1955, several of its former members would become prominent among those who lined up with the Ayatollah Khomeini (1900–89) to mastermind the Islamic Revolution of 1979.

Khomeini himself first took a political stand in 1962, joining other ayatollahs to oppose the shah's plans for land reform and female suffrage. At this point, Khomeini was not a revolutionary but a traditionalist alarmed by modernization and anxious to defend the privileges of his clerical caste. When his followers staged an urban uprising in June 1963, he was arrested and subsequently exiled, first to Turkey, then to Iraq. The turning point came in 1970, when Khomeini, still in Iraq, became one of the very few Shi'ite religious authorities to switch from traditionalism to totalitarianism. Much like Mawdudi,[13] he called for a revolution to create an Islamic state, and inspired by Qutb, he condemned all nontheocratic regimes as idolatrous. His followers in Iran were active in Islamist cultural associations that spread, among others, the ideas of Qutb and Mawdudi. Qutb's ideology was used by Khomeini's students to recapture for the Islamist movement a whole generation influenced by the world's predominant revolutionary culture—Marxism-Leninism.

Khomeini became a major figure in the history of Islamist terrorism because he was the first truly eminent religious figure to lend it his authority. For despite all its influence on the young, Islamism before the Iranian Revolution was a marginal heterodoxy. Qutb and Mawdudi were theological dabblers whom Sunni scholars had refuted and dismissed. Even the Muslim Brothers had officially rejected Qutb's ideas. As an established clerical scholar, Khomeini gave modern Islamist totalitarianism a religious respectability that it had sorely lacked.

Once in power, the onetime opponent of land reform and women's suffrage became a "progressivist," launching a massive program of nationalization and expropriation and recruiting women for campaigns of revolutionary propaganda and mobilization. The Leninist characteristics of his rule—his policy of terror, his revolutionary tribunals and militias, his administrative purges, his cultural revolution, and his accommodating attitude toward the USSR—alienated the majority of his fellow clerics but also gained him the active support of the Moscow-aligned Iranian Communist Party, which from 1979 to 1983 put itself at the service of the new theocracy.

Khomeini's revolution was not an exclusively Shi'ite phenomenon. Not accidentally, one of the first foreign visitors who showed up to congratulate him was the Sunni Islamist Mawdudi; before long, Qutb's face was on an Iranian postage stamp. Khomeini's successor, Ali Khamenei, translated Qutb into Persian.[14] Khomeini's own interest in creating an "Islamist International"—it would later be known by the hijacked Koranic term Hezbollah ("party of God")—was apparent as early as August 1979.

The Islamist "Comintern"

As these ties suggest, Islamism is a self-consciously pan-Muslim phenomenon. It is a waste of time and effort to try to distinguish Islamist terror groups from one another according to their alleged differences along a series of traditional religious, ethnic, or political divides (Shi'ite versus Sunni, Persian versus Arab, and so on). The reason is simple: *In the eyes of the Islamist groups themselves, their common effort to strike at the West while seizing control of the Muslim world is immeasurably more important than whatever might be seen as "dividing" them from one another.*

The Lebanese-based, Iranian-supported Hezbollah is a case in point. Its Iranian founder was a hardcore Khomeini aide who drew his inspiration from a young Egyptian Islamist—an engineer by training, not a theologian—who was the first to politicize what had been a purely religious term. A closer look at the organization reveals the strong influence of Marxism-Leninism on the ideology of its founders and leadership. The group's current leader, Mohammad Hosein Fadlallah, influenced by Marx's and Nietzsche's theories on violence,[15] has openly advocated terrorist methods and tactical alliances with leftist organizations.[16] Hezbollah is a successful creation of the Islamist "Comintern." "We must," says Sheikh Fadlallah, "swear allegiance to the leader of the [Iranian] revolution and to the revolutionaries as to God himself," because "this revolution is the will of God."[17] One indication of the extent of this allegiance is the fact that all the negotiations over the fate of the hostages held in Lebanon ended up being carried out by Tehran. Similarly, the head of Iran's Revolutionary Guards boasted about having sponsored the attack against

French and American peacekeeping forces in Lebanon.[18] Hezbollah's chief military planner, Imad Mughaniyyah, is an Arab who operates from Iran. Western intelligence agencies suspect that Hezbollah has been working with bin Laden on international operations since the early 1990s.[19] Hezbollah's terrorist network in Lebanon contains both Shi'ite and Sunni groups, and there is also a Saudi Arabian wing that was involved in the Khobar Towers bombing, which killed 19 U.S. troops in 1996.

Also inspired by the Iranian Revolution was the independent Sunni terrorist network that later became the basis of al-Qaeda. The Tehran regime began forming propaganda organs to sway opinion among Sunni religious authorities as early as 1982.[20] Among the supranational institutions created was the World Congress of Friday Sermons Imams, which at one time had a presence in no fewer than 40 countries. The overarching goal of these efforts has been to mobilize the "Islam of the people" against the "reactionary Islam of the establishment."[21] For a variety of reasons this network has remained loosely organized, but all of its branches spring from and are fed by the same ideological taproot.

The influence of Iran's Islamist revolution was also cited by the members of Egyptian Islamic Jihad who gunned down President Anwar Sadat in October 1981. Their theoretician was an engineer, Abdessalam Faraj, who was also fond of quoting Qutb to justify terror.[22] The conspirators—including the junior army officers who did the actual shooting—were inspired by the Iranian model, and expected the death of Sadat to trigger a mass uprising that would replay in Cairo the same sort of events which had taken place two years earlier in Tehran[23] (where the Iranian authorities would subsequently name a street after Sadat's killer). Among those imprisoned in connection with the plot was a Cairo physician named Ayman al-Zawahiri. He became Egyptian Islamic Jihad's leader after serving his three-year prison term, met bin Laden in 1985, and then joined him in Sudan in the early 1990s. Zawahiri, who would become al-Qaeda's top operational planner, is reported to have said publicly that Osama is "the new Che Guevara."[24]

The Islamization of the Palestinian question is also partly due to Khomeini's influence on the Palestinian branch of Islamic Jihad. Its founder was another physician, this one named Fathi Shqaqi. His 1979 encomium *Khomeini: The Islamic Alternative* was dedicated to both the Iranian ruler and Hassan al-Banna ("the two men of this century"). The first press run of 10,000 sold out in a few days.[25] Shqaqi, who was of course a Sunni, had nonetheless traveled to Tehran to share the Friday sermon podium with Ali Khamenei, denouncing the Mideast peace process and accusing Yasser Arafat of treason.[26]

Distorting Islam's History and Teachings

As these examples show, such distinctions as may exist among these terrorist groups are overshadowed by their readiness to coalesce and collaborate according to a common set of ideological beliefs. These beliefs are properly called "Islamist" rather than "Islamic" because they are actually in conflict with Islam—a conflict that we must not allow to be obscured by the terrorists' habit of commandeering Islamic religious terminology and injecting it with their own distorted content. One illustration is the Islamists' interpretation of the *hijra*—Mohammad's journey, in September 622 C.E., from Mecca to Medina to found the first fully realized and autonomous Islamic community *(ummah)*. Despite a wealth of historical and doctrinal evidence to the contrary, half-educated Islamists insist on portraying this journey as a revolutionary rupture with existing society that licenses their desire to excommunicate contemporary Muslim societies in favor of their own radically utopian vision.

The Islamic Republic of Iran also rests on heterodoxy, in this case Khomeini's novel and even idiosyncratic theory of the absolute power of the single, supreme Islamic jurisprudent *(faqih)*. It was not a coincidence that one of the first uprisings against Khomeini's regime took place under the inspiration of a leading ayatollah, Shariat Madari.[27] Officials of the regime have admitted that most Iranian clerics have always taken a wary view of Khomeinism. It is important to realize that the religious references which Khomeini used to justify his rule were literally the same as those invoked a century earlier by an eminent ayatollah who was arguing for the legitimacy of parliamentarism and popular sovereignty on Islamic grounds.[28] Koranic verses lend themselves to many different and even contradictory interpretations. It is thus to something other than Islamic religious sources that we must look if we want to understand Islamism and the war that it wages on its own society, a war in which international terrorism is only one front.

In a brief article on bin Laden's 1998 declaration of *jihad* against the United States, Bernard Lewis showed brilliantly how bin Laden travestied matters not only of fact (for instance, by labeling the invited U.S. military presence in Saudi Arabia a "crusader" invasion) but also of Islamic doctrine, by calling for the indiscriminate butchery of any and all U.S. citizens, wherever they can be found in the world. Reminding his readers that Islamic law *(shari'a)* holds *jihad* to be nothing but a regular war and subject to the rules that limit such conflicts, Lewis concluded, "At no point do the basic texts of Islam enjoin terrorism and murder. At no point do they even consider the random slaughter of uninvolved bystanders."[29]

What gives force to the terrorist notion of *jihad* invented by the Iranians and later embraced by bin Laden is not its Koranic roots—there are none—but rather the brute success of terrorist acts. Bin Laden has spoken with particular admiration of the Iranian-sponsored suicide truck bombing that killed 241 U.S. Marines and others in Beirut on 23 October 1983, precipitating the U.S. withdrawal from Lebanon.[30] Bin Laden was also not the first to think of setting up training camps for international terrorists—the Tehran authorities were there before him.[31]

A Friday sermon given in 1989 by one of these authorities, Ali Akbar Hashemi Rafsanjani, then president of the Islamic Parliament, reveals better than any other the logic of Islamist terrorism. Attacking the existence of Israel as another front in the pervasive war of unbelief *(kufr)* against Islam, Rafsanjani added:

> If for each Palestinian killed today in Palestine five Americans, English, or French were executed, they would not commit such acts anymore. . . . [T]here are Americans everywhere in the world. . . . [They] protect Israel. Does their blood have any value? Scare them outside Palestine, so that they don't feel safe. . . . There are a hundred thousand Palestinians in a country. They are educated, and they work. . . . [T]he factories that serve the enemies of Palestine function thanks to the work of the Palestinians. Blow up the factory. Where you work, you can take action. . . . Let them call you terrorists. . . . They [the "imperialism of information and propaganda"] commit crimes and call it human rights. We call it the defense of rights and of an oppressed people. . . . They will say the president of the Parliament officially incites to terror. . . . [L]et them say it.[32]

There is no reference here to religion; Rafsanjani's appeal is purely political. The West's offense he calls human rights; against it he urges Muslims to wield terror as the best weapon for defending the rights of an oppressed people. Rafsanjani, moreover, proudly commends "terror" by name, using the English word and not a Persian or Arabic equivalent. Thus he employs the very term that Lenin had borrowed from *la Terreur* of the French Revolution. The line from the guillotine and the Cheka to the suicide bomber is clear.

With this in mind, let us look for a moment at the French Revolution, where the modern concept of political terror was invented, to find the explanation that the Islamic tradition cannot give. When it announced its policy of terror in September 1793, the "virtuous minority" which then ran the revolutionary government of France was declaring war on its own society. At the heart of this war was a clash between two understandings of "the people" in whose name this government claimed to rule. One was a group of 25 million actually existing individuals, each endowed with inherent rights. The other was an essentially ideological construct, an abstraction, an indivisible and mystical body, its power absolute. The Terror of the French Revolution was neither a mistake nor an unfortunate accident; it was meant to purify this mystical body of what the terrorist elite regarded as corrupting influences, among which they numbered the notion that individual human beings had unalienable rights.[33]

The spokesmen of the Islamist revolution echo the terrorists of Jacobin France. The denigration of human rights marks the spot where the internal war on Muslim society meets the terrorist war against the West. Suffice it to hear bin Laden's comments on the destruction of the World Trade Center: "Those awesome symbolic towers that speak of liberty, human rights, and humanity have been destroyed. They have gone up in smoke."[34] Every Islamist terror campaign against Westerners during the last 20 years has had as its cognate an Islamist effort to tyrannize over a Muslim population somewhere in the world. Think of the ordeal to which the Taliban and al-Qaeda subjected the people of Afghanistan, or of what ordinary Algerians suffered during the savage Islamist civil wars of the 1990s. Or think of the state terror that daily labors to strangle any hope for recognition of human rights in Iran. To explore fully this correlation between terror against the West and tyranny against Muslims would take a separate essay. Yet we can get an idea of its nature by considering the first instance of Islamist terrorism against the United States, the 1979 hostage-taking in Tehran.

Holding Democracy Hostage to Terror

As they released the hostages in January 1981, the Tehran authorities crowed over their victory, which Prime Minster Mohammad Ali Rajai called "the greatest political gain in the social history of the world" and an act that "had forced the greatest Satanic power to its knees." At first glance this claim might seem foolish, for the United States had said no to the revolutionary government's demands to hand over the shah and unfreeze Iranian assets. But a closer look shows that the Iranian Islamists had in fact scored a big political and ideological victory over both the United States and their domestic opponents, and thus had ample cause for jubilation.

The seizure of the U.S. embassy took place at a time when Khomeini and his allies had not yet consolidated their tyrannical regime. An Assembly of Experts was drafting the constitution of the Islamic Republic. Opposition was gaining strength daily in religious as well as in moderate secular circles. The Marxist-Leninist left, angered by a ban on its press, was growing restive. Open rebellions were breaking out in sensitive border regions populated by ethnic Kurds and Azeris. By sending in its cadres of radical students to take over the U.S. embassy and hold its staff hostage, the regime cut through the Gordian knot of these challenges at a single blow and even put itself in a position to ram through its widely criticized Constitution. Rafsanjani's assessment of what the act meant is instructive:

> In the first months of the revolution, the Washington White House decided in favor of a coup d'état in Iran. The idea was to infiltrate Iranian groups and launch a movement to annihilate the revolution. But the occupation of the embassy and the people's assault against the U.S.A. neutralized this plan, pushing the U.S. into a defensive stand.[35]

One could describe this version of the facts as a parody: The U.S. government in 1979 clearly had neither the will nor the ability to stage a coup against the Islamic Republic. But totalitarians typically speak an esoteric language of their own devising. Those who administered the Terror in revolutionary France painted some of their country's best-known republicans with the label "monarchist" before sending them off to be guillotined. The Bolsheviks called striking workers and the sailors of Kronstadt "bandits" and "counterrevolutionaries" before slaughtering them. In 1979, promoting human rights was a prominent aspect of how the United States described its foreign policy. By Rafsanjani's logic, therefore, any Iranian group that spoke of human rights was thereby revealing itself as a tool of the United States.

And indeed, as muddled negotiations over the hostages dragged on, the administration of President Jimmy Carter dropped any talk of supporting democracy in Iran[36]—the very cause for which Carter had taken the risk of ending U.S. support for the shah. Meanwhile, the revolutionary regime began using the Stalinist tactic of claiming that anyone who spoke in favor of a more representative government was really a U.S. agent.[37] With the hostage crisis, the Islamist regime was able to make anti-Americanism such a leading theme that Iranian Marxists rallied to its support, while Moscow extended its tacit protection to the new theocracy.

After the failure of the U.S. military's "Desert One" rescue attempt on 25 April 1980 and eight more months of negotiations, the United States at last succeeded in obtaining the release of the hostages. To do so, it had to agree to recognize the legitimacy of the Iranian revolutionary regime, and it had to promise not to file any complaints against Iran before international authorities, despite the gross violations of human rights and international law that had occurred. Though these concessions may have appeared necessary at the time, in retrospect we can see that they emboldened the Islamists to sink to new levels of hatred and contempt for the West and its talk of human rights. For had not the revolutionary students and clerics in Tehran forced the Great Satan to abandon its principles and brought it to its knees?

The terrorists accurately assessed the extent of their victory and drew conclusions from it. They used terror to achieve their goal, and upon the continued use of terror their survival depends. "[America] is on the defensive. If tomorrow it feels safe, then it will think to implement its imperialistic projects."[38] Among these projects are human rights, which a representative of the Islamic Republic denounced before the UN Human Rights Committee as an "imperialist myth."[39]

From the taking of the hostages in Tehran in 1979 until the terrorist attacks of last September, Western policy makers too often implicitly downgraded the claims of justice and shirked their duty both to their own citizens and to the cause of human rights by refusing to pursue the terrorists with any real determination. Considerations of "pragmatism" and "prudence" were put forward to justify a sellout of justice which, in one of the cruelest ironies revealed by the harsh light of September 11, proved not to have been prudent at all.

Since the impunity granted to the hostage-takers of Tehran, terrorist outrages have increased both in frequency and in scale. In addition to all the questions raised about security measures, intelligence failures, accountability in foreign-policy decision making, and the like, the atrocity of September 11 also forces citizens of democratic countries to ask themselves how strongly they are committed to democratic values. Their enemies may believe in a chimera, but it is one for which they have shown themselves all too ready to die. In the mirror of the terrorists' sacrifice, the citizens of the free world are called to examine their consciences; they must reevaluate the nature of their loyalty to fragile and imperfect democracy. In particular, the strongly solidaristic networks that the Islamist totalitarians have created should make citizens in democratic societies ask how much they and their governments have done to help prodemocracy activists who have been persecuted for years in Iran, in Algeria, in Afghanistan, in Sudan, and elsewhere. Unarmed, they stand on the front lines of the struggle against terror and tyranny, and they deserve support. Here is a moral, political, and even philosophical challenge upon which the minds and hearts of the West should focus.

Whither the Muslim World?

Islamist terror poses a different but no less grave problem for those of us (including the authors of this essay) who come from Islamic countries, and it carries a special challenge for Muslim intellectuals. Public opinion in the Muslim world has largely—if perhaps too quietly—condemned the massacres of September 11. In Iran, young people poured spontaneously into the streets, braving arrest and police violence in order to hold candlelight vigils for the victims. But there were also outbursts of celebration in some Muslim countries, and sizeable anti-American demonstrations in Pakistan. Perhaps more disturbing still have been the persistent and widespread rumors going around Muslim societies that somehow an Israeli conspiracy was behind the attack. The force and pervasiveness of this rumor are symptoms of a collective flight from an uncontrollable reality. It is true that the Palestinian question is a painful and complicated one that requires an equitable solution. But it is equally true that reaching for foreign conspiracies has become an easy way of evading responsibility for too many of us from Muslim countries.

For the last several centuries, the Islamic world has been undergoing a traumatizing encounter with the West. Since this encounter began, our history has been a story of irreversible modernization, but also of utter domination on the one side, and humiliation and resentment on the other. To Muslim minds the West and its ways have become a powerful myth— evil, impenetrable, and incomprehensible. Whatever the Western world's unfairness toward Muslims, it remains true that Western scholars have at least made the effort to learn about and understand the Islamic world.

But sadly, the great and brilliant works of the West's "Orientalists" have found no echo in a Muslim school of "Occidentalism."

We have been lacking the ability or the will to open up to others. We have opted for an easy solution, that of disguising in the clothes of Islam imported Western intellectual categories and concepts. In doing so we have not only failed to grasp the opportunity to understand the West, we have also lost the keys to our own culture. Otherwise, how could a degenerate Leninism aspire today to pass itself off as the true expression of a great monotheistic religion? The Islamists see themselves as bold warriors against modernity and the West, but in fact it is they who have imported and then dressed up in Islamic-sounding verbiage some of the most dubious ideas that ever came out of the modern West, ideas which now—after much death and suffering—the West itself has generally rejected. Had we not become so alien to our own cultural heritage, our theologians and intellectuals might have done a better job of exposing the antinomy between what the Islamists say and what Islam actually teaches. They might have more effectively undercut the terrorists' claim to be the exclusive and immediate representatives of God on earth, even while they preach a doctrine that does nothing but restore human sacrifice, as if God had never sent the angel to stop Abraham from slaying his son.

Our incapacity to apprehend reality lies at the root of our paranoia. If we were to take a clear and careful look at the West, we would see that it draws its strength from its capacity for introspection and its intransigent self-criticism. We would know that Western culture has never stopped calling on us, on the figure of the stranger, to help it understand itself and fight its vices. When it could not find the other, it invented it: Thomas More imagined a faraway island called Utopia to mirror the social problems of his time; Michel de Montaigne couched his criticisms of French politics in the form of a conversation with an Indian chief from Brazil; and Montesquieu invented letters from a Persian tourist to denounce the vices of Europe.

Had we had our own eminent experts on Western civilization, we might know that the West is a diverse, plural, and complex entity. Its political culture has produced horrors but also institutions that protect human dignity. One of these horrors was the imperialism imposed on Muslim and other lands, but even that did as much harm to the Europeans themselves as it did to us, as anyone familiar with the casualty figures from the First World War will know. Our experts might have helped us understand that Qutb and Khomeini's denunciations of human rights were remarkably similar to Pope Pius VI's denunciation of the French Declaration of the Rights of Man of 1789. We might have grasped that, not long ago, Westerners faced the same obstacles that we face today on the road to democracy. Citizens in the West fought for their freedoms; in this fight they lost neither their souls nor their religion. We too must roll up our sleeves to fight for freedom, remembering that we are first and foremost free and responsible human beings whom God has endowed with dignity.

NOTES

We would like to thank Hormoz Hekmat for his useful comments and critiques and Laith Kubba for providing some useful information.

1. Bernard Lewis, *The Assassins: A Radical Sect in Islam* (New York: Oxford University Press, 1987), 133–34.

2. On the heterodoxy of the Islamists' references to Muslim jurisprudent Ibn Taymiyya (1263–1328), see Olivier Carré, *Mystique et politique: Lecture révolutionnaire du Coran par Sayyid Qutb, Frère musulman radical* (Paris: Cerf, 1984), 16–17. On Ibn Taymiyya's theology and life, see Henri Laoust, *Pluralisme dans l'Islam* (Paris: Librairie Orientaliste Paul Geuthner, 1983).

3. This account of the Saleh case is based on reports in *Le Monde* (Paris), 8 and 10 April 1992.

4. For an overview of the career of Islamist terror networks, see Xavier Raufer, *La Nebuleuse: Le terrorisme du Moyen-Orient* (Paris: Fayard, 1987); Roland Jacquard, *Au nom d'Oussama Ben Laden: Dossier secret sur le terroriste le plus recherché du monde* (Paris: Jean Picollec, 2001); Yossef Bodansky, *Bin Laden: The Man Who Declared War on America* (Rocklin, Calif.: Prima, 1999); Gilles Kepel, *Jihad: Expansion et déclin de l'islamisme* (Paris: Gallimard, 2000); and Yonah Alexander and Michael S. Swetnam, *Usama Bin Laden's al-Qaida: Profile of a Terrorist Network* (New York: Transnational Publishers, 2001).

5. To confront Western colonialism, Muslim intellectuals and religious scholars such as Sayyid Jamal al-Din 'al-Afghani of Iran and Muhammad Abduh of Egypt concluded that a reformation and a new interpretation of Islam were needed in Muslim societies. The reforms that they advocated were aimed at reconciling Islam and modernity. They sought to promote individual freedom, social justice, and political liberalism. After the First World War, however, this movement was succeeded by one that was hostile to political liberalism. On Afghani, see Nikki K. Keddie, *An Islamic Response to Imperialism: Political and Religious Writings of Sayyid Jamal al-Din 'al-Afghani* (Berkeley: University of California Press, 1983). On Abduh, see Yvonne Haddad, "Muhammad Abduh: Pioneer of Islamic Reform," in Ali Rahnema, ed., *Pioneers of Islamic Revival* (London: Zed, 1994), 31–63.

6. This section draws on David Dean Commins, "Hassan al-Banna (1906–49)," in Ali Rahnema, ed., *Pioneers of Islamic Revival,* 146–47; as well as Richard P. Mitchell, *The Society of the Muslim Brothers* (London: Oxford University Press, 1969). See also Gilles Kepel, *Muslim Extremism in Egypt* (Berkeley: University of California Press, 1993).

7. Richard P. Mitchell, *The Society of the Muslim Brothers,* 29.

8. The widespread but mistaken impression that a Shi'ite cult of martyrdom serves as a religious inspiration for suicide attacks is one of the illusions about themselves that the terrorists skillfully cultivate. It is true that Shi'ites revere Hussein (d. 680 C.E.), the third Imam and a grandson of the Prophet, as a holy martyr. Yet Shi'ite teaching also enjoins the avoidance of martyrdom, even recommending *taqieh* ("hiding one's faith") as a way of saving one's life from murderous persecutors. Moreover, Sunnis are not noted for devotion to Hussein, and yet when it comes to suicide attacks, there is little difference between the Sunnis of al-Qaeda and the mostly Shi'ite cadres of Hezbollah. There are striking similarities between the Islamist justification for violence and martyrdom and the discourse of German and Italian Marxist ter-

rorists from the 1970s. On this subject see Philippe Raynaud, "Les origines intellectuelles du terrorisme," in François Furet et al., eds., *Terrorisme et démocratie* (Paris: Fayard, 1985), 65ff.

9. On Sayyid Abu'l-A'la Mawdudi, see Seyyed Vali Reza Nasr, *The Vanguard of the Islamic Revolution: The Jama'at-i Islami of Pakistan* (Berkeley: University of California Press, 1994); and Seyyed Vali Reza Nasr, *Mawdudi and the Making of Islamic Revivalism* (New York: Oxford University Press, 1996).

10. Olivier Carré, *Mystique et politique*, 206–7.

11. Muhammad Qutb, Sayyid Qutb's brother, was among the Muslim Brothers who were welcomed in Saudi Arabia. He was allowed to supervise the publication and distribution of his brother's works, and became ideologically influential in his own right: The official justification for the Saudi penal code uses his definition of secular and liberal societies as a "new era of ignorance." Exiled Muslim Brothers became influential in Saudi Arabia. Wahabism, the intolerant and fanatical brand of Islam that prevails in Saudi Arabia, was not in its origins a modern totalitarian ideology, but it provides fertile ground for the dissemination of terrorist ideology and facilitates the attraction of young Saudis to terrorist groups. See Olivier Carré, *L'utopie islamique dans l'Orient arabe* (Paris: Presses de la Fondation Nationale des Sciences politiques, 1991), 112–14; and Gilles Kepel, *Jihad,* 72–75.

12. Banna's followers recalled that he often said, "Each of the four schools [of Islam] is respectable," and urged, "Let us cooperate in those things on which we can agree and be lenient in those on which we cannot." Richard P. Mitchell, *The Society of the Muslim Brothers,* 217.

13. Sayyid Abu'l-A'la Mawdudi, *The Process of Islamic Revolution* (Lahore, 1955).

14. See Baqer Moin, *Khomeini: Life of the Ayatollah* (London: I.B. Tauris, 1999), 246.

15. Cited in Olivier Carré, *L'utopie islamique dans l'Orient arabe,* 197.

16. Cited in Olivier Carré, *L'utopie islamique dans l'Orient arabe,* 231–32.

17. Olivier Carré, *L'utopie islamique dans l'Orient arabe,* 232.

18. The then-head of the Iranian Revolutionary Guards, Mohsen Rafiqdoust, said that "both the TNT and the ideology which in one blast sent to hell 400 officers, NCOs, and soldiers at the Marine headquarters have been provided by Iran." *Resalat* (Tehran), 20 July 1987.

19. On 22 March 1998, the *Times of London* reported that bin Laden and the Iranian Revolutionary Guards had signed a pact the previous February 16 to consolidate their operations in Albania and Kosovo. Roland Jacquard adds that in September 1999, the Turkish intelligence services learned of an Islamist group financed by bin Laden in the Iranian city of Tabriz. See Roland Jacquard, *Au nom d'Oussama Ben Laden,* 287–88.

20. The first conference on the unification of Islamist movements was organized under Iranian auspices in January 1982. See the speeches of Khamenei and Mohammad Khatami (who is now the elected president of the Islamic Republic) in *Etela'at* (Tehran), 9 January 1982.

21. Xavier Rauffer, *La Nebuleuse,* 175.

22. Charles Tripp, "Sayyid Qutb: The Political Vision," in Ali Rahnema, ed., *Pioneers of Islamic Revival,* 178–79.

23. Gilles Kepel, *Jihad,* 122–23.

24. Roland Jacquard, *Au nom d'Oussama Ben Laden,* 76.

25. Gilles Kepel, *Jihad,* 187 and 579.

26. As reported in *Jomhouri-e Islami* (Tehran), 5 March 1994 (14 esfand 1372), 14 and 2.

27. Reported in the daily *Khalq-e Mosalman,* 4 and 9 December 1979.

28. M.H. Nad'ni, *Tanbih al-Omma va Tanzih al-mella* 5th ed. (Tehran, 1979), 75–85.

29. Bernard Lewis, "License to Kill: Usama bin Ladin's Declaration of Jihad," *Foreign Affairs* 77 (November–December 1998): 19. Bin Laden's declaration of *jihad* mentions Ibn Taymiyya's authority and yet clearly contradicts the latter's ideas on *jihad.* Ibn Taymiyya explicitly forbids the murder of civilians and submits *jihad* to strict rules and regulations. See Henri Laoust, *Le traité de droit public d'Ibn Taimiya* (annotated translation of *Siyasa shar'iya*) (Beirut, Institut Français de Damas1948), 122–35.

30. See "Declaration of war against the Americans occupying the land of the two holy places: A Message from Usama Bin Muhammad bin Laden unto his Muslim Brethren all over the world generally and in the Arab Peninsula specifically" (23 August 1996), in Yonah Alexander and Michael S. Swetnam, *Usama Bin Laden's al-Qaida,* 13.

31. In 1989, the vice-president of Parliament, Hojatol-Eslam Karoubi, proposed the creation of training camps for the "anti-imperialist struggle in the region." Quoted in the daily *Jomhouri-e Eslami* (Tehran), 7 May 1989, 9.

32. *Jomhouri-e Eslami,* 7 May 1989, 11.

33. In this connection, it is worth noting that after the end of the Terror, the Declaration of the Rights of Man and the Citizen was not officially restored to constitutional status in France until 1946.

34. Howard Kurtz, "Interview Sheds Light on Bin Laden's Views," *Washington Post,* 7 February 2002, A12. Bin Laden gave this interview to Tayseer Alouni of the Arabic-language satellite television network al-Jazeera in October 2001.

35. Ali Akbar Hashemi Rafsanjani, *Enqelabe va defa'e Moqadass* (Revolution and its sacred defense) (Tehran: Press of the Foundation of 15 Khordad, 1989), 63–64.

36. Russell Leigh Moses, *Freeing the Hostages: Reexamining U.S.-Iranian Negotiations and Soviet Policy, 1979–1981* (Pittsburgh: University of Pittsburgh Press, 1996), 174–75.

37. In an interview that ran in the Tehran daily *Jomhouri-e Eslami* on 4 November 1981 to mark the second anniversary of the embassy seizure, student-radical leader Musavi Khoeiniha remarked that the neutralization of Iranian liberals and democrats was the hostage-taking's most important result.

38. Ali Akbar Hashemi Rafsanjani, *Enqelabe va defa'e Moqadass,* 64.

39. *Amnesty International Newsletter,* September 1982. The representative was Hadi Khosroshahi, another translator of Sayyid Qutb.

EPILOGUE: DOES DEMOCRACY NEED RELIGION?

Hillel Fradkin

Hillel Fradkin, *a senior fellow and director of the Project on the Muslim World at the Hudson Institute, has taught at the University of Chicago, Columbia, and Yale. He served as president of the Ethics and Public Policy Center from 2001 to 2004, and has written widely on the relationship between religion and politics. This essay originally appeared in the January 2000 issue of the* Journal of Democracy.

"On my arrival in the United States the religious aspect of the country was the first thing that struck my attention," Tocqueville reports in *Democracy in America* (I, 308). Tocqueville's wonder embraces admiration as well as surprise. Though religion is not formally a part of the American political system, Tocqueville goes so far as to describe it as the first of America's political institutions by virtue of its indirect effects upon political life (I, 305). For him, only one other extrapolitical factor is more important—that when America became a political democracy it already enjoyed "equality of conditions." Yet he regards the latter as almost certain to endure under any and all foreseeable future political arrangements; the future vitality of religion he sees as far less certain. Accordingly, the role of religion forms one of the most important themes of his reflections on the blessings, problems, and prospects of democracy as such. He not only devotes several chapters and even groups of chapters to the subject but also presents observations about it throughout the rest of the work.

Tocqueville considers this theme to be of special importance to his French and other European readers. It goes to the very heart of the "great problem of our times"—"the organization and the establishment of democracy in Christendom" (I, 325). The project of establishing political democracy in Europe had heretofore been, in Tocqueville's opinion, a failure. Among the principal causes of that failure was that "the spirit of religion and the spirit of freedom [were almost always] marching in opposite directions." In America, by contrast, "they were intimately united" (I, 308). Though the Americans have not entirely resolved the problem of democracy and religion, "they furnish useful data to those who undertake to resolve it" (I, 325). Of course, Tocqueville was chief among those who aimed at a solution. It was, in fact, his duty, one impossible for decent men not to face.

Reconciling Democracy and Religion

The problem for the rest of Christendom was manifold. Many religious forces and institutions in Europe, and the French Catholic Church in particular, were inclined to see democracy as the inevitable and implacable enemy of religion and hence were opposed to the establishment of democratic republics. Tocqueville, on the other hand, citing the American experience, proposes that democracy can indeed become a friend to religion and may even be crucial to its future vitality. The first objective of Tocqueville's discussion of religion in America is to persuade the partisans of religion and of democracy to join forces.

But the simple establishment of democracy in Europe is not his most fundamental concern, nor is the support that American religion gives to democracy its only, or even its chief, virtue. In his introduction to *Democracy in America,* Tocqueville argues that the inexorable advance of equality of conditions has made the march of democracy through Europe inevitable. It is, Tocqueville concludes, of divine provenance. No action, however intended, fails to abet it. European Christianity cannot stop the democratic movement and will only succeed in destroying itself if it proceeds on its present course.

Yet increasing equality of conditions will not necessarily lead to freedom and liberal democracy. It could as easily result in a new form of despotism, unprecedented in its capacity for oppression, evil, and degradation. The only possible historical precedent is the tyranny of the Caesars, though Tocqueville seems to think that modern democratic despotism will surpass it in evil (I, 328). In this, he was, as we now know, remarkably prescient.

Hence the most fundamental question is whether one can prevent democracy from degenerating into despotism. Here is where the study of America was indispensable: The United States had avoided that outcome and offered fair promise of continuing to do so. According to Tocqueville, religion had been crucial to this success. "If it does not impart a taste for freedom, it facilitates the use of it" (I, 305). This is vital because democratic despotism and the temptation to succumb to it are the result of certain features of democratic life, among them individualism and materialism; when these are taken to an extreme, they lead to conditions in which citizens either are forced to surrender their freedom or do so happily. Although religion cannot destroy individualism and the pursuit of material well-being, which are inevitable consequences of equality, it offers the chief means of moderating and educating these tendencies. Indeed, Tocqueville goes so far as to suggest that religion may even be necessary to sustain (as well as to moderate) individualism and material prosperity and thus may be doubly necessary to the future success of democracy.

All this suggests that, practically speaking, there is a "natural" harmony between religion and democracy. More precisely, Tocqueville asserts that there is a necessary relationship between Christianity and modern democracy. Only the appearance of Jesus in the world and the proclamation of the universal equality of all men makes true democracy possible (II, 15). It is partly in that sense that the modern democratic movement is providential.

But Christianity, in Tocqueville's account, is critical in another sense as well. Its distinction between that which belongs to Caesar and that which belongs to God makes possible the rise of democratic conditions as well as democratic sentiments (II, 23). Christianity denies to political and military force a sovereign claim to complete authority in all human affairs. Without that, Europe would have retained its feudal character indefinitely. The strict and aristocratic hierarchy of feudalism was not easily assailable, being perhaps the natural form of human rule. Yet Christianity prepared its demise by, among other things, permitting men of low origins to rise to high station and thus setting an example for other challenges to the feudal hierarchy. Although many of these challenges had their motives in the personal ambitions of kings, merchants, lawyers, and scholars, their fundamental opportunity and perhaps their fundamental justification derived from Christian teaching.

In addition, certain changes within Christianity abetted the delegitimization of aristocratic hierarchy. Though he describes himself as an observant Catholic, Tocqueville credits Protestantism with encouraging a kind of individualism and freedom with respect to authority that, when translated into political terms, served to support political democracy. Moreover, certain forms of Protestantism, having their home among the middle classes, united politically democratic inclinations with social equality. Nowhere was this combination clearer or more compelling than in the case of the founders of New England. Among the New England settlers, an equality based on religion was joined together in a particularly fortuitous mixture with equality of middle-class station, the great social factor underlying American success.

The Benefits of Separation

Yet although Christianity may have been the source of the equality of conditions that increasingly characterized Europe, only in America had the true harmony between Christianity and democracy been realized. This triumph rested on the principle of the separation of church and state. The separation of church and state in America has two great benefits. First, it has prevented the development of vested religious interests in the fortunes of particular political forces and parties, as had occurred in Europe. Thus in America religion had little to fear from the inevitable variability of political fortunes in a democracy. Neither did democratic political institutions have anything to fear from religion; hence they were entirely favorable to religious freedom. In turn, all sects were favorable to the political liberty that protected their religious liberty. Everything in this arrangement conspired to support respect for liberty, the principle of democratic life (I, ch. 17). It is especially important that religion should lend its support to the principle of separation of church and state. According to Tocqueville, democracy rests not on constitutional arrangements, or even on laws, but on what he calls the mores of society, which embrace both the "habits of the heart" and opinions. Religion is the most powerful source of both. The liberty characteristic of democracy permits individual habits and opin-ions to acquire great force in the aggregate. Religion is therefore bound to have a great, if indirect, influence (I, 303).

This is the second great benefit of the separation of church and state. Prevented by law from engaging in politics, religion in America devotes itself to its proper sphere: the cultivation of opinion and habit, especially moral habits. The focus on moral instruction, even if it comes at the expense of doctrine, is a wonderful characteristic of American religion. Inasmuch as all American religious sects "agree in respect to the duties which are due from man to man" and "preach the same morality in the name of God," they share a common interest, even though "each sect worships God in its own fashion." This interest is identical to the interest of democracy. For religion "never instructs the Americans more fully in the art of being free than when it says nothing about freedom" (I, 303). Americans are in great need of this art, as are all citizens of democracies.

Tocqueville is admirably blunt about the reason why: "How it is possible that society should escape destruction if the moral tie is not strengthened . . . as the political tie is relaxed? And what can be done with a people who are their own masters if they are not submissive to the Deity?" he asks (I, 303). "While the law permits the American people to do as they please, religion prevents them from conceiving, and forbids them to commit, what is rash or unjust" (I, 305). Tocqueville's bluntness is directed at European friends of democracy who "sincerely desire to prepare man to be free" but often "attack religious opinions." In this, Tocqueville argues, "they obey the dictates of their passions and not of their interests." For while "despotism may govern without faith . . . liberty cannot" (I, 307).

The message, then, seems to be clear and simple: Successful political democracy will inevitably require moral instruction grounded in religious faith. The American political system—and in particular the separation of church and state—has shown how all democratic republics may enjoy the moral benefits of religious faith while avoiding its potential curse, hostility to liberty.

How Democracy Influences Religion

Tocqueville's account of the moral situation and dynamics of democracy is more complicated, however. He goes on to describe how religion itself undergoes a transformation, and perhaps even a deformation, under the impact of democracy. To begin with, in America religion's emphasis on moral teaching amounts to a deemphasis of theological considerations. This not only has contributed to social peace among Christian sects but amounts to a moral change as well. Christianity's natural moral impulse, an austere indifference to the things of this world, was still reflected to some degree in the America of Tocqueville's time. Yet as he points out, the dynamics of democracy undermine otherworldliness and can only continue to do so. "Of all the passions which originate in or are fostered by equality, there is one which it renders peculiarly intense, and which it also infuses into the heart of every man; I mean the love of well-being. The taste for well-being is the prominent and indelible characteristic of democratic times" (II, 26). Tocqueville provides vivid examples of this characteristic, which has certainly not diminished over time.

Given the otherworldly character of Christianity, American religion could easily have found itself in opposition to democracy and thus have been regarded as an enemy by its partisans. This did not happen, because Christian ministers and preachers have wholly adapted themselves to democratic life. "While they never cease to point to the other world as the great object of the hopes and fears of the believer, they do not forbid him honestly to court prosperity in this [world]" (II, 27). Tocqueville commends this attitude of American ministers. They should not attempt to conquer the love of well-being, for they would not succeed. The only result would be that "the minds of men would at length escape [religion's] grasp, to plunge into the exclusive enjoyment of present and material pleasures." Rather, religion should work to "purify, regulate, and restrain" this passion and to persuade people to "enrich themselves by none but honest means" (II, 26).

This modification of the traditional religious stance toward wealth is not the only adaptation that religion must make. Democratic circumstances demand simplicity in religious dogma and ritual, although these (especially dogma) remain vital as a bulwark against democratic despotism. ("When there is no longer any principle of authority in religion . . . men are speedily frightened at . . . this unbounded independence" and are likely to hand themselves over to a master [II, 22].) Thus religion must take into account that people in democratic ages are loath to accept dogmatic beliefs and are impatient with the details of worship.

But this leads to a problem of which Tocqueville is well aware: "As all religions have general and eternal truths for their object, they cannot shape themselves to the shifting inclinations of each age without forfeiting their claim to certainty in the eyes of mankind." Doing so would not only harm religion, it would also sacrifice precisely those benefits to democracy that Tocqueville attributes to religious dogma. Tocqueville's answer is that religions must hold fast to the essentials (what "theologians call articles of faith"), while leaving room for flexibility in everything else (II, 25).

These difficulties call into question the natural harmony between religion and democracy. Tocqueville implicitly admits this by declaring that "religious nations are . . . naturally strong on the very point on which democratic nations are weak" and by stating that religion's greatest advantage is that it inspires principles diametrically opposed to the individualism and materialism that are the characteristic passions of a democratic age (II, 22). The relationship between religion and democracy would thus appear to require very careful management. Despite the adaptations religion must make, it has a substantial interest in maintaining a harmonious relationship. In America, "by respecting all democratic tendencies not absolutely contrary to herself and by making use of several of them for her purposes, religion sustains a successful struggle with that spirit of individual independence which is its most dangerous opponent" (II, 28).

Nevertheless, one cannot help but wonder whether this success will continue or whether there is a need to find other, nonreligious means of moral and intellectual regulation. Tocqueville addresses this possibility by taking up the theme of "self-interest rightly understood," a moral doctrine that is neither new nor unique to the United States, although it is "among the Americans of our time that it finds universal acceptance" (II, 122). Essentially this doctrine teaches that one's "private interest is to do good" or, as the popular adage goes, that "honesty is the best policy." Although this doctrine is not sublime, it is clear and definite, and Americans have put it into practice to good effect. "Each American knows when to sacrifice some of his private interests to save the rest" (II, 123). Although this doctrine cannot make a man virtuous by itself, its discipline can train people to become orderly, temperate, moderate, careful, and self-controlled citizens. If it does not lead the will directly to virtue, it establishes habits that unconsciously turn it in that direction.

Tocqueville's discussion here suggests that self-interest rightly understood may prove wholly adequate to the moral requirements of democracy, thus implying that religion may ultimately be unnecessary. Unlike religion, it is "within the reach of all capacities; everyone can without difficulty learn and retain it. By its admirable conformity to human weaknesses, it easily obtains great dominion; nor is that dominion precarious, since the principle checks one personal interest by another and uses, to direct the passions, the very same instrument that excites them" (II, 123). Indeed Tocqueville goes so far as to say that "the principle of self-interest rightly understood appears to me the best suited of all philosophical theories to the wants of the men in our time, and that I regard it as their chief remaining security against them-selves" (II, 123).

In the very next chapter, however, he takes up the issue of whether this "philosophical theory" is compatible with religious doctrine, and he uses the American experience to prove that it is and to show how they can be reconciled (II, ii, ch. 9). Here, the implication seems to be that this reconciliation *must* be achieved; in other words, the "philosophy" of self-interest rightly understood is ultimately insufficient to serve as the sole basis for the future of democracy and must be supplemented by religion. This prepares Tocqueville's discussion of his final reasons for insisting on the indispensability of religion in democracy, reasons having to do with the role that the question of "the future" plays in human life, for individuals, nations, and mankind as a whole.

Religion, Democracy, and the Future

All human life is somehow oriented toward the future, but this is especially true of democratic life. Citizens in a democracy exhibit a high level of activity because of the freedom they enjoy and the passions that democracy liberates. Democracy requires this activity in order to maintain itself and its freedom. Yet to sustain such activity, democratic citizens must orient themselves toward some future goal. Only the prospect of some future good will induce men to subordinate their selfishness to common purposes. Without it, men would soon tire of activity, becoming enervated, passive, and ripe for despotic rule. Given the fact of human mortality, only religion can persuasively ground the future and its prospective goods. Only religion can speak of "eternity" or "the future" without qualification. Moreover, as Tocqueville delicately puts it, there are "many sacrifices that can find their recompense only in another [world]" (II, 125).

Although religion may speak elaborately of the "next world," it suffices if men believe in a "supersensual and immortal principle, united for a time to matter" (II, 146). "Most religions are only general, simple, and practical means of teaching men the doctrine of the immortality of the soul" (II, 145). Hence most religions will do.

As always, Tocqueville emphasizes the direct political utility of religion, but this is not his only or deepest concern. Religion's political necessity also points to a more profound human need, one that is especially threatened in democratic ages, when there is a real danger that an excessive concentration on the pursuit of material well-being could lead to the loss of the most sublime human faculties—in effect, to human degradation. Tocqueville calls on democratic legislators and on "virtuous and enlightened men" in general to "raise the souls of their fellow citizens and keep them lifted up towards heaven" (II, 145).

This is no idle or sentimental hope. According to Tocqueville, it is supported by something deeply rooted in human nature: "It was not man who implanted in himself the taste for what is infinite and love of what is immortal; these lofty instincts are not the offspring of his capricious will; their steadfast foundation is fixed in human nature and they exist in spite of his efforts. He may cross and distort them; destroy them he cannot" (II, 134). This is true always and everywhere. In a democracy, the pursuit of material well-being may for a time distract men from these loftier needs. But as this pursuit becomes ever more successful and absorbing, it prepares the way for a backlash. America offers substantial evidence of this through its periodic outbursts of "a fanatical and almost wild spiritualism" (II, 134).

Tocqueville's account of religion in America necessarily focuses on Christianity. What are the implications of his analysis for democracy in non-Christian lands? Tocqueville himself raises the question of Muslim countries (II, 23), predicting that democracy will not fare well under Islam because the latter's teaching makes it much harder to separate religion and politics. To date, history has confirmed this prediction. On the other hand, Tocqueville's treatment of Christianity itself shows how much it had to be transformed (and even deformed) in order to work in a democracy. At the same time, his discussion of both religious morality and the immortality of the soul show how little might be required of a religion in a democracy.

The continued strength of religiosity in America compared to all other Western democracies and the relative success of the United States tend to support Tocqueville's understanding of the role of religion in democracy. So too does the current character of that religiosity, which reflects the religious transformations Tocqueville observed, predicted, or recommended. The failure of the communist movement, which made the propagation of atheism a principle of the regime, also seems to support his view. Tocqueville was careful to insist that the exact form taken by democracy in America would not be necessary or appropriate for other countries. It may be the case, however, that over the long run other democracies will not thrive unless religion plays a role similar to that which it has played in America.

INDEX